"In this remarkable book, Darrow Miller reaffirms the greatness of the Great Commission. Given the clash of civilizations and the war of worldviews we are now witnessing, that reaffirmation could not have come at a better time. This is a book to read. It is a book to put into practice. And it is a book to give away to every pastor, teacher, and leader you know."

GEORGE GRANT, author of *The Micah Mandate*

"Darrow Miller offers us a fresh and biblically sound understanding of the Great Commission. In particular, Miller enables thoughtful Christians to respond wisely to the worldwide challenge from Islamic radicalism. I hope this volume is widely read by the church for its instruction and mobilization."

DAVID DENMARK, executive director, The Maclellan Foundation

"For activists like me who seek understanding, here comes a three-in-one treat. With refreshingly profound insights into the Great Commission, Darrow Miller equips the church to understand, love, and serve radical Muslims and secularists."

VISHAL MANGALWADI, author of *The Book That Made Your World*

"Darrow Miller has written extensively on worldviews, and *Emancipating the World* is Miller at his best. The book reads well, is as challenging as it is inspiring, and deals with timely issues of the culture wars in the West and the war with jihadists from the East. Given this context, he offers a renewed and fresh examination of the Great Commission in response to fundamentalist atheism and militant Islam. I highly recommend this book."

TETSUNAO YAMAMORI, senior advisor, Lausanne Committee for World Evangelization

"Sizzling with significant truth about our task as Christ-followers for the times in which we live with the emergence of the twin towers of radical Islam and fundamentalist atheism. This is a book for every dedicated disciple of Jesus."

LUIS BUSH, international facilitator, Transform World Connections

Books by Darrow L. Miller

Against All Hope: Hope for Africa
(with Scott D. Allen and the African Working
Group of Samaritan Strategy Africa)

Discipling Nations: The Power of Truth to Transform Cultures
(with Stan Guthrie)

*The Forest in the Seed: A Biblical Perspective
on Resources and Development*
(with Scott D. Allen)

LifeWork: A Biblical Theology for What You Do Every Day
(with Marit Newton)

*Nurturing the Nations: Reclaiming the Dignity
of Women in Building Healthy Cultures*
(with Stan Guthrie)

On Earth As It Is in Heaven: Making It Happen
(with Bob Moffitt)

Servanthood: The Vocation of All Christians

Kingdom Lifestyle Bible Studies (with Scott D. Allen and Bob Moffitt)
God's Remarkable Plan for the Nations
God's Unshakable Kingdom
The Worldview of the Kingdom of God

DARROW L. MILLER

EMANCIPATING
THE
WORLD

a

CHRISTIAN RESPONSE

to

RADICAL ISLAM

and

FUNDAMENTALIST
ATHEISM

YWAM Publishing
Seattle, Washington

YWAM Publishing is the publishing ministry of Youth With A Mission (YWAM), an international missionary organization of Christians from many denominations dedicated to presenting Jesus Christ to this generation. To this end, YWAM has focused its efforts in three main areas: (1) training and equipping believers for their part in fulfilling the Great Commission (Matthew 28:19), (2) personal evangelism, and (3) mercy ministry (medical and relief work).

For a free catalog of books and materials, call (425) 771-1153 or (800) 922-2143.
Visit us online at www.ywampublishing.com.

Emancipating the World: A Christian Response to Radical Islam and Fundamentalist Atheism
Copyright © 2012 by Darrow L. Miller

Published by YWAM Publishing
a ministry of Youth With A Mission
P.O. Box 55787, Seattle, WA 98155-0787

This title is available as an e-book. Visit www.ywampublishing.com.

Unless otherwise noted, Scripture quotations are taken from the Holy Bible, New International Version®, NIV® Copyright © 1973, 1978, 1984, 2011 by Biblica, Inc.™ Used by permission. All rights reserved worldwide. Verses marked ESV are taken from The Holy Bible, English Standard Version® (ESV®), copyright © 2001 by Crossway, a publishing ministry of Good News Publishers. Used by permission. All rights reserved. Verses marked NASB are taken from the New American Standard Bible®, Copyright © 1960, 1962, 1963, 1968, 1971, 1972, 1973, 1975, 1977, 1995 by The Lockman Foundation. Used by permission.

Library of Congress Cataloging-in-Publication Data

Miller, Darrow L.
    Emancipating the world : a Christian response to radical Islam and fundamentalist atheism / Darrow L. Miller.
        p. cm.
    Includes bibliographical references (p.   ) and indexes.
    ISBN 978-1-57658-716-4 (alk. paper)
    1. Missions—Theory. 2. Mission of the church. 3. Great Commission (Bible) 4. Christianity and other religions. 5. Islam. 6. Atheism. I. Title.
    BV2063.M54 2012
    261.2—dc23   2012002565

First printing 2012

Printed in the United States of America

[The kingdom of God] is the most radical proposal ever proposed to the mind and allegiance of man. . . . It gathers up everything good in any system of thought and every religion anywhere, fulfills the good, cleanses the evil, and goes beyond anything ever thought or dreamed anywhere.

E. STANLEY JONES, *The Unshakable Kingdom and the Unchanging Person*

CONTENTS

ACKNOWLEDGMENTS

Any writing project is a group effort. Countless people ask profound questions or make stimulating observations. News headlines and current events are writing history. These and other influences push a writer's attention in new directions. A written acknowledgment always risks forgetting someone's valuable input. From anyone so overlooked, I ask forgiveness.

First, I would like to thank my friends at the YWAM base in Puerto Rico. Thanks to Yarley Niño's invitation, I have the privilege of engaging with them every year. They have given me a place to wrestle with new ideas and new materials and have provided excellent feedback. They also tend to take the things I teach and immediately use their creativity to put what they have heard into innovative practice.

Thank you to Mandie Miller, one of the Disciple Nations Alliance (DNA) editorial team members, who gave critical feedback on the manuscript, did yeoman's work on the original draft, and then labored to assemble the indexes and other supplemental materials. Mandie also chaired the evaluation team that gave input on the content of a workshop that formed the basis of the book. Thank you, Mandie!

Thanks to the evaluation team in Puerto Rico who spent many hours during the evenings of the "Great Commission" workshop critiquing what they had heard, giving ideas for improving the content, and suggesting many of the stories and illustrations found in the book's final form. These people are Miguel Rodriguez, Nelson Peres Resto, Natalia Park, Veronica Alegria, Alyssa Boehm, Marcela Plaza, Bob Evans, and Samuel Alcaraz.

My profound thanks to Gary Brumbelow! Gary is a dear friend, a coworker, and a gifted writer and editor. He spent many hours over a six-month period poring over the manuscript, bringing good and hard questions to the text, and using his artistry to make the book much more readable. In some mysterious way he was able to keep up with my pace when I was in writing mode and return his work to me within a few hours, or a day or so at most. Gary, this book would not have reached the light of day without your encouragement and thoughtful work.

The DNA owes profound thanks to YWAM Publishing. Tom Bragg, the executive director, and Warren Walsh, the editorial and production manager, have believed in the DNA messages and partnered with us for most of our publishing endeavors. Thank you for believing in us when no one showed interest in unknown authors whose message was often a challenge to mainstream thinking about the church, missions, poverty, and development.

Thanks particularly to Ryan Davis, my editor at YWAM Publishing, for his excellent and timely editing of the manuscript. Your work has immensely improved the structure, flow, and substance of the narrative.

Thank you to my friend Joyce Ditzler for your critical feedback at a time when I was thinking about expanding an earlier manuscript into what became this book. Thanks to Pastor Tyler Johnson of Redemption Church in the Valley of the Sun for challenging me on some important points that I needed to revise. Thanks to Timothy Friberg, linguist and Greek scholar, for helping me parse "Therefore go."

Thanks to AF, PA, JT, and JB, who have backgrounds in the Middle East and North Africa. These friends have spent hours poring over what I have written on Islam. Their lifetime of experience in the Islamic world has made their analysis, feedback, and suggestions for how to improve this section of the book invaluable.

Thank you to Scott Allen, president of the DNA and a friend and coworker for over twenty-five years. Thank you for your love for ideas, our long discussions over the years, and your encouragement in this and other writing projects.

As ever, I must thank the bride of my youth, Marilyn, for her patience as I spent hours bent over my computer. Thank you for your partnership in life and for your support of God's calling upon our life together.

Above all, my thanks to our living God, Creator of the universe, who made us to live in freedom and redeemed us through his Son to live in freedom. Without God and the freedom he has granted us, we would not be able to write our signatures on the universe or contribute to the building of nations.

Without all these, and others, this book would not have been born. Thank you.

Any errors in substance or detail belong to the author alone. Please feel free to write me with corrections and critique. My heart's desire is to be part of a growing and learning community.

FOREWORD

The post-9/11 international order finds itself in the grip of a global struggle "for the hearts and minds of people and the souls of nations." So writes author, speaker, teacher, and activist for the poor and hungry Darrow Miller in this vitally important new book.

The aggression launched on a fateful September day would blast into contemporary consciousness the knowledge that jihadists are waging what Miller describes as a "war from the East." Islamic tyranny is spreading as "holy warriors" fight to subjugate every tribe and nation to Islamic power by any means necessary, including the barrel of a gun, the edge of a sword, and the explosions of homicide bombers. If we take Islamists at their word, the use of nuclear devices and other weapons of mass destruction is far from unthinkable.

One would expect that the Western nations, out of a sense of self-preservation, would rise up to defend themselves against this onslaught. But, alas, this has not been the case. Instead, we see halting, stumbling, and outright denial.

What is the reason for such a weak response? Miller explains that the "war *from* the East" is being facilitated by a "war *in* the West." Atheism and secularism have produced a moral anarchy that is eviscerating the West's ability to rise up to meet even so basic a challenge as self-preservation.

Atheist ideologies have unleashed an assault on truth, goodness, and beauty. Truth is reduced to subjectivity—whatever works for you at a particular moment. Goodness is dissolved into moral relativism—what is right for you may not be right for me. And beauty is lost in the banality and coarseness of the advertising and entertainment culture.

Though this breakdown of Western culture is couched by the liberal and secularist PR machine in glowing terms of liberation, Miller is more clear-sighted: he diagnoses this internal breakdown as the source of the West's suicidal vulnerability to external aggression. Indeed, jihadist groups often justify their violence by pointing to the cultural and moral degradation in the West. Thus the two wars are united at a deep level.

What can be done? Can the West mount an effective resistance? Or has the struggle already reached a point of no return?

Darrow Miller argues that the situation is desperate but not hopeless. America and the West still possess the spiritual capital needed to meet the twin challenges of Islamic tyranny and morally debilitating secularism. The crucial question is whether the West will avail itself of these resources to combat, repulse, and overcome this two-pronged assault on human freedom and dignity.

After diagnosing the problem, Miller deploys the second half of *Emancipating the World* to argue that a robust, authentic understanding of historic Christianity is key to winning both battles. This section of the book is dedicated to the proposition that the Christian community has an ongoing biblical calling to face precisely this kind of challenge, here and now in this life, instead of turning away to concentrate on a private spirituality while awaiting a future in heaven.

That scriptural calling is expressed in the intrinsic connection between the known but much-misunderstood "Great Commission" (Matt. 28:18–20) and the neglected but foundational "Cultural Mandate" (Gen. 1:28). The Cultural Mandate reminds us that human beings, created in the image of God, are called to exercise caring stewardship over the whole of creation. In other words, the content in Genesis 1:28 to "be fruitful and multiply" and "subdue" the earth is not a simplistic call to reproduce and run the show. Rather, it communicates the Creator's challenge to humanity to go forth into the world, exercising creativity to develop his creation in ways that demonstrate love and respect for the human race and for nature.

Furthermore, this most basic and expansive of human tasks remains in effect even though the world is now fallen and broken. The God-proclaimed goodness of creation has not been destroyed by evil.

And neither is life in this world to be disrespected as lacking "eternal value" and therefore treated as a meaningless waste of time when compared to "the things of God." This devaluation smacks of ancient Greek culture, with its low regard for the material world and the physical body, which is unholistically viewed as a prison house of the soul from which one seeks to escape.

In fact, this world and human life upon it, including existence in its material and physical aspects, are precisely "things of God." To use the vernacular, they are a "God thing." To act and think otherwise is to embrace not historic Christianity and not the *Great* Commission, but instead a sub-version of Christianity devitalized by a kind of "*Greek* Commission" (as Miller describes it).

Evident in *Emancipating the World* is Miller's incisive, grassroots understanding of worldviews, a product of years of hard-won experience in nations around the globe. He has personally witnessed the power of ideas to elevate and improve a society—or to enslave and impoverish it. He has traveled, lectured, and worked face-to-face with Africans and Haitians holding animist and voodoo worldviews and with Muslims submitting to an Islamic worldview.

Miller has witnessed firsthand the way ideas shape not only how people think but also the social and political institutions they create. His burden in *Emancipating the World* is to communicate the gospel's humane and revolutionary power to create societies that foster liberty and prosperity. It is love of neighbor released into the fullness of creation, unbounded by privatized spiritualities or by inward-looking ecclesiastical applications.

"True spirituality," to use Francis Schaeffer's phrase, covers the whole of life. Or, as Miller writes, life in community with our Father in heaven is a life in which humanity works and prays, farms and philosophizes, loves and protects, so that his will is done . . . where? "On earth as it is in heaven."

Unfortunately, Miller notes, some in the Christian community run too quickly past that first phrase: "on earth." Yet the Creator calls his people to steward this creation and to love our neighbors in this present life, here and now, and not just in the life to come. To meet that call, each generation must address the real-world threats and questions that arise in their particular moment of history.

The church, therefore, as a living community of renewed humanity, has the potential to become nothing less than a training ground to educate and equip frontline responders to act effectively and concretely in the present struggle on both fronts of the two wars. As a matter of humanity, as a matter of love, as a matter of neighborliness, secularists and jihadists should be challenged here, today, this moment, "on earth."

The resistance stems not from a rebranded paganism (autonomous licentiousness or the secularized state) or from a soft-focus religiosity (you have your private "truth," I have my private "Jesus"). The pushback, instead, emerges from the self-sacrificing love and wisdom of human beings who embrace a public and verifiable Christ who defeated hatred and death in space and time.

In the course of human history, truth can be won but truth can also be lost. Civilizations rise and fall. But whatever the present condition of a particular society, newness of life for the individual and for a people is ever at the door.

But none of this will occur without an effective cause. For in this world, freedom is axiomatic but never automatic. A key is needed to activate the givens embedded in God's good creation. Fortunately for the poor and the hungry, for the rich and the bored, and for those strong in power but weak in love, meaning, and humanness, the freedom narrative for man has always been an eternal imperative from God.

In *Emancipating the World*, Darrow Miller has written a particularly timely and necessary book. It pulses with the author's desire to free and elevate, to enrich and liberate. It offers a stereotype-shattering way to cast aside forms of spirituality that are too small for the full flourishing of human life, too limiting for the human being created in the image of God. And it gives a true and humane basis for overcoming evil with the true, the good, and the beautiful.

It is encouraging to imagine what a nation or a people might look like if they took seriously the lessons of this book and applied them to their daily lives, corporate structures, mission works, and public institutions. This we know: the West would begin rediscovering its ultimate rationale for a free and humane way of life. As for advocates of Islamist tyranny and atheistic fundamentalism, they might not know what hit them at first, but their bewilderment would likely last for only a little while. It is impossible to contain really Good News.

J. RICHARD PEARCEY
Bloomington, Minnesota
January 14, 2012

J. Richard Pearcey is editor and publisher of *The Pearcey Report* (www.pearcey report.com) and the blog *Pro-Existence*. Formerly managing editor of Human Events, he is a published writer, book editor, and on the faculty of Rivendell Sanctuary, where he team teaches with his wife, Nancy Pearcey.

A Clash of Civilizations

Freedom is a common grace. All human beings are hardwired to live freely. But free societies do not fall from heaven. They are born within the hearts of people, grounded in biblical principles, and established through obedience to all that Christ commanded. For nations to remain free, the lessons of freedom must be passed on to our children and grandchildren. That's why I wrote this book. May God be pleased to use it thus.

I was in the shower, listening to National Public Radio, when the program was interrupted for a breaking news announcement: at 8:46 a.m. a plane had crashed into the north tower of the World Trade Center in New York City. Quickly I wrapped a towel around myself and ran, dripping wet, to turn on the television. The picture snapped into focus just in time for me to witness an unbelievable scene: a second plane, a commercial jet, plowed into the south tower. This was no accident! The date was September 11, 2001, and I was witnessing a turning point in history.

From a cave somewhere near the Khyber Pass in the rugged Tora Bora region of Afghanistan, Osama bin Laden, founder of the jihadist organization al-Qaeda, was waging war against the United States. The world would never be the same.

Unknown to many, this attack did not come without warning. Osama bin Laden had sent a "Declaration of War" to then US Secretary of Defense William Perry five years earlier, on August 23, 1996. But before the planes crashed into the towers, few people had even heard of al-Qaeda or of bin Laden, much less his declared war.

Three Competing Narratives

The politically correct view is to frame this conflict in criminal terms: terrorists like bin Laden are criminals who must be brought to justice. But this is war, not just criminal activity. Soldiers, terrorists, and civilians—innocent mothers and children, including Muslims, Buddhists, Hindus, secularists, Jews, and Christians—are being killed. Cities are being bombed.

The clash we are facing is a battle for the hearts and minds of people and souls of nations. It is a *clash of civilizations,* to borrow from the provocative title of Dr. Samuel Huntington's book.[1] It is a battle of conflicting visions shaped by three metaphysical big ideas: moral anarchy, tyranny, and freedom.

Moral anarchy, or license, is the product of the atheistic materialism and secular humanism of the West.[2] This ideology regards truth, morals, and beauty as relative; people are free to do what is right in their own eyes, without moral or sexual restraints. A dimension of this worldview is hedonism: "Eat, drink, and be merry, for tomorrow we die." The symbol of this way of life is the condom.

Another big idea, one that has enveloped many nations throughout history, is *tyranny.* This was the reality of communism and fascism in the twentieth century and is currently espoused by the jihadist minority of fundamentalist Islam.[3] Tyrants rule over others in oppressive and often violent ways. The symbol of tyranny is the sword.

Secularists and jihadists are not irrational. They are functioning rationally but from faulty assumptions. They may be sincerely motivated, thinking that they are advocating and working toward "good for mankind," but sincerity does not make their convictions or actions right.

The third big idea, *freedom*, comes from Judeo-Christian theism—the biblical worldview—which is the root of Euro-American civilization. Freedom is the foundation of all thriving cultures and nations. It flows from the gospel of Jesus Christ, lived and proclaimed.[4] The symbol of this way of life is the self-sacrificial cross of Christ.

Looking at these three narratives, we understand that this clash of civilizations is a struggle between the disorder (license without order) of modern and postmodern atheism, the tyrannical order (without freedom) of the jihadists, and the freedom (the order of internal self-government based on biblical principles) found in the kingdom of God.

This war will not be won by swords, bullets, or bombs. It will be won by the side most convinced of the truth of their moral vision. It will be won by lives lived well and even sacrificed for others. It will be won by truth over falsehood, justice over corruption, freedom over tyranny, liberty over license, love over hate, and beauty over vileness. It will be won by those with the best set of ideas or "theology," a theology fleshed out in the midst of our poor and broken world.

Two Views of the Great Commission

For most of the twentieth century, the church was dominated by a dualistic worldview that separated the spiritual realm from the physical realm. This separation created a framework for the church's understanding of her nature and mission, of the Scriptures, and of what it means to be a Christian. But the universe, as revealed in both creation and the Bible, was not founded with this dichotomy. In the true Judeo-Christian worldview, God is the Lord of all of life, not merely of spiritual life, and humans are created by God to be in relationship with him and rule over the earth. The mission and nature of the church and what it means to be a Christian are integrative and comprehensive.

The church's two worldviews create two very different understandings of the Great Commission, the final command of Christ given to his disciples. The first view, shaped by dualism, values the spiritual over the material, leading to a mission concerned only with the future—a mission to save individual souls for heaven. The second view, shaped by the biblical paradigm, understands that the blood of Christ was shed "to reconcile to himself all things" (Col. 1:20), leading to a comprehensive mission to restore individuals, nations, and all of creation.

In the first view, the Great Commission is not "great"; it is limited. The purpose of this book is to put the "great" back into the Great Commission.

The Great Commission is first and foremost *God's* mission. It reflects God's "big agenda" for the world. It is a reflection of God's heart for all nations to be blessed and to flourish. The completion of the mission will be celebrated by the return of Jesus Christ, the coming of the New Jerusalem, and the ingathering of the nations at the end of history.

While the Great Commission is God's mission, he has delegated certain responsibilities for its completion to his people, the body of Christ, expressed in both the universal and local church. This is why it is called a "*co*-mission." It is both God's mission *and* our mission.

The Structure of This Book

This book has two parts. In Part 1, "The Twin Wars," we will examine the contemporary context of the Great Commission. Every generation has its own context in which it is to represent Christ and carry out his commission. The context of the Great Commission at the beginning of the twenty-first century is that we are at war. At its heart, this war is a rebellion in the heavens between Satan and God, between the forces of darkness and light. And yet this war is played out on earth. In our generation, the war is manifesting itself on two fronts, the *war in the West* and the *war from the East*.

The war in the West is the conflict for the soul of the West—the culture war. This is an engagement between a domineering atheism and a sleeping Judeo-Christian theism. The war from the East is that declared by a small band of jihadists. This is first a war for the soul of Islam between jihadists and moderate Muslims. The winner will determine the nature of Islam's future and her relationship with the world. Currently the jihadists are on the offensive both at home among Muslims and in their assault on the West.

In Part 2 we will unpack the Great Commission as expressed in Matthew 28:18–20. We will see that Christ is king of both heaven *and* earth. He has a task for all Christians, wherever they are deployed, and that task is nothing less than the discipling (might we even say the building?) of nations. This primary responsibility has two secondary tasks: to baptize nations, overwhelming them with the nature and character of God; and to teach them to be obedient to all that Christ has commanded them, transforming them to reflect the truth, goodness, and beauty of God's kingdom.

The Great Commission is God's comprehensive movement to bring about the restoration of all things that have been broken by man's rebellion against God and his order; it is to be the church's response to the conflicts raging in the West and from the East.[5]

My Motivation

In 2004 the draft of the European Constitution was completed. Conspicuously missing was any reference to the role of Christianity in laying the historic foundation of European civilization. When a people sever themselves from their roots, whether by neglect or choice, that people and their culture die. As I write, we are witnessing the cultural suicide of Europe and are approaching a tipping point that will determine whether the United States will survive as a nation of freedom.

As an American citizen who loves the freedom and wonder derived from Judeo-Christian principles, and as a resident of our global community, my heart is broken to see nations dying, moving toward disorder, and languishing in poverty.

For nations to flourish, they must be bound within the framework of God's created order. To be so permeated and transformed by this order, a nation's people must be wise. Her people must be students of God's self-revelation both through creation and his Word. They must understand the first principles that will nourish a nation's soul and enable it to flourish.

On a recent trip to Asia, I read *The American Cause* by American historian and social critic Russell Kirk. In the editor's introduction, Gleaves Whitney tells a story that motivated Kirk to write his book. The story took place in the early 1950s during the Korean War. The chief of intelligence of the Chinese People's Volunteer Army based in North Korea was reflecting on how little American prisoners of war knew of the founding impulses that shaped their nation's freedom. This intelligence officer wrote to his commander in Beijing of the American POWs: "There is little knowledge or understanding, even among United States university graduates, of American political history and philosophy; of federal, state, and community organizations; of state rights and civil rights; of safeguards to freedom; and of how these things supposedly operate within [their] own system."[6]

Sadly, more than sixty years since these words were penned, things have not improved. Rather, they have deteriorated. As the fortieth president of the United States, Ronald Reagan, said, "Freedom is a fragile thing and is never more than one generation away from extinction."[7]

If the United States and Europe are to remain free, we need to reflect on the gospel roots of our Western civilization. Those living in countries struggling with poverty, corruption, and enslavement need to understand that the foundation of free and just societies is found in the Great Commission. We need to be people who *think* from biblical paradigm and principle.

Russell Kirk notes that Greece died because her people refused to think: "Demosthenes, the great Athenian patriot, cried out to his countrymen when they seemed too confused and divided to stand against the tyranny of Macedonia; *'In God's name, I beg of you to think.'* For a long while, most Athenians ridiculed Demosthenes' entreaty. . . . Only at the eleventh hour did the Athenians perceive the truth of his exhortations. And that eleventh hour was too late. So it may be with Americans today. *If we are too indolent to think, we might as well surrender to our enemies tomorrow."*[8]

In the West, Christians and non-Christians alike have not thought seriously about the foundations of the Western order and thus have unknowingly acted to sever our nations from their roots. We must wake up before it is too late.

In recent years, many Christians have loved Christ with all their hearts but have failed to love him with all their minds. We are faced with secular and jihadist ideologues who know who they are and what they are about. They have a narrative that guides their lives; they want to impose these ideas on the world. American writer Paul Berman states, "The terrorists speak insanely of deep things. The antiterrorists had better speak sanely of equally deep things. . . . Who will defend liberal ideas against the enemies of liberal ideas?"[9]

The founders of the United States were Christian. Most were Puritans or influenced by Puritan thinking. The Puritans crossed the Atlantic with the Bible in their hands and a biblical worldview in their minds; biblical principles informed their concept of governance. They thought theologically, so the language of America's founding was theological, not psychological, as is the language that governs national discourse today. The Puritans were *consciously Christian.*

Many Christians today function from *near memory.* They unconsciously function from biblical principles but make no connection between their faith and the way they live in the marketplace.[10]

Other Christians, and non-Christians as well, function from a *distant memory*. They function from their legacy (e.g., work hard or live frugally) but have no idea why. They live as they do because this is how their parents lived.

I am compelled to call Christians, for God's sake and for the health and prosperity of their nations, to consciously *think* and *act* from a biblical framework.

Following the 1973 *Roe v. Wade* Supreme Court decision, I was actively involved in the effort to secure the dignity of women and rescue their unborn babies from the abortionists' knives and chemicals. Three times I was arrested and jailed for these activities. It was during these experiences that I felt most alive and most consciously Christian.

It must be noted that I am not a scholar; I am a social activist who has come to see the power of ideas. I have had a lifelong interest in mission, issues of poverty and hunger, and the power of the biblical worldview and biblical principles to lift communities and even nations out of poverty.

I am quite comfortable writing on the culture wars in the West because I have lived through them, participated in them, and seen the profound impact they have had on Europe and are having on the United States. Likewise, I have studied the Scriptures all my adult life, and the Great Commission[11] and the Cultural Commission[12] (or Cultural Mandate) have been among my favorite subjects.

Regarding Islam and the jihad movement, however, I write strictly as a layman. I have done considerable reading in this area since 9/11, but I am certainly not an expert. I have, however, had the help and input of several people with intimate knowledge of Islam.

The purpose of this book is to provide a renewed and comprehensive examination of the Great Commission in light of the modern context of the culture wars in the West and the war with jihadists from the East, and to call the church to engage in these great conflicts of our time.

It is to call the church to think and to act. She needs once again to function consciously from biblical conviction, to engage in the conflicts that are dominating and transforming (or deforming) the world today. It is to call the sleeping church to wake from slumber and engage in the battle for the souls of our nations and the future of our world—before it is too late. It is to encourage the church to engage as partners with moderate (reasonable) Muslims and secularists for the sake of free and just societies. It is to call the church to begin to create love cells to comprehensively serve and minister to Muslims, jihadists, atheists, and neo-pagans in their own communities.

I am writing first for thoughtful global Christians who are interested in what it takes to build free and just nations and who are committed to being nation builders. Second, I'm writing for Christians with a heart for missions who want to have a better understanding of the mission of the church and specifically the meaning of the Great Commission. Third, I'm writing for Christians everywhere who are witnessing the moral and spiritual disintegration of their own society or the coming jihad, and who are needing a fresh framework for responding well to these conflicts.

We will be exploring issues that are hotly debated today. My intention is to write substantively and respectfully. I'm not concerned that my words may not be politically correct as determined by the current Western academic establishment and media. If my words are not always "nice," I have nevertheless tried to speak with candor, not rancor—to write from conviction but with civility.

Optimism and Opportunity

People often ask me, "In light of the poverty in the world; the growing moral and spiritual bankruptcy in the United States and Europe; and the advances of Islam in Europe and of jihadists throughout Asia, the Middle East, and parts of Africa, how can you be so optimistic?"

Though at some points this book may seem discouraging or even overwhelming, we need not be discouraged. We are reminded of what our attitude should be as we consider the words of Hebrews 12:2–3: "Let us fix our eyes on Jesus, the author and perfecter of our faith, who *for the joy set before him* endured the cross, scorning its shame, and sat down at the right hand of the throne of God. *Consider him* who endured such opposition from sinful men, *so that you will not grow weary and lose heart*" (NIV 1984).

We can take courage from Christ's example. We can also be optimistic because we know that Christ already won the battle that marked the turning point in the whole spiritual conflict,[13] and thus we know how the conflict will end. Knowing the end of the glorious story, we can live with hope in the midst of all the conflicts that we face.

Crisis creates opportunity, and great crises create great opportunities. The church in the West is confronted with two great crises. The war in the West creates an opportunity to restore Christian *orthodoxy*—a wholistic biblical worldview[14]—to the church. It calls the church to speak the truth to lies, to create beauty in a society that is increasingly ugly and vulgar, and to be good and do good,[15] challenging evil and injustice in society. The war from the East can propel the church to *orthopraxy*—the practice of orthodoxy—by loving all Muslims and caring for those who are trapped in poverty, both physical and spiritual.

Will we rise to these opportunities, or will we stick our heads in the sand, ignoring the twin wars until their consequences come knocking at our doors? Our response to both of these crises has the potential to reengage the church in fulfilling the Great Commission. It is my hope that all Christians will recognize and seize the opportunities before them, for the sake of our communities, our nations, and our world.

PART 1

The Twin Wars

CHAPTER 1

The War from the East: Is This War?

Two global civilizations appear to be poised in a complex confrontation on various levels of human activity. One is based in Muslim countries and the other in the West.
—AKBAR S. AHMED

War has been declared on the nations and the moral vision of the West. On September 11, 2001, four US commercial jets were hijacked by jihadists and used as bombs. Two attacked the World Trade Center, the symbol of America's economic prosperity. One flew into the Pentagon, the symbol of America's military power. The fourth jet was prevented from attacking the third target, thought to be a symbol of America's political power such as the United States Capitol or the White House, when the passengers of United Airlines Flight 93 attacked the hijackers, forcing the plane to crash in a Pennsylvania field.

The nineteen hijackers were militant Muslims directed by Osama bin Laden to kill as many Americans as possible. Nearly

13

three thousand innocent victims died on 9/11, including people from over fifty countries, surpassing the number of people who died at Pearl Harbor. This event shocked the world and has surely changed the course of history.

In this chapter we will examine the historical and religious nature of the war that jihadists have declared on the West and what is at stake for those who value freedom.

The Prelude

Before 9/11 very few people had ever heard of Osama bin Laden and his al-Qaeda organization. Yet long before 9/11, the exiled Saudi had declared war on the United States and had begun attacking American interests. On February 26, 1993, jihadists attacked the same World Trade Center with a truck bomb, killing six and injuring 1,042. On November 13, 1995, five Americans were killed when a car bomb exploded in Riyadh, Saudi Arabia. On June 25, 1996, the US base at Khobar Towers in Saudi Arabia was bombed, wounding hundreds and killing nineteen.

Finally, on August 23, 1996, when these attacks had apparently not gained the attention of the US government, Osama bin Laden issued his multipage "Declaration of War against the Americans Occupying the Land of the Two Holy Places." Writing from a cave somewhere in the rugged mountains of Afghanistan, he addressed the document to then US Secretary of Defense William Perry. "These youths [the jihadists] love death as you love life," he wrote. "Those youths will not ask you for explanations, they will tell you singing there is nothing between us [that] need[s] to be explained, there is only killing and neck smiting."[1] These chilling words go to the heart of the conflict between the jihadists and the West: they love death as much as we love life!

I consider myself to be widely read, keeping up with major global events, and yet I had never heard of this "Declaration of War" until I began doing research for this book. How could I have been so unaware of something so significant? Did the Western press and Western governments consider this declaration too insignificant to warrant public mention? Associate Professor of Criminal Justice at Appalachian State University, Dr. Matthew Robinson, documents dozens of reports going back to 1994 of attempts by Islamic terrorists plotting to use commercial airplanes as bombs.[2] How could the United States government have been so asleep? How could the world have been so surprised?

Because bin Laden's 1996 "Declaration of War" did not get the world's attention, bin Laden and the leader of the Egyptian Islamic Jihad, exiled Egyptian physician Ayman al-Zawahiri, formally merged their organizations. On February 23, 1998, they issued a *fatwa* (Islamic religious ruling) in the name of the World Islamic Front. The fatwa, "Jihad against Jews and Crusaders," included a ruling that

> to kill the Americans and their allies—civilians and military—is an individual duty for every Muslim who can do it in any country in which it is possible to do it, in order to liberate the al-Aqsa Mosque and the holy mosque [Mecca] from their grip, and in order for their armies to move out of all the lands of Islam, defeated and unable to threaten any Muslim. This is in accordance with the words of Almighty Allah, "and fight the pagans all together as they fight you all together," and "fight them until there is no more tumult or oppression, and there prevail justice and faith in Allah.[3]

Following the issue of the fatwa, on August 7, 1998, hundreds of people were killed in simultaneous bombings of the US Embassies in Nairobi, Kenya, and Dar es Salaam, Tanzania. Following this, bin Laden was put on the Federal Bureau of Investigation's (FBI) Ten Most Wanted List. The US government identified the Saudi refugee as a "criminal" and the violence he had perpetrated as criminal acts, but refused to categorize his actions as acts of war.

Less than a year before 9/11, on October 12, 2000, the jihadists struck again, this time against the American destroyer the USS

Cole. The attack, in the Yemeni port of Aden, killed seventeen US sailors and wounded thirty-nine.

Is This World War III?

September 11, 2001, was clearly a turning point in human history. One of the leading American scholars of Islam, Dr. Bernard Lewis, professor emeritus of Near Eastern studies at Princeton University, marks the dramatic nature of 9/11 with these words: "There are times in the long history of the human adventure when we have a real turning point, a major change—the end of an era, the beginning of a new era. I am becoming more and more convinced that we are in such an age at the present time—a change in history comparable with such events as the fall of Rome, the discovery of America, and the like."[4]

Likewise, journalist and author Thomas Friedman, three-time winner of the Pulitzer Prize, writes of his thoughts as he watched the collapse of the Twin Towers: "As I watched live on CNN as the Twin Towers imploded and collapsed onto the streets of Manhattan, it was equally obvious to me that history, wherever it had been heading before the morning of September 11, had just taken another sharp right turn, and a whole new history would flow from this towering inferno."[5]

Author, historian, and fifty-eighth Speaker of the US House of Representatives, Newt Gingrich, likens the current conflict to a World War III: "I am now firmly convinced that the world confronts a situation that is frighteningly similar to a Third World War, one every bit as serious and dangerous as the two great conflicts of the 20th Century."[6]

While 9/11 is certainly a pivotal point in world history, perhaps as significant as the fall of Rome or World Wars I and II, it does not mark the beginning of a new war. It is rather a continuation of a war that is known as the Long War, which began with Muhammad and has roots in ancient history.

History of the Conflict

The three great monotheistic religions—Judaism, Christianity, and Islam—all descend from Abraham. Jews and Christians trace their ancestry to Abraham through Isaac (non-Jewish Christians are spiritually grafted into the line of Isaac's descendant Judah).[7] Arabs trace their ancestry to Abraham through Ishmael.

When Sarah, Abraham's wife, could not conceive, she arranged for her handmaiden, Hagar, to sleep with Abraham. When Hagar conceived a son, Sarah, in a jealous rage, drove Hagar into the desert.[8] In this history we find two significant words of prophecy: Hagar's descendants will be "too numerous to count" (Gen. 16:10), and Ishmael will be a "wild donkey" who will "live in hostility toward all his brothers" (16:12; 25:18). The first prophecy has been fulfilled, and so has the second. Ishmael's descendants (Arabs, not all Muslims) have lived in hostility toward each other for generations. Arabs have a proverb, "Myself against my brother, my brother and I against my cousin, my cousin and I against the stranger."[9]

A descendant of Ishmael, Islam's founding prophet, Muhammad, conquered Arabia in AD 630. Upon Muhammad's death, Arab nomads left the Arabian Peninsula, challenging the *kuffar*, "unbelievers," in Persia, Syria, Armenia, Egypt, and North Africa from 632 to 661. In 637 Muhammad's followers conquered Jerusalem, the capital of the Jews and birthplace of Christianity. The Arabs built the Dome of the Rock, Islam's third-holiest site, to demonstrate the supremacy of Islam over Judaism and Christianity. The Dome of the Rock was built on Mount Moriah, the Temple Mount, the Jews' holiest site. The inscription on the Dome of the Rock assails the Christian doctrine of the deity of Christ: "He is God, One, God the Everlasting, who has not begotten and has not been begotten."[10]

After conquering the home of the Jews and Christians, Muslims swept across North Africa, then across the Strait of Gibraltar into Spain and Portugal, then over the Mediterranean into southern Italy, with the extent of their control reaching to the border areas of

France. At the same time, Islam was also spreading eastward as far as today's Afghanistan, Uzbekistan, and Pakistan. Ultimately, with the contributions of the *dhimmis* (non-Muslim residents under Islamic law), they established the Golden Age of Islam.

Between 1096 and 1204, four waves of Roman Catholic crusades, each lasting several years, pushed back against Islam's march. The behavior of the "Christian" armies was not unlike the conduct of the Muslim armies, which fuels hatred among Muslims toward Christians to this day.

With the creation of the Ottoman Empire in 1299, Muslims advanced to southeastern Europe and the rest of southwestern Asia over the next three centuries. Constantinople, the eastern capital of Christendom, fell to the Muslim Turks in 1453.

The Muslim advance in Europe came to an end on September 11, 1683, when the Muslims were defeated at the gates of Vienna.[11] Islam continued to expand southward and eastward, however, farther into Africa and India and into Southeast Asia as far as the Philippines. Then, with the demise of the Mughal and Safavid empires in the 1700s and the Ottoman Empire at the end of World War I, the spread of Islam slowed and Muslim influence declined politically.

While Westerners may have forgotten this history, Muslims have not. That is why a small group of jihadists, exiled in the caves of Afghanistan, chose September 11, 2001—the 318th anniversary of their defeat at Vienna—to attack the homeland of the world's mightiest military and economic power. Islam is on the march again; the Long War continues.

Resistance against the West

Muslims enjoyed unbroken government from 632 to 1924, something almost unprecedented in the history of the world. The last caliphate (the rulership of Muhammad's successor) was established by the Ottoman Empire in 1517. On July 24, 1923, the new "secular" Turkey was established, and the caliphate was constitutionally abolished on March 3, 1924.

Sunni Muslims were devastated by the abolishment of the caliphate. Four years later, Egyptian schoolteacher Hasan al-Banna founded the first modern Sunni fundamentalist movement, the Muslim Brotherhood (al-Ikhwan al-Muslimun). Thus began the resistance against moderate Muslims and the West.

Yale University professor Dr. Joanne Meyerowitz relates al-Banna's description of his reaction to the West:

[I was] appalled by "the wave of atheism and lewdness [that] engulfed Egypt" following World War I. The victorious Europeans had "imported their half-naked women into these regions, together with their liquors, their theatres, their dance halls, their amusements, their stories, their newspapers, their novels, their whims, their silly games, and their vices." . . . Suddenly the very heart of the Islamic world was penetrated by European "schools and scientific and cultural institutes" that "cast doubt and heresy into the souls of its sons and taught them how to demean themselves, disparage their religion and their fatherland, divest themselves of their traditions and beliefs, and to regard as sacred anything Western."[12]

One can easily imagine the bewilderment and anger of pious Muslims viewing the advance of an amoral, atheistic culture sweeping the world.

The next major challenge for Muslims came after the Jewish holocaust of World War II, with the European-sponsored birth of Israel. For generations, three faith communities—Jews, Christians, and Muslims—had lived in relative peace in the land of Palestine. This changed with the 1947 United Nations Resolution 181, which partitioned Palestine into Arab and Jewish states and divided Jerusalem. This created a Jewish state in the heart of the Muslim world. While the Jews celebrated having a homeland, the Palestinians were distressed.

With the influx of Jews from Europe, Jewish communities in Palestine were expanding and new communities were being birthed. After UN 181, violence broke out between Palestinians and the Jewish communities. On May 15, 1948, the day after Israel's declaration of independence, the neighboring Arab armies attacked the fledgling Jewish state. The ensuing defeat of the Arab armies was officially recognized by the 1949 Armistice Agreement, which also created 650,000 Palestinian refugees. In 1956, 1967, and 1973, the Arabs launched additional unsuccessful attacks against Israel.

How could the tiny nation of Israel vanquish powerful Arab armies? While many Arabs believed the answer lay in bigger and more modern armies, some framed the question itself differently: How could the armies of the Jewish and Christian God defeat the armies of Allah? Many Muslims believed that Islam had become impure, corrupted by modern secularism. Perhaps Allah was punishing Arabs and Muslims for their infidelity. Thus emerged a new fundamentalist and jihadist goal to purify the faith and overcome the "near enemy" of secularized, apostate Muslims.

On December 19, 1989, the Kuwait newspaper *Al-Qabas* reported that Hashemi Rafsanjani, president of Iran (1989–97), took the long view. This conflict was not modern but ancient. "Every problem in our region can be traced to this single dilemma: the occupation of Dar al-Islam [the House of Islam] by Jewish infidels or Western imperialists. . . . The everlasting struggle between Ishmael and Isaac cannot cease until one or the other is utterly vanquished."[13]

The battle to rid Palestine of the Jews remains the focus of the conflict with the West. But the larger war is over the ideals and moral vision that will shape the world. On October 7, 2001, Osama bin Laden stated: "These events [of 9/11] have divided the whole world into two sides—the side of believers and the side of infidels, may God keep you away from them. Every Muslim has to rush to make his religion victorious. The winds of faith have come."[14]

A Religious War

Will we take people like bin Laden and Rafsanjani at their word and recognize this as a war of sacred belief systems? Most Western media, news, and university elites are cultural relativists; they are tone-deaf to the pronouncements of the jihadists. They see the poverty of and injustices committed against Muslim societies as the primary source of jihadists' rage against the West. And yet, as we have seen, this is not the rhetoric fueling al-Qaeda. The elites of the Western world are in a Neville Chamberlain mode, in denial of the dangers we face.

Dr. Mary Habeck, associate professor of strategic studies at Johns Hopkins University, has written:

> The consistent need to find explanations other than religious ones for the attacks says, in fact, more about the West than it does about the jihadis. Western scholars have generally failed to take religion seriously. Secularists . . . discount the plain sense of religious statements made by the jihadis themselves. To see why jihadis declared war on the United States and tried to kill as many Americans as possible, we must be willing to listen to their own explanations. To do otherwise is to impose a Western interpretation on the extremists, in effect to listen to ourselves rather than to them.[15]

We have witnessed this over and over again in the politically correct statements of President Obama and his administration. In November 2009 US Army major Nidal Malik Hasan, a Muslim radical, cried "Allahu Akbar" as he murdered fourteen people and wounded thirty-one at the Fort Hood army base. Janet Napolitano, secretary of homeland security, commented on the rampage: "This was an individual who does not, obviously, represent the Muslim faith."[16] In February 2010 the Department of Homeland Security's Quadrennial Homeland Security Report "failed to make any reference to the Islamist nature of the threat."[17]

Today many academics, reporters, and government officials view the world through an atheistic and materialistic set of glasses. They see all problems and their solutions through political and economic lenses. They cannot understand how jihadists can be motivated by religious belief. Robert Spencer, American author and director of Jihad Watch, writes:

> Even at the *Wall Street Journal* they don't understand that the primary motivation of the jihadists is a religious ideology, not resentment born of economic injustice or marginalization. Economic injustice and marginalization are things they understand; a religious ideology that can move men to give up good lives and devote themselves to murder and destruction is so far out of their purview that they cannot even imagine it, and take all the evidence of it that is in front of their faces as indications of something else.[18]

A Wake-up Call

Today's conflict between the West and Islam is a renewed battle of an ancient war that began with enmity between Abraham's sons. This Long War is a clash of visions and ideals. Originally it was a clash between the followers of Muhammad and pagans, Jews, and Christians. Now it is a conflict between jihadists and *modernity*. It has been rightly identified as a clash of civilizations.

Muslims correctly see the West today as largely functioning from an atheistic-materialist worldview, without moral standards. They are witnessing an infectious outpouring of secular and materialist ideology onto the world through movies, television, and the Internet. In a recent demonstration in one Muslim country, participants carried placards of pornographic pictures from the Internet. Their heading read, "This is the kind of freedom the West offers," insinuating that immoral Western society is completely broken.

The West was long considered Judeo-Christian. While it was founded on a biblical worldview and principles, many now consider it to be post-Christian. European governments operate from an overwhelmingly secular worldview, and the United States is following suit. The modern West lives in the present. Ours is the period of narcissism, an obsession with self. Today's generation disregards history, living a material life in the present and spending as if there were no tomorrow.

Spanish philosopher, poet, and novelist George Santayana (1863–1952) famously said, "Those who cannot remember the past are condemned to repeat it."[19] The late Daniel J. Boorstin, Librarian of Congress, author, historian, lawyer, and professor, voiced a similar wake-up call to the West:

> In our schools today, the story of our nation has been replaced by social studies. . . . In our churches, the effort to see the essential nature of man has been displaced by the social gospel—which is the polemic against the pet vices of today. Our book publishers no longer seek the timeless and the durable, but spend most of their efforts in a fruitless search for à la mode social commentary. . . . Our merchandisers frantically devise their new year models, which will cease to be voguish when their sequels appear three months hence. . . . We have become a nation of short-term doomsayers. In a word, we have lost our sense of history.[20]

Boorstin and Santayana are telling us that we cannot grasp our present or future without understanding our past. Christians, and all who embrace the Judeo-Christian freedoms, must wake up. We are in a battle for the future of our nations and the future of the world. Our continued freedom rests in part on our grasping and responding to the war from the East.

Muslims have a strong interest in history. Their long memories fuel the attitudes and actions of the fundamentalist and jihadist communities. Jihadists are living the current moment of a historical conflict. Not only is this conflict between jihadists and people in the West; it is also between Muslim groups as they fight for the soul of Islam.

CHAPTER 2

The Fight for the Soul of Islam

This is not a film about Islam. It is about the threat of radical Islam. Only a small percentage of the world's 1.3 billion Muslims are radical. This film is about them.
—M. Zuhdi Jasser, *The Third Jihad*

While most of the religions of the world are local and regional, three vie for global dominance. The largest is Christianity with 2.1 billion adherents; atheism is the third largest "religion" with 1.1 billion.[1] Islam is the second largest with 1.5 billion adherents—23 percent of the world's population.[2]

According to a research study by the Pew Forum on Religion and Public Life, Indonesia, with 203 million Muslims, is the country with the largest Muslim population.[3] While we think of the Middle East and North Africa as the home of Islam, because of their smaller populations they represent only about 20 percent of the world's Muslims. Asia-Pacific has the largest percentage of the world's Muslims with more than 60 percent. Sub-Saharan Africa has 15.3 percent, Europe 2.4 percent, and the Americas 0.3 percent.[4]

In this chapter I will provide a brief overview of Islam, then look at the conflict going on within Islam—the fight for the soul of Islam—and finally examine the current state of Muslims around the world.

Overview of Islam

Islam, along with Judaism and Christianity, is one of the world's well-known monotheistic religions. Monotheism stands in contrast to the belief systems of atheism, monism (e.g., Hinduism), and polytheism (e.g., African traditional religions). Muslims believe in one God who is the creator of the heavens and the earth. All three monotheistic religions trace their spiritual genesis back to Abraham.

The term *Islam* is derived from the Arabic word *salama* with the root letters S-L-M ("seen-laam-meem"), meaning "safety" and "peace." *Islam* itself means "accept," "surrender," or "submit." Peace in life can only come from complete submission or surrender to Allah (God Almighty) and Islam. Allah is identified by ninety-nine different names, among them the Creator, the Sustainer, the Merciful, the Compassionate, the Judge, the Transcendent, and the Eternal.

Islam was founded by Muhammad ibn Abdullah, the "final prophet." Muhammad was born in Mecca in the Arabian Peninsula in AD 570 and died sixty-two years later, AD 632, in the city of Medina. Muhammad served as a comprehensive leader of his people, functioning as a religious, political, and military figure. He was appalled by the idols and polytheism of his day and taught the worship of Allah as the one true God.

Muslims, like Jews and Christians, are "People of the Book." They believe that Adam, Nuh (Noah), Ibrahim (Abraham), Musa (Moses), Dawud (David), and Isa (Jesus)—among others—were prophets. They recognize the Torah, the Psalms, and the Gospels as divine revelation. The Qur'an, given to Muhammad, is God's final revelation, superseding the other scriptures.

There are two primary sources of authority for Muslims: the Qur'an and the Sunnah. The Qur'an means "The Recitation" and consists of the revelation of the angel Gabriel to Muhammad over a period of twenty-two years in Mecca and in Medina. The second source of authority is the Sunnah, "The Trodden Path." This "way of the prophet" provides the everyday application of Qur'anic principles through the sayings and lifestyle of Muhammad himself.

The Five Pillars of Islam

The Five Pillars of Islam (*Arkan al-Islam*) are the five common duties of all devout Muslims. By fulfilling these duties a Muslim has a better chance of getting into heaven. They are:

Al-Shahadah—Testimony of Faith. The testimony is: "I bear witness that there is no God but Allah, and I bear witness that Muhammad is his messenger." This is the Muslim declaration of faith. It explicitly establishes a Unitarian, not Trinitarian, nature of God and thus is one of the main points of disagreement with Christianity. It also institutes Muhammad as the final revelation of God.

Al-Salat—Prayer. The Muslim's prayer is an act of worship of Allah. A devout Muslim prays toward the Holy City of Mecca five times a day: before dawn, at noon, afternoon, after dusk, and in the evening.

Al-Zakat—Almsgiving. Almsgiving is seen as a means to purification and growth. It is a combination of tax and charity to help maintain equality in society; a suggested 2.5 percent of a person's accumulated net worth is given to help the poor. In addition, the most devout Muslims will give more in secret.

Al-Sawm—Fasting. Ramadan is the ninth month of the Islamic calendar and is the month of fasting for devout Muslims. During this month Muslims avoid eating, drinking, smoking, and sex from dawn to sundown. The fast is a time for purification and the rededication of one's life to Allah, a time of discipline to help strengthen Muslims against sin.

Al-Hajj—Pilgrimage. The lifetime goal of every Muslim is a pilgrimage to Mecca. The heart of the pilgrimage is to walk around the *Kaaba* (Cube), Muhammad's first place of worship. Tradition has it that Abraham erected the stones here to sacrifice his son. About two million Muslims from every corner of the world complete the hajj each year. Muslims believe that a person who performs the hajj properly will return home as innocent as a newborn baby, free from all sins committed to that point in life.

Branches of Islam

Islam, like Christianity and Judaism, is monotheistic but not uniform. All Muslims share essential beliefs but are divided by theological distinctions, ideas of governance, and religious practice. The two main branches of Islam—Sunni and Shia—make up over 99 percent of all Muslims. Sunnis represent about 85 percent, and Shiites (followers of Shia Islam) about 15 percent. Sunni and Shia Islam also have many subdivisions.

The separation between Sunni and Shia Islam is not primarily about theology but about governance. One group of Muhammad's followers believed that at time of his death, Muhammad had not appointed a replacement. They thought the successor should be a "pious leader" and selected Abu Bakr al-Siddiq, a companion of Muhammad, to be the first caliph (successor). This group became known as the Sunnis, "the followers of [the Prophet's] custom."[5] A second group of Muhammad's followers believed succession should be through bloodline and recognized Muhammad's cousin and son-in-law, Ali ibn Abi Talib, as the rightful heir. Claiming that Ali was appointed before fifty thousand people, they became known as Shiites, from *shi'at Ali*, "supporters or helpers of Ali."

Sunnis are prominent throughout the Islamic world. Al-Sunnah means "principle" or "path," and they follow the path of Muhammad their prophet, believing that the Muslim people should be led by the *khalifah* (caliph) as the head of state, a political leader. Sunnis had a caliphate from 632 until 1924, when it was abolished by the secular Turkish parliament.

Shiites are found in Iran, Yemen, Iraq, Azerbaijan, Lebanon, and Pakistan. They do not honor the caliph as head of state; instead they believe that Islam is to be led by an *imam*, a hereditary descendant of Muhammad from the fourth imam, Ali. The twelfth imam disappeared in 939, and Shiites are waiting for his return as the *Mahdi*, the redeemer of Islam who will rid the earth of evil, injustice, and tyranny.[6]

One minority branch of Islam worth mentioning here is Sufism. Sufis are mystical in their orientation and are viewed as heretics by most Sunnis and Shiites. Sufis devote themselves to developing a personal spirituality and prayer life, focusing on internal aspects rather than the social, economic, and political aspects of Islam.

The Fight for the Soul of Islam

In March 2003 a group of Muslim professionals from Phoenix, Arizona, organized the American Islamic Forum for Democracy to call Muslim Americans away from "political Islam," that is, Islam as a religio-political ideology. Dr. M. Zuhdi Jasser, an internal medicine physician and leader of this initiative, later identified the goal of this movement: "Until the majority of American Muslims can reform their theo-political ideas against the growing global power of the Islamist movement, homegrown terror will only increase as it has. There must be a public war of ideas within the Islamic consciousness promoting liberty over Islamism, freedom over theocracy and secular law over Sharia law."[7]

Dr. Jasser's efforts are commendable. Will Islam coexist with other faiths? Or will it instead demand a society that fuses Islam and politics? A fight for the soul of Islam rages over this very question. On one side are the moderates who believe in revelation and reason and want to engage with the rest of the world on the playing field of ideas. On the other side are the jihadists who reject reason and want to destroy the modern world. The moderates say the jihadists have hijacked a peaceful religion. To the jihadists, the moderates are false

Muslims who have been co-opted by modernity. The more literally a Muslim takes Muhammad's revelation from his time in Medina, the more militant he or she will be.

Before we look at the fight within Islam, the following points must be understood:

- Most Muslims are pragmatists (moderates), not fundamentalists.
- Most fundamentalist Muslims are not terrorists.
- Today most terrorists are Muslims.

Jihadists are fighting and killing Muslims in Sudan, Iraq, Lebanon, and Palestine, to name a few places. They are killing more of their fellow Muslims than of any other group. According to a 2009 West Point study, "The fact is that the vast majority of al-Qa'ida's victims are Muslims: . . . only 15% of the fatalities resulting from al-Qa'ida attacks between 2004 and 2008 were Westerners."[8] In addition, jihadists are killing secularists in Europe and the United States; Christians in Africa, Indonesia, Pakistan, the Philippines, and the United States; Jews in the Middle East; Buddhists in Thailand; and Hindus in Kashmir and India. The jihadists are highly motivated: if they are killed while carrying out "holy war," their reward is an instant pass to heaven. Martyrs don't have to wait for judgment day.

In this section we will examine five conflicting schools of thought within Islam. Then we will track the progression of Muhammad's ideas from his time in Mecca to his time in Medina. Lastly, we will examine the Golden Age of Islam and the return to Islam's fundamentalist past.

The Five Schools of Thought

We have already seen that Islam is monotheistic and contains two major groups: Sunni and Shia. Islam may also be divided into five schools of thought: the pragmatists, the reformers, the secularists, the fundamentalists, and the jihadists.

The *pragmatists* are the majority of the Muslim world. Like other human beings, they want to live and raise their families in a secure environment and have enough to eat. They may have vague objections about conflict between Islam and the rest of the world, but out of fear or desire for security they are silent; they "go along to get along." Pragmatists can be described as "moderate."

The *reformers*, such as Dr. Jasser, believe in both reason and revelation. They view Islam as a progressive, rational, and reforming faith. They want to relate to the world without giving up their faith. They follow Muhammad's Mecca teaching (more on this below) and are natural allies of their fellow monotheists, reasonable Jews and Christians. The reformers are a small but courageous minority. Like the pragmatists, reformers can be described as "moderate."

The *secularists* are Muslims by birth, name, and background, but not by faith. They have rejected Islam as a religion and operate, consciously or subconsciously, from atheistic assumptions. They believe in reason, deny revelation, and typically function from a secular-materialist value system and lifestyle. The brilliant Ayaan Hirsi Ali is an example. She grew up in a strict fundamentalist Muslim home and eventually rejected Islam. After immigrating to Holland, she wrote the provocative book *Infidel* and became a member of the Dutch Parliament.[9] Ali fled Holland after a jihadist fatwa threat was issued against her life. She moved to the United States as an intellectual refugee where she has worked as a resident fellow at the American Enterprise Institute, a conservative think tank.

The *fundamentalists* are literalists who seek to live by the Qur'an and Sunnah. They believe in God's divine revelation through the Qur'an, but deny reason and engagement with the world. Fundamentalists believe the current problems of Islam stem from modernization. They see the moral and spiritual bankruptcy of the West and its polluting effect on the world—especially Islamic nations—and utterly reject it. They are also called restorationists; they want to restore Islam to how it was at the time of Muhammad and his companions. Unlike the jihadists, they are generally nonviolent, but may give sympathy and support to their violent jihadist brothers.

While certainly not as large as the pragmatist community, fundamentalists are greater in number and influence than the reformers or secularists.

The *jihadists* (or Islamists), like their fundamentalist brothers, are also restorationists. They want to return to "true" Islam. They believe in God's divine revelation in the Qur'an but have no place for reason in their faith. Jihadists spring from a minority of Islam's fundamentalists and follow Muhammad's Medina-era teachings, believing that all good Muslims need to raise the sword and destroy moderate Muslims (reformers and secularists who are viewed as kuffar, "infidels"), Israel, and the West.[10] For them, faith relates to every area of life, including social, economic, and political institutions. Islam is to be imposed on the heathen by the sword. Christian author Joel Rosenberg has effectively captured the spirit of this school of Islam: "Islam is the answer and jihad is the way."[11]

My focus in this book is not the silent majority of Muslims but the radicalized jihadists.

Mecca and Medina

As mentioned above, Muhammad's teaching changed after leaving Mecca for Medina. This change has weighty implications and is thus important to understand.

Muhammad was born in Mecca in AD 570 and made his home there for fifty-two years. He claimed to have begun to receive the angel Gabriel's revelation in 610 and launched his mission in 613. This revelation was progressive and continued until Muhammad's death in 632, eventually becoming collected as the Qur'an. His time in Mecca is known as the "building the faith" years. He viewed Christians and Jews as fellow "people of the book" and engaged in peaceful debate with them, seeking to persuade them of the truth of Islam as God's final revelation. Few were persuaded, and Muhammad became frustrated.

In 622 Muhammad, facing opposition, fled Mecca for the city of Medina. This change of location accompanied a transformation in his thinking. Persuasion had produced little fruit, so Muhammad chose a new conversion strategy: coercion. He would now regard the "people of the book" as "infidels" to be converted through warfare.

The move or emigration (*Hijrah*) was a defining moment for the prophet and his religion. Islam changed from a peaceful, persuasive religious movement to a militant religious-political-military movement. The Hijrah was so significant that it marks the first year of the Islamic calendar.

Muhammad and his army conquered Mecca in 630. After his death in 632, his followers, nomadic Arabs, began to sweep out of the Arabian Peninsula into Iraq, Syria, Iran, the Holy Land, and Egypt and the rest of North Africa. Muhammad's Medina teachings were unequivocal: Islam would advance by conquest. The era of peaceful persuasion had ended.[12]

These two distinct periods of Muhammad's life are reflected in the Qur'an. Revelation received in Mecca calls Muslims to enlightenment, whereas the Medina-era revelation commands more strident, less reasoned behavior.

Today moderate Muslims emphasize the "Mecca texts" of the Qur'an. They see Jews and Christians as "people of the book" to be converted through persuasion. Islam is a religion of peace; jihad is a struggle within the believer's soul. The small group of reformers base their views on these portions of the Qur'an. They seek freedom, enlightenment, and peace in a pluralistic society.

The more strident Muslims, the fundamentalists and jihadists, emphasize the Medina parts of the Qur'an. Islam spreads by conquest. Christians and Jews are infidels to be conquered and forced to choose between three alternatives. They can become Muslims, they can submit to *dhimma* (a pact which allows them to live in utter subjugation to Muslim rule and taxation), or they will die. Uniformity and tyranny characterize nations ruled by Islamic law (*sharia*).

This tension between Mecca and Medina thinking has left Islam with two very different concepts regarding reason (*ijtihad* in Arabic). From Mecca, ijtihad emphasizes free enquiry, "rational thinking, and the quest for truth . . . covering science, rationalism, human experience, critical thinking and so on."[13] From Medina, ijtihad adopted a very narrow and legalistic sense, that is, "a process of juristic reasoning employed to determine the permissibility of an action when primary sources, namely the Koran and Sunnah (Tradition of the Prophet), are silent and earlier scholars of shari'a (Islamic law) had not ruled on the matter."[14]

Both sides begin with revelation, but only the reformers have a view of reason and freedom of thought that allows Islam to engage the world in discovery and discourse. Discrepancies within the Qur'an are resolved by fundamentalists through the doctrine of *naskh,* or "abrogation." Ibn Warraq (a pseudonym), a Pakistani-born secularist author and founder of the Institute for the Secularization of Islamic Society, describes the naskh: "When there is a contradiction between verses in the Koran, the later verse supersedes the earlier verse."[15] Thus the jihadists believe that the revelations of Muhammad in Medina supersede the revelations of Muhammad in Mecca. By this method of naskh, conquest takes precedence over persuasion.

It was the Mecca understanding of ijtihad, free inquiry, that led to the Golden Age of Islam.

The Golden Age of Islam
Historian Will Durant, in *The Age of Faith,* describes Islam's glory days: "For five centuries, from 700–1200, Islam led the world in power, in refinement of manners, in standards of living, in human legislation and religious tolerance, in literature, scholarship, science, medicine, and philosophy."[16] This bright period flowed from the caliphates of Damascus, Baghdad, and Córdoba. Muslims, along with Christian and Jewish scholars (the dhimmis), compiled the best thought from the outside world—China, India, Egypt, Persia, North Africa, and Greece—and translated it into Arabic.

During this period, "the peoples of the book" led the world in architecture (Moorish in Spain, the Taj Mahal in India); literature (the tales of Aladdin, Sinbad, and others in *The Thousand and One Nights*); and the visual arts (Persian carpets, ceramics and tiling, painting, metalwork, silk art). In medicine, Avicenna, "the father of modern medicine," developed *The Canon of Medicine,* a million-word systematic summary of the world's medical knowledge of the day. In math, Arabic numerals, algebra (founded by al-Khawarizmi), and algorithms were introduced. In science, Islamic thinkers contributed to experimental physics, optics, experimental psychology, astronomy, and chemistry (Jabir ibn Hayyan was known as the "father of chemistry"). In technology, they contributed to the camera, coffee, the hang glider, hard soap, the suction piston pump, the mechanical clock, the crankshaft, the combination lock, valves, the windmill, the fountain pen, and eyeglasses.

English historian Dean Derhak writes of the primacy of Andalusia, the celebrated region in southern Spain where Europe and Moorish Africa met: "During the end of the first millennium, Cordova was the intellectual well from which European humanity came to drink. Students from France and England traveled there to sit at the feet of Muslim, Christian and Jewish scholars, to learn philosophy, science and medicine. . . . In the great library of Cordova alone, there were some 600,000 manuscripts."[17] Here Muslims, in the true spirit of ijtihad, joined Jewish and Christian scholars to think together.

Missionary, educator, and historian Kenneth Scott Latourette describes the impact of the meeting of Arab, Jewish, and Christian minds in Andalusia: "In the portions of Spain ruled by Moslems were schools controlled by the Arabs in which Christians and Jews as well as Moslems studied. Partly through them more of Greek thought became available to the Christian scholars of Western Europe. . . . Under the impact of this Greek thought, either coming directly or through Moslem Arab intermediaries, the active and eager minds of the Christian scholars of Western Europe were stimulated and shaped as they addressed themselves to theology."[18]

A Return to the Past

The death of the Andalusian vision and the battle for the soul of Islam began anew with the rise of Genghis Khan in the thirteenth century in Central Asia. In 1221 Genghis Khan and his Mongol armies marched into Persia. In 1258 the Mongols captured and destroyed Baghdad and killed the Abbasid caliph.

Ibn Taymiyyah (1263–1328), a Sunni Islamic scholar from Syria, dropped the curtain on the Golden Age of Islam by leading a movement to restore the narrow fundamentalist—Medina—understanding of ijtihad. Revelation remained; reason was confined to its narrowest interpretation. Andalusia faded and died. The irony is that jihadists long for a return to the Golden Age of Islam, but they repudiate the very asset that produced that age: *freedom of thought*, with Muslims, Jews, and Christians reasoning together.

There is a move today among fundamentalist Muslims to return to the tenets of Islam's founding fathers. Salafism is a term used by Sunni theologians to refer to the first three generations of Muslims known as the *Salaf al-Salih* ("Pious Predecessors"), who are considered to reflect Muslim orthodoxy. The Salafis, and the similar Wahhabis, want to return to these predecessors' understanding of the texts and tenants of Islam. Any variation of creed or practice from the Islamic founders is to be avoided.

Today we are witnessing a battle for the soul of Islam. It is the battle between the mind and methods of Mecca and Medina. The strident fundamentalists are in ascendancy; the jihadists are on the march through Muslim lands and beyond in a conflict that has impoverished millions of Muslims around the world.

The Decline of Islam

Islam has declined from its Golden Age of Andalusia into bleakness. The religion that led the world in art, science, medicine, and influence has fallen behind the West and eastern Asia. A friend who has worked among Arabs for years told me, "I can't count how many conversations I have had with people in Muslim nations who bring up this point. They themselves don't understand it. They wonder what went wrong since Andalusia, realizing that the Qur'an and

Hadith haven't changed—so how could the glory of those days have changed so drastically? It is a powerful question/doubt within the religion of Islam."[19]

The reason for this is a change in mindset, figuratively from Mecca to Medina, from the power of persuasion to power of the sword, from revelation and reason to revelation without reason. Generally, shortage of resources does not cause poverty. Rather, poverty is rooted in cultural influences and limited metaphysical capital. The *Arab Human Development Report 2002* proves helpful: "Culture and values are the soul of development . . . instrumental in the sense that they help to shape people's daily hopes, fears, ambitions, attitudes and actions, but they are also formative because they mould people's ideals and inspire their dreams for a fulfilling life for themselves and future generations. . . . Values are not the servants of development; they are its wellspring."[20]

Several essential concepts are absent in Muslim cultures: humans made in the image of God; the dignity of women; free will (Islam is fatalistic); the dignity of labor; freedom of religion, conscience, and speech; the importance of reason and free inquiry; and justice and transparency.

We should weep over the poverty of the Islamic people, especially in light of the glorious days of Andalusia and the immense oil wealth in many Muslim nations. Theirs is not simply material scarcity but another form of human poverty, caused not by lack of ability or resources but by fundamentalist culture and the resulting jihadist violence.[21]

Below we will briefly consider some of the causes and effects of Islam's decline.

Restricted Religious, Economic, and Political Freedom

After the most basic liberties—the right to life and to freedom of conscience—the next is freedom of worship. Fundamentalist Islam opposes pluralism in society and produces religious tyranny. The institution of *mutaween* (religious police), tasked with the enforcement of Islamic law, began in Saudi Arabia, spread to the Taliban in Afghanistan, and is growing in fundamentalist communities in other Muslim states.

A strong corollary exists between religious liberty and economic and political freedom. Countries with the least religious freedom also have the least economic and political liberty. Arab countries are overwhelmingly poor, as Lebanese-born American, Middle East scholar Dr. Fouad Ajami states: "The combined gross national product of twenty-two Arab states . . . was less than that of Spain."[22] Consider these employment and income figures: "About 15 percent, average unemployment across Arab countries is among the highest rates in the developing world. . . . One out of every five people lives on less than $2 per day."[23]

The *Arab Human Development Report* provides a wealth of information on the state of Islam in Arab countries. According to the 2009 *Report in Numbers*, "The vast majority of the Arab regional GDP falls into the high and lower middle income country groups, while over 80 per cent of the Arab population live in the low and lower middle income countries."[24]

The report continues: "The Arab region is one of the two world regions where the number of undernourished has risen since the 1990s. The 25.5 million undernourished people in the region represent nearly one in every 10 people in the Arab countries."[25]

Freedom House's *Freedom in the World 2012* report reveals that 45 percent of the world's population lives in free countries, 31 percent in partly free countries, and 24 percent in not free countries.[26] Most Muslim countries are rated "not free."

The *Arab Human Development Report 2002* catalogues the dearth of freedom in Islamic countries: "This *freedom deficit* undermines human development. . . . While de jure acceptance of democracy and human rights is enshrined in constitutions, legal codes and government pronouncements, de facto implementation is often neglected and, in some cases, deliberately disregarded."[27]

Public trust in government institutions is weak. "The Human Security Survey conducted for the Arab Human Development

Report 2009 found that those who express a strong level of trust in state institutions are in the minority in all four Arab countries included in the study."[28]

"In six Arab countries, there is outright prohibition on the formation of political parties. In others, restrictions and extended emergency rule often amount to *de facto* prohibition. Thousands of political prisoners are incarcerated across the Arab region."[29]

"The rule of law indicator rates the Arab region as the second worst in the world [better only than sub-Saharan Africa]. Performance on that indicator deteriorated in that region between 1998 and 2007."[30]

Restricted Freedom of Inquiry

Freedom of inquiry reflects a people's liberty to engage with ideas from abroad. Dr. Fouad Ajami speaks of educational limitations in Muslim lands: "Approximately 40 percent of adult Arabs were illiterate; only 1.6 percent of the population had access to the Internet, a figure lower than in the states of sub-Saharan Africa. The entire Arab world translated fewer foreign books than Greece."[31] Some sixty-five million Arabs are illiterate, two-thirds of them women.[32] "No more than 10,000 books were translated into Arabic over the entire past millennium, equivalent to the number translated into Spanish each year."[33]

What does Islamic free expression look like? "In the Arab world, restrictions imposed on freedom take the form of legal constraints on publications, associations, general assemblies and electronic media, which prevent those from carrying out their communicative and cultural roles."[34]

A friend who has worked for years in the Middle East tells of talking with some neighbor girls who attended the Qur'anic school. "I asked them what they were learning and got the standard answer 'Qur'an' or 'There is no god but Allah, and Muhammad is his messenger.' I asked them if they ever have questions that they ask their imam. With faces aghast they exclaimed that they could never ask questions. If they do they get hit with the stick or sent home in shame to face the harsher sentence of their parents."[35] Andalusian spirit has been purged from Arab cultures.

Corruption

Corruption is a major barrier to economic and political freedom. Historically, countries birthed in the Judeo-Christian worldview of northern Europe and North America have been the least corrupt. According to the Transparency International 2007 Corruption Perception Report, in the ranking of 179 countries "there are no Muslim countries in the top 10 (least corrupt) countries. There are none in the top 20. There are none in the top 30. The least corrupt Muslim country on the list is Qatar, number 32."[36]

Technological Deficit

During Islam's Golden Age, Arabs and dhimmi scholars led the world in science and technology; today Muslims are falling behind. One measure is that of scientific publications. Dr. Athar Osama, engineer and public policy researcher, writes of the dearth of scientific publications in the Islamic world: "Muslim countries contribute just 2.5 percent of more than 11.5 million papers published worldwide each year. This reflects the low value placed on scientific research in general, and publishing research findings in particular, within much of the Islamic world."[37]

The Unknown Future

Again, we should weep at the poverty in the Muslim world. In addition, Christians should remember that in terms of basic beliefs, we have more in common with our fellow monotheists than we have with atheists. Among other things, we believe there is a Creator who has revealed himself to mankind through a book, and we believe in a moral universe. These and other monotheistic commonalities stand in stark contrast to atheism's naturalistic, impersonal, and amoral concept of reality. Whether Christians' and Muslims' sense of mutuality grows or fades depends on the outcome of the current battle for the soul of Islam.

At this writing, revolution is in the air throughout North Africa and the Middle East. Called "the Arab Spring" by Western media, this is a largely a generational conflict between the older autocratic order and those who are younger and who express a longing to "breathe free." At this point, however, it looks like the Arab Spring will become an "Arab Winter." It seems the young reformers and secularists at the front of the revolt are being replaced by jihadists and fundamentalists. Instead of freedom and the rule of law, sharia is becoming the law of the land. Old autocrats are being replaced with new religious tyrants. We must understand that it takes more than a revolution to bring freedom. Freedom, as we shall see later, is born out the narrative of Judeo-Christian theism, out of a biblical worldview and principles.

As the fight for the soul of Islam continues, radical Muslims are seeking to conquer the world through violent means. They are actively engaged in jihad, which we will now examine.

CHAPTER 3

The Tyranny of Jihad

We shall never call for, nor accept, peace. We shall only accept war
and the restoration of the usurped land. We have resolved to drench
this land with our blood, to oust you, aggressors, and to throw you
into the sea for good.

—HAFEZ AL-ASSAD

To Muslims the world can be divided between those who are faithful to Allah and those who do not know him. Sayyid Qutb (1906–66), author, poet and intellectual father of modern Muslim militancy, identifies two kinds of societies: Islamic and *jahil* (ignorant).[1]

Stated another way, the world is divided between *Dar al-Islam* and *Dar al-Harb*—the House of Islam and the House of War. The House of Islam is governed by Muslims under sharia (Islamic law). Most faithful Muslims share one mission: to bring the whole world into a system of governance marked by the religious-political authority and uniformity of Islam. As we have seen, some Muslims seek to accomplish this through persuasion, while others employ tyranny.

All people not living by sharia are *jahiliyya* (the ignorant) and as such comprise Dar al-Harb, the House of War. Whole nations—those such as the United States and England and moderate Muslim countries such as Morocco and Jordan—are *jahiliyya*. Therefore, they are in a perpetual state of war with Dar al-Islam until they either submit to Islamic faith or are conquered by the sword.

The House of War is engaged in a battle with only one acceptable end. The war will be fought until every person and nation joins the House of Islam and the ignorant proclaim the Shahadah: "I bear witness that there is no god but Allah, and Muhammad is his messenger" (English translation).

Based on Muhammad's life, Sayyid Qutb speaks of several stages of Islamic war: "a peaceful time of preparation, a migration, the creation of an Islamic state, and finally open warfare."[2]

Throughout history, civilizations have sought to restrain war's most heinous practices. The Geneva Convention, developed after the atrocities of World War II, was a major modern attempt to "humanize" warfare. So, too, Muslims have set boundaries. As Mary Habeck points out, "Islamic jurisprudents used the Qur'an, hadith, and life of Muhammad to determine the Islamically correct way to conduct war. The majority determined that noncombatant women, children, and monks or nuns could not be killed; the captives should not be slaughtered outright; and that even animals and trees had certain rights."[3]

Jihadists, however, reject such restrictions, whether proposed by international communities or by moderate fellow Muslims. To jihadists, sharia takes precedence over international law. They advocate terrorizing both civilians and nations into submission. Their war is a no-holds-barred conflict.

The Meaning of Jihad

The word *jihad* occurs throughout the Qur'an and means "to strive, to struggle, to strive in the way of Allah." Jihad has three traditional understandings, two of which reflect the Mecca texts and one of which reflects the Medina texts of the Qur'an. Almost a hundred percent of the time, jihad refers to violent conflict and is understood as such, not simply by extremists but by the vast majority of all Muslims. The tiny minority of Sufi, the mystical impulse within Islam, understands jihad as an inner striving for perfection. Reformers and other moderates see jihad—their "sixth pillar of Islam"—as persuading non-Muslims of the veracity of their faith.

The West stumbles when she fails to note these distinctions. Sufis and reformers may interpret jihad as something other than violence, but these groups are seen as infidels and are not taken seriously by the jihadists and other fundamentalists who understand jihad as violence and fighting for the true religion.

In 1981 extremist Ayatollah Ruhollah Musavi Khomeini called Muslims to war against infidels: "Muslims have no alternative if they wish to enforce those in power to conform to the laws and principles of Islam. Holy war means the conquest of all non-Muslim territories, and *this war is the duty of all Muslims*."[4]

Holy War is declared against the *kuffar,* people or states that do not recognize Allah or Muhammad, the prophet of Allah. *Kuffar* (singular *kafir*) comes from the Arabic root meaning "to cover" and refers to those who cover up truth. There are two types of *kuffar.* The first is all non-Muslims, including people of other faiths, atheists, and pagans. The second is Muslims who become apostate. The action of one Muslim declaring another Muslim apostate is called *takfir,* and for jihadists it is right to kill apostates.[5] Muslims may be declared apostate if they become too closely aligned with the West.[6] Often the declaration of takfir is followed by a fatwa (usually the ruling of a *mufti,* an Islamic scholar of law). Such an injunction amounts to putting out a contract on a person's life, allowing jihadists to kill with impunity.

Two Jihadist Visions

While jihadists are attacking the West and moderate Muslims, it is important to understand that they also attack each other. This is the result of the historical division between Shia Islam and Sunni Islam (see chapter 2). The division between Shia and Sunni has resulted in bloodshed at various times throughout history. The Iran-Iraq War (1980–88) is a tragic example of this feud, in this case between secular Sunnis of Iraq (who ruled over a majority Shiite population) and religious Shiites of Iran.

Two jihadist visions have sprung from the division between Sunni and Shia Islam. While both Sunni and Shiite jihadists want to see Islam rule the world, Sunni jihadists strive to fulfill their vision by violent purification of the world, whereas Shiite jihadists seek to begin a global military conflict. Both visions stand in contrast to more moderate Muslims who seek to spread Islam through nonviolent means.

Of the various Sunni jihadist groups, perhaps the most well known is al-Qaeda, led by the late Osama bin Laden and Dr. Ayman al-Zawahiri. Their goal is "to establish the truth, get rid of evil, and establish an Islamic nation."[7]

The Shiite front of jihad is led by the spiritual Supreme Leader of Iran, Ali Khamenei, and the radical Iranian president, Mahmoud Ahmadinejad. Their goal is world domination, as expressed by Ayatollah Khamenei: "We shall export our revolution to the whole world. Until the cry 'Allah Akbar' resounds over the whole world, there will be struggle. There will be Ji'had. . . . Islam is the religion of militant individuals. . . . Islam will be victorious in all the countries of the world, and Islam and the teachings of the Koran will prevail all over the world."[8]

The Culture of Death

The Judeo-Christian worldview promotes a culture of life. Because humans are made in the image of God, every individual has intrinsic worth and a God-given right to life. All human life, from conception to natural death, at any level of society, is sacred. I firmly believe that living things are hardwired for life and instinctively regard death as an enemy.

A single human life is of absolute significance. This is the message of Stephen Spielberg's 1998 award-winning film, based on a true story, *Saving Private Ryan*. During the allied invasion of Normandy in World War II, a small group of US soldiers was sent to rescue Private Ryan, whose three brothers had already been killed in the war. These young men put their own lives in extreme jeopardy to save the life of one man, the last living son of his family.

Jihadists are raised in a culture of death. They are trained to deny their natural hardwiring in favor of death. As bin Laden said in his "Declaration of War": "These youths [the jihadists] love death as you love life."[9] The widespread practice of suicide bombing reveals that jihadists hate moderate Muslims, Israel, and the West more than they love life.

Israeli Prime Minister Golda Meir captured with unforgettable clarity this culture of death in a 1957 statement to the National Press Club in Washington, DC. "Peace will come when the Arabs will love their children more than they hate us," she said, implying that many Palestinian mothers hate Israel more than they love their own children.[10] A dozen years later at a London Press conference Meir said, "When peace comes we will perhaps in time be able to forgive the Arabs for killing our sons, but it will be harder for us to forgive them for having forced us to kill their sons."[11]

Sheikh Yusuf al-Qaradawi, the Muslim "theologian of terror," has stated, "The Israelis might have nuclear bombs but we have the children bomb and these human bombs must continue until liberation."[12] Middle East expert Walid Phares writes that jihadists "praise death as a weapon to bring about victory, but they also worship the concept of killing for the sake of ideology. *'Naashaq'ul maout kama taashaqun al hayat' ('we are in love with death')*."[13]

The Hamas website proclaims: "With Allah's grace, we have raised an ideological generation that loves death as much as our enemies love life."[14]

Martyrdom in the service of Allah guarantees immediate access to paradise. The death of Ibn Omar Muhammad, a volunteer commander in the Popular Defense Forces of Northern Sudan, was followed, not by a funeral, but by his "wedding." His family dressed the corpse as a bridegroom and seventy-two virgins were the brides.[15]

Jihad's symbol is the sword: conquering the world for Allah. The symbol of Christianity is the cross: sacrificing self that others may live. Jihad calls her sons to kill for Allah to achieve salvation. Christianity's God sent his only Son to die for our salvation. Jihad achieves righteousness by works: entering paradise by killing infidels. Christianity teaches righteousness by grace: salvation by faith in the finished work of Christ on the cross.

Jihadist Tactics

Islam is spread through both nonviolent and violent means. Most Muslims abhor violence, choosing words and life-affirming actions to further their religion. Jihadists, on the other hand, use any means, including violence, to reach their desired goal.

Technology and Propaganda

Jihadist groups use the Internet and digital technology to engage Muslims in the struggle. Without the constraints of government structures, jihadists can quickly mobilize Muslims through the Internet and satellite television. In September 2005, when a Danish newspaper printed political cartoons of Muhammad, word spread on Islamic news sites, and riots erupted almost instantly throughout the Muslim world and Europe.

Education

Another jihadist tactic has been an explosion in the founding of *madrassas*, Islamic religious schools. Madrassas do not teach math, science, art, history, literature, or reasoning, but focus rather on Islamic religious instruction. Pulitzer laureate Thomas Friedman writes: "For many young Pakistani boys, the only way to get an education and three meals a day was by going to one of these madrasas. In 1978 there were three thousand madrasas in Pakistan and now there are thirty-nine thousand—the vast majority of them factories churning out young men who are unprepared for modernity, have little exposure to women and are hostile to everything the West stands for."[16]

Saudi oil wealth has funded Wahhabi schools around the world as well as Islamic studies departments at major Western universities. Alex Alexiev, senior fellow of the Center for Security Policy notes, "While nobody knows for sure how much the Saudis have spent on getting a foothold in non-Muslim regions and especially in Western Europe and North America, the sums are clearly huge. According to official information, the Saudis have built over 1,500 mosques, 210 Islamic centers, 202 Islamic colleges and 2,000 schools for educating Muslims in non-Muslim countries."[17] In addition to Islamic Cultural Centers, mosques are being built on the campuses of major US universities all over the country.

Sharia

Fundamentalists seek to create "parallel societies" in their adopted lands around the world not only through the maintenance of their ethnic language and culture, but also through the use of sharia in their own communities. Sharia allows for "honor killing" by the males in the family of a female family member who has been adulterous, flirtatious, or raped. Such acts break the family honor. The offending party must die to restore the honor. Honor killings are now happening in the United States and Europe. On October 20, 2009, Noor Almaleki died in Peoria, Arizona, after her father, Faleh Hassan Almaleki, ran over her with the family car. Noor had brought shame on her family by becoming too Westernized, refusing an arranged marriage back in Iraq, and living with an American boyfriend and his mother, all grounds for murder under sharia.[18] Almaleki was convicted of second-degree murder in February 2011.

Deception

Deception (*taqiya*) is a virtue in Dar al-Islam, a tactic in the jihadist struggle against its enemies. To distort, conceal, or lie for the advancement of Islam is a good thing. In many parts of the world, politicians are rarely known for their integrity; this is similarly true of Muslim leaders. As an example, Yasir Arafat, the late secularist Palestinian president, often took taqiya to new levels. When addressing the English-speaking world, Arafat claimed to support peace with Israel to end the Palestinian-Israeli conflict. But when speaking in Arabic to the Muslim world, he called for endless jihad until Israel was removed from the face of the earth. The Judeo-Christian heritage of trust and honesty, so critical for a free and prosperous society, is despised and rejected by jihadists. No wonder so many Islamic societies are poor in the midst of plenty.

Tactical Peace

Tactical peace (*hudna*) is not a permanent peace but a cease-fire or temporary end to hostilities, allowing jihadists to rearm, regroup, and prepare to fight again. Dr. David Bukay, professor of Middle East studies at the University of Haifa, writes: "Arabs view peace as a tactical means for achieving their strategic objective, by defeating the enemy. Peace constitutes a temporary break in the ongoing war against the enemy, until Islam controls the whole world."[19] We have seen such hudnas countless times in the Middle East conflict. The ceasefire in the 2006 Israel-Hezbollah War was the occasion for the jihadists to rebuild and rearm their forces, preparing for their next attack.

Extremists have little hope of an outright military defeat of the United States and her Western allies. But if they can create terror in the hearts of civilian populations, perhaps Western governments will capitulate to jihadists' demands. Such a pattern has been repeatedly seen in Europe and in the United States.

Bombings

We have already mentioned some of the bombings that were part of the pre- and post-9/11 tactics. Since 9/11, bombings in Bali, Madrid, and London claimed numerous Western lives. The Mumbai bombing also took many lives in India. Almost weekly a terrorist bomb explodes somewhere, though many other plots are thwarted.

Hijacking

One of the earliest terrorist tactics was hijacking planes and ships. The four planes commandeered on 9/11 were the most dramatic example.

Kidnapping and Hostage Taking

Perhaps the most famous example of the taking of hostages occurred November 4, 1979, when a group of Iranian students and Islamic militants overwhelmed the US embassy in Tehran and held fifty-three Americans hostage for 444 days. Islamists have also taken hostages in other countries, such as the Philippines and Yemen.

Executions

On January 23, 2002, al-Qaeda jihadists snatched American Jewish journalist Daniel Pearl in Karachi, Pakistan. During the following week he was beaten and tortured before being decapitated on camera.

Use of Children

Jihadists routinely use women, children, and seniors as human shields, often taking firing positions behind crowds of civilians, or placing military equipment on or near school grounds, hospitals, and mosques, daring the infidels to attack them. On March 20, 2007, a car approached a military checkpoint in Baghdad. US soldiers, noting two children in the back seat, cleared the vehicle. Once through the checkpoint, the adults jumped out of the front seat and detonated a bomb, which destroyed the car with the children still inside.[20]

Until the whole world is the House of Islam, jihadists will combat the rest of the world, the House of War. They are fighting for a religious-political empire, a global caliphate.

The Global Caliphate

The Arabic term *ummah,* "community of believers" or "nation," refers to the global Muslim community. Islamists seek an ummah without frontiers. While reformed and other moderate Muslims are content to live in a pluralistic society, fundamentalists and jihadists want nothing less than a global caliphate.

As mentioned before, the word *caliphate* comes from the Arabic *khalifah,* which denotes the head of state, or caliph. The caliph is a religious and political leader who applies sharia throughout society, not simply in the religious arena. Jihadists are not content to govern their own nations; as globalists, they intend to replace all states with one Islamic empire. They want not a union of diverse nations but uniformity under sharia. Their goal is Dar al-Islam.

Lebanese-born American Dr. Walid Phares is an expert on Middle Eastern affairs and global terrorism. He states, "The Caliphate wasn't just an office to interpret holy texts but it was also a real Governance and power position; the equivalent to the Papacy and Emperor rolled into one."[21]

Islam once had caliphates from Afghanistan in the east to Portugal in the west, from North Africa in the south to southern Europe in the north. Christian Byzantine emperor Justinian I built the Hagia Sophia, one of the world's most beautiful cathedrals. When the Muslims conquered Constantinople (present-day Istanbul, Turkey), they converted the Hagia Sophia into a mosque. A friend told me of her visit to this sixth-century structure, which was converted to a museum in the 1930s by Atatürk, the secularist president of Turkey. She recalled the guides pointing with pride to the medallions with the inscribed names of the first four caliphs and speaking of their expectation that one day caliphs will rule again.

Jihadists are engaged in a threefold mission, or *dawa,* relative to the caliphate. The first goal is to restore to Islam all lands that were once part of a caliphate. This precludes peace with Israel; Israel as a nation-state must disappear. Second, they want to expand the caliphate to include the fifty-seven Islamic nations of the world. The final stage is ridding the world of Western moral and spiritual bankruptcy by finishing the dawa and establishing a global caliphate.

These sobering words from Dr. Walid Phares effectively summarize this section:

> The term "Caliphate," with all its linguistic and doctrinal derivatives in today's Salafi terminology, is as charged and politicized as the "Third Reich" was to the National-Socialists during WWII. The "Caliphate" epitomizes all that the Jihadists are preparing for, working towards, and killing for. This word IS at the center of the War with Terrorism. . . . The bringing back of the "Caliphate" is the chief reason why Osama Bin Laden, Ayman Zawahiri, Zarqawi, and Adam Gadahn have declared and waged a war against the people of the United States. Given its centrality to the Jihadist activities, the term must be treated seriously.[22]

Presently, the United Nations recognizes 192 sovereign states and their territories. Another eleven entities claim, or are seeking, statehood but are not universally recognized. Examples include the State of the Vatican City, a sovereign entity which is widely but not universally recognized; Taiwan, which claims sovereignty but is recognized by the UN as a territory of the People's Republic of China; and the Palestinian people, who long to emerge from their state of limbo into nationhood.

The jihadists want to change all this. In their vision, the world's 203 states would cease to exist. Jihadists decry nationalism. They reject borders of any nation, seeking instead for one global caliphate, Dar al-Islam—the House of Islam.

Which leads to an important question: Is Islam a religion of peace?

A Religion of Peace?

Within a week after September 11, President George W. Bush visited the Islamic Center of Washington, DC, to build bridges with the Islamic community and calm the fears of the American people. During his brief talk he identified Islam as a religion of peace: "The face of terror is not the true faith of Islam. That's not what Islam is all about. Islam is peace. These terrorists don't represent peace. They represent evil and war."[23]

Is Islam a religion of peace? More importantly, is the Western concept of peace, derived from the Bible and rooted in the Messiah of Peace, equivalent to the Muslim view of peace?

Examining the root of the Western concept of peace as established by the Old and New Testament scriptures allows us to compare it with the Islamic concept of peace.

In the Old Testament, the word translated "peace" is *shalom*. Its range of meanings include: prosperity (favorable circumstances); completeness (the fullness of a collection); safeness/salvation (free from danger); health (well-being or wholeness); satisfaction/contentment; and blessing (giving kindness to another).[24] We often speak of shalom as the fulfillment of human existence: welfare, health, and freedom from worry. In the New Testament, the word translated "peace" is *eirēnē*. It means harmony, tranquillity.[25]

These biblical concepts are reflected in Webster's 1828 *American Dictionary of the English Language*, which defines peace this way: "To be at peace, to be reconciled; to live in harmony. Heavenly rest; the happiness of heaven. Public tranquillity; that quiet, order and security which is guaranteed by the laws."[26] In the West, then, peace means harmony, communion, completeness, tranquillity, serenity, health, welfare, and security—freedom from war or danger and freedom from anxiety or worry.

We must avoid the temptation to assume that Islam shares our Western understanding of peace. As we saw before, the term *Islam*, derived from the Arabic root translated "safety" or "peace," literally means "accept," "surrender," or "submit." Peace comes only in complete submission or surrender to Allah and Islam.

Just as the Unitarian concept of God in Islam differs from the Trinitarian concept of the Bible, so also the Muslim and Christian concepts of peace are very different. Dr. Syed Kamran Mirza, member of the Institute for the Secularization of Islamic Society, describes the nature of Islamic peace: "Islamic understanding of peace means submission or surrender. Peace comes (according to Islam) only after one surrenders or submits one's self. Submission or surrender to whom? Submission to only Allah and his messenger Muhammad. Therefore peace (Islamic) exists only inside the *Dar-ul-Islam*—the house of submission, after the conversion to Islam."[27]

In correspondence with non-Muslim contemporaries, Muhammad used the Arabic phrase *Aslim Taslam,* "accept Islam and you will be saved."[28] Islamic peace is derived from surrender to Allah and the Qur'an.

Syrian-born Muslim reformer Bassam Tibi, professor of international relations at Göttingen University, warns of the need to differentiate between the Western and Islamic concepts of peace: "First, both sides should acknowledge candidly that although they might use identical terms these mean different things to each of them. The word 'peace,' for example, implies to a Muslim the extension of the Dar al-Islam—or 'House of Islam'—to the entire world."[29]

Uwe Siemon-Netto, a United Press international religion correspondent, comments on Professor Tibi's work: "According to Tibi, the quest of converting the entire world to Islam is an immutable fixture of the Muslim worldview. Only if this task is accomplished—if the world has become 'Dar al-Islam'—will it also be a 'Dar a-Salam,' or a house of peace."[30] The goal of Islamists is to expand the borders of Dar al-Islam at the expense of Dar al-Harb.

Islamists equate the terms "sword" and "surrender." Conversion in jihad is by force, at the edge of the sword. This contrasts with Judeo-Christian conversion through persuasion and emancipation. As the symbol of Islam, the sword appears on the flags of several

Muslim nations and societies, including Oman, Afghanistan, and Hamas. The Saudi flag has the sword, as well as an abbreviated version of the Islamic Shahadah, testimony of faith: "No God but Allah and Muhammad is his messenger."

Is Islam a religion of peace? Yes and no. Yes, Islam believes in peace, but no, not peace as defined by the West. Peace in the view of Islam means surrender, a head bowed before the sword. One cannot grasp Islam without understanding how it uses terms like "peace."

A Beachhead in the West

Islam is establishing a beachhead in the West, filling the profound spiritual vacuum that already characterizes Europe and that is growing in the United States. A British university estimates that one hundred thousand people in England have converted to Islam.[31] NBC News reports that in the United States twenty thousand people convert each year, with four female converts for each male.[32] The Judeo-Christian culture of the West promotes freedom of religion, but Islam knows nothing of this freedom. In many Islamic countries a Muslim comes to Christ on pain of death.

The FBI recently reported that "of the two thousand mosques in the United States, 10% preach Jihad."[33] These sermons, it appears, are bearing fruit. Hezbollah, al-Qaeda, and smaller, less-known groups have cells throughout the United States. These cells enlist and train home-grown terrorists for US and global attacks. Reformist Muslim and physician Dr. M. Zuhdi Jasser has documented the jihadist vision and movement in the United States in his groundbreaking documentary film *The Third Jihad*.[34]

An article titled "American Jihadist Cell Planned Attacks in Israel, Jordan, Kosovo" reported on the arrest and indictment of a terrorist group led by Daniel Boyd, a native of North Carolina, in July 2009: "Eight men, including seven living in North Carolina, were indicted Monday by a U.S. Federal Grand Jury for planning . . . to carry out 'violent jihad' . . . in Israel, Jordan and Kosovo. To this end members of the cell stockpiled weapons, trained at a camp set up in North Carolina, traveled to the Middle East and Kosovo, and recruited fellow Muslims. They are also charged with providing assistance to terrorists, including weapons training, fundraising and travel arrangements."[35]

In October 2002 John Allen Muhammad and Lee Boyd Malvo—the Beltway Snipers—began a random shooting spree in Virginia, Maryland, and Washington, DC. Over three weeks, they killed ten people and seriously injured three. After they were apprehended, the press largely ignored the fact that both men were Muslims and the possibility that their acts could be jihad. In jail, Malvo, the younger of the two killers, drew a portrait of himself and Mr. Muhammad with the statement, "We will kill them all. Jihad . . . Allahu Akbar!" Another drawing included a poem written by the current prime minister of Turkey, Recep Tayyip Erdogan, which reads, "Our minarets are our bayonets, Our mosques are our barracks, Our believers are our soldiers."[36] Also largely ignored by the media was that Muhammad was convicted "under a previously untested terrorism law" in which "the killing was 'pursuant to the direction or order' of someone engaged in an act of terrorism."[37]

Major Nidal Malik Hasan, a US Army psychiatrist, attended one of the largest mosques in the United States, Dar al-Hijrah in Falls Church, Virginia. Authorities believe Hasan was a student of the radical cleric Anwar al-Awlaki, who taught at this mosque.[38] In June 2007 Hasan shocked his fellow physicians when, instead of the scheduled lecture on a medical topic, he gave a presentation entitled *A Koranic World View as It Relates to Muslims in the U.S. Military.*[39] On November 6, 2009, Major Hasan opened fire at Fort Hood, Texas, reportedly shouting, "Allahu Akbar" (God is great), as he systematically killed fourteen (including an unborn baby) and wounded thirty.

Islamists find America's prisons fruitful territory for proselytizing young inmates from impoverished and dysfunctional backgrounds. Prison Fellowship founder Chuck Colson has raised the issue as has FBI Director Robert Mueller, who called America's prisons "fertile ground for extremists."[40] In a hearing before the Committee on Homeland Security and Governmental Affairs, Senator Susan M. Collins spoke of "the prison population [being] particularly ripe for radicalization."[41] Attorney General Alberto Gonzales has stated, "The threat of homegrown terrorist cells— radicalized online, in prisons and in other groups of socially isolated souls—may be as dangerous as groups like al Qaeda, if not more so."[42]

These examples should be enough to show that the threat of jihad is very real, whether or not Westerners recognize it or want to believe it. Those who value freedom must wake up to the reality of the war from the East. Christians, as we will see in the second part of this book, have an opportunity to demonstrate the power of love over hate in this battle of worldviews.

But before we get to that point, we must face another reality: we are in the midst of another war, one going on within our own culture. And this war, we will see, bears directly on the war from the East.

CHAPTER 4

The War in the West:
The Culture Wars

Our country is founded on a sham: our forefathers were slave-owning rich white guys who wanted it their way. So when I see the American flag, I go, "Oh my God, you're insulting me." That you can have a gay parade on Christopher Street in New York, with naked men and women on a float cheering, "We're here, we're queer!"—that's what makes my heart swell. Not the flag, but a gay naked man or woman burning the flag. I get choked up with pride.
—Janeane Garofalo

Generations of Americans have thrilled at the sight of the Stars and Stripes; Janeane Garofalo's goose bumps are created by naked homosexuals burning the American flag. A fight is on for the soul of the West. At stake is the very essence of Western society as a whole and the United States of America in particular.[1]

In the first three chapters we examined the external threat to the Western world, the war from the East. Now we turn to an internal crisis. The war in the West is a battle of ideas, ideals, and vision, rooted in opposing worldviews. It is a culture war. One side will win and one will lose. The battle was lost in Europe as the cultural consensus steadily denied the rich Christian heritage that founded Western civilization. In the United States, the battle is still being fought. The worldview that wins will decide the nature of American society and whether we will continue to live as a free nation. It will also determine the way in which the West responds to the war from the East.

The Foundation of a Nation

John Adams, who became America's second president, noted in January 1776: "The foundation of every government is some principle or passion in the minds of the people. The noblest principles and most generous affections in our nature, then, have the fairest chance to support the noblest and most generous models of government."[2]

Similarly, the great Russian novelist Aleksandr Solzhenitsyn wrote, "The strength or weakness of a society depends more on the level of its spiritual life than on its level of industrialization. Neither a market economy nor even general abundance constitutes the crowning achievement of human life. If a nation's spiritual energies have been exhausted, it will not be saved from collapse by the most perfect government structure or by any industrial development."[3]

Nations are founded on religious ideals and convictions, which, in turn, shape the culture. In other words, culture is a manifestation of worship. The *cult* (system of worship), be it atheistic, demonic, or theistic, will produce the *culture* of a people. The culture, in turn, establishes the first principles upon which the social, economic, and political structures, institutions, and laws of a society are established. Thus, the spiritual realm impacts the natural realm through culture.

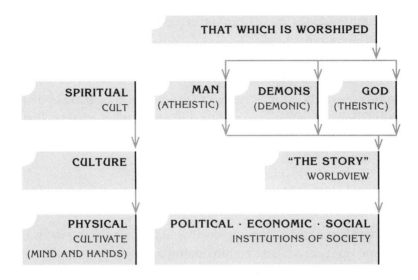

Figure 1. The spiritual impacts the physical through culture

Dr. Bruce Frohnen, law professor and senior fellow at the Russell Kirk Center for Cultural Renewal, explains:

> Culture comes from the cult. This is no mere wordplay. Culture and cult share a common root in the Latin, colere, which means to cultivate, as in cultivating one's garden or one's character, developing the proper, elevated habits. . . . A people grow together from its common worship. As a people develop common liturgical habits . . . they also develop social habits concerning things like cuisine, art, and daily ritual. These common habits bind them together as a people into a common culture. They also tie, forever, the culture of a people with its common religion.[4]

Historian Russell Kirk confirms that "culture arises from the cult; . . . when belief in the cult has been wretchedly enfeebled, the culture will decay swiftly. The material order rests upon the spiritual order. . . . The culture can be renewed only if the cult is renewed;

and faith in divine power cannot be summoned up merely when that is found expedient."[5]

The cultures we create reflect the gods we worship. A society cannot be founded except religiously. When the religious foundations of a society crumble, either the society will collapse or a new foundation will be laid to create a different kind of society. This is the situation we are currently facing in America.

Two Nations, One Geography

America is one nation geographically, but it is two nations in vision. Author, political advisor, commentator, and syndicated columnist Pat Buchanan is one of the West's "culture warriors." His account of the current division in America is on target: "We no longer inhabit the same moral universe. We are no longer a moral community. We are two countries. One part of America has seceded, and the other has no interest in re-establishing the Union."[6] Likewise, in his book *America's Real War*, Rabbi Daniel Lapin writes, "We are no longer one nation under God. We are two separate nations with two distinct and incompatible moral visions."[7]

We see this polarization in many dimensions of life in the United States: the Supreme Court, the electorate, a trove of issues including the sanctity of life and the nature of marriage, liberals vs. conservatives, Republicans vs. Democrats, rural Americans vs. urban Americans.

During the 2000 presidential election, the late television journalist Tim Russert popularized the terms "red states" and "blue states"—those leaning Republican and those leaning Democrat. News anchors referred to maps showing the vast mid-section of America, dubbed the "flyover states," in red. The large cities and media centers were blue. Pundits portray this as political reality, but I argue that it lies at the deeper level of worldview. Political platforms build on deeper principles such as the "sacredness of life" versus a "woman's right to choose."

These principles derive from paradigms. For example, the biblical paradigm affirms that people are made in the image of God; thus, life is sacred. It follows that policies and parties grounded in the Judeo-Christian worldview seek to protect human life. Atheistic materialism, on the other hand, sees human beings simply as animals; the Darwinian principle of the survival of the fittest prevails. Such a paradigm leads inevitably to abortion: an adult has the power (and deserves the right) to end the life of her weaker baby. From this perspective derive policies, parties, and laws that support abortion.

Too often in the struggle for a nation, however, we confuse *issues* with *the* issue. We should be concerned about abortion, cohabitation, out-of-wedlock births, racism, economic and political corruption, sexual slavery, divorce, school violence, drug addiction, and the destruction of the environment. We need to resist such evils in our programs and policies. These issues are important, but none of these is *the* issue. They reveal the true issue. We must not settle for winning individual battles while losing the war. *The* issue is a clash of worldviews, one theistic and the other atheistic. We must address the above concerns through programs and policies, yes. But if we fail to fight the battle at the level of principle and paradigm, we will ultimately lose the war.

Two Worldviews

This battle transcends differences in politics, race, or gender. It lies deeper than Republican vs. Democrat, black vs. white, women vs. men. This is a battle of sacred belief systems, worldviews, and ideologies. Opposing faith systems are competing for the soul of the West. Theism, on one side, recognizes the Creator and transcendent reality. Judeo-Christian theists believe in reason and revelation (see chapter 15). They affirm one nation under God; whether they will fight for it remains to be seen. Atheism, on the other side, denies God. Nature is all that exists. Man is the center of the universe. There is no revelation, only reason. These are children of the Enlightenment.

The same divide exists between Europe and North America. François Heisbourg, director of the Paris-based Foundation of Strategic Research, reflects on the gap of moral vision: "The biblical references in politics, the division of the world between good and evil, these are things that we [Europeans] simply don't get. . . . In a number of areas, it seems to me that we are no longer part of the same civilization."[8] The two continents had a common history and culture, but Europe has already severed her roots and America is hacking away.

The outcome of this conflict will decide which moral and metaphysical framework will govern life in the United States and influence the rest of the West and the world. One set of beliefs will form the basis of national laws. One, as we will explore later, will decide what is true, good, and beautiful.

Over 150 years ago Abraham Lincoln understood this conflict of visions. He gave his "House Divided" speech on June 16, 1858, in Springfield, Illinois, as he accepted the Republican nomination for the US Senate. In it he paraphrased Jesus' words in Matthew 12:25: "Every kingdom divided against itself will be ruined, and every city or household divided against itself will not stand." The United States was divided over slavery. This rift appeared when one side dismissed the Declaration of Independence's affirmation that "all men are created equal." Lincoln's prophetic words endure:

> "A house divided against itself cannot stand." I believe this government cannot endure, permanently, half slave and half free. I do not expect the Union to be dissolved; I do not expect the house to fall; but I do expect it will cease to be divided. It will become all one thing, or all the other. Either the opponents of slavery will arrest the further spread of it and place it where the public mind shall rest in the belief that it is in the course of ultimate extinction, or its advocates will push it forward till it shall become alike lawful in all the states, old as well as new, North as well as South.[9]

Lincoln proved correct: the nation did not dissolve. It went through the bloody Civil War (1861–65), in which 620,000 soldiers perished in the fight to save the union and affirm that "all men are created equal."

Today we face a new conflict of moral vision. Francis Schaeffer describes this clearly in his book *A Christian Manifesto*:

> These two world views [Judeo-Christian theism and secular humanism] stand as totals in complete antithesis to each other in content and also in their natural results—including sociological and governmental results, and specifically including law. It is not that these two world views are different only in how they understand the nature of reality and existence. They also inevitably produce totally different results. The operative word here is *inevitably*. It is not just that they happen to bring forth different results, but it is absolutely *inevitable* that they will bring forth different results.[10]

America stands at a place similar to Lincoln's America 150 years ago. War is under way for the soul of the nation. Either God will be recognized as sovereign, or man will pretend to be sovereign. We will be "one nation under God" or "one nation under man." It is a *culture* war. May God keep us from *civil* war.

Changing the Story

The culture wars, we have seen, are the result of shifts in worship and worldview. Western civilization was born out of Judeo-Christian theism. This worldview gave way to the deism of the French Revolution, which in turn gave way to the atheism of modernism, which embraced Darwin's survival-of-the-fittest narrative. Now we are moving into a postmodern era of neo-paganism, the worship of nature.[11]

In *The Book of Laughter and Forgetting*, Czech-French novelist Milan Kundera depicts the power of changing the story in order to transform the nation: "'You begin to liquidate a people,' Hübl said, 'by taking away its memory. You destroy its books, its culture, its history. And then others write other books for it, give another culture to it, invent another history for it. Then the people slowly begins to forget what it is and what it was.'"[12] This is exactly what happened in Europe and is taking place in America today. Our history is being deconstructed and a new history is being written. Western intellectuals argue that the deistic Enlightenment, not Judeo-Christian theism, produced Western civilization.

James Kurth, professor of political science at Swarthmore College, makes the following argument: "The real clash of civilizations will not be between the West and one or more of the Rest. It will be between the West and the Post-West, within the West itself. This clash has already taken place within the brain of Western civilization, the American intellectual class. It is now spreading from that brain to the American body politic."[13]

With the shift from theism to atheism, from revealed truth to man-made "truth," a new metanarrative has invaded the intellectual elite of the West. From that intellectual stronghold, it is now working its way into the broader life of Western nations. Hollywood is one avenue by which that happens. William Lind, director of the Center for Cultural Conservatism, states: "The entertainment industry . . . has wholly absorbed the ideology of cultural Marxism [atheism] and preaches it endlessly . . . in parables: strong women beating up weak men, children wiser than their parents, corrupt clergymen thwarted by carping drifters . . . manly homosexuals who lead normal lives. It is all fable, and inversion of reality."[14]

Language is another avenue. Over the last fifty years in the West, changes of language have preceded culture change. The phrase "quality of life" has replaced "sacredness of life." The language of psychology has replaced that of theology: "sin" became "sickness." Authority was taken from the pastor and priest and given to the psychiatrist.

The Public Square

What led to these cultural changes in the West? How did biblical morality give way to atheistic immorality? Jim Nelson Black, senior analyst for Sentinel Research Associates, explains:

> One of the greatest reasons for the decline of American society over the past century has been the tendency of Christians who have practical solutions to abandon the forum at the first sign of resistance. Evangelicals in particular have been quick to run and slow to stand by their beliefs. In reality, most Christians had already vacated "the public square" of moral and political debate by their own free will, long before civil libertarians and others came forth to drive us back to our churches.[15]

The church has a unique role in affirming and securing the virtues and habits of civilization. Tragically, the Western church has largely failed to influence culture over the past several decades. In the United States and Europe, many Christians have abandoned a conscious commitment to the Creator, to Christ as Lord and Savior, and to a biblical worldview. Many have abandoned objective truth for subjective experience. Many have retreated from the marketplace and the public square into the privacy of their own homes.

For the West to survive, those who value freedom and morality must return to the truth, beauty, and goodness of Judeo-Christian culture and courageously reengage the society. If they do not, the opposing side will win the culture war by default, and life in the West will change dramatically. It is essential for us to understand that free societies come not from deistic or atheistic philosophy but from Judeo-Christian theism.

CHAPTER 5

The Freedom of
Biblical Theism

*In my youth I stressed freedom, and in my old age I stress order. I
have made the great discovery that liberty is a product of order.*
—WILL DURANT

The Chinese Academy of Social Science (CASS) was tasked
with discovering what accounted for the West's ascendancy
over the rest of the world. What they found surprised them and
challenged the assumptions of Western intellectuals. In a lecture in
Beijing in 2002, a member of the Academy known as Dr. Wu presented the CASS's findings:

> One of the things we [Chinese scholars] were asked to look into
> was what accounted for the success, in fact the pre-eminence of
> the West over the world. We studied everything we could from
> the historical, political, economic, and cultural perspective. At
> first, we thought it was because you [the West] had more pow-
> erful guns than we had. Then we thought it was because you

had the best political system. Next we focused on the economic system. But in the past twenty years, we have realized that *the heart of your culture is your religion: Christianity.* That is why the West is so powerful. *The Christian moral foundation of social and cultural life* was what made possible the emergence of capitalism and then the successful transition to democratic politics. We don't have any doubt about this.[1]

The battle for the soul of the West will decide which narrative explains the story of the West. Modern Western scholars, steeped in naturalistic Darwinism, are rewriting the narrative of the United States and Europe and argue that America's freedom is rooted in the European Enlightenment: there is no God, no revelation; man is sovereign; reason is our only means for discovering truth.

On the other side is the historical record, which affirms that America's freedom is rooted in biblical theism. This is what Dr. Wu and his colleagues discovered.

This chapter will focus on the United States, my country, as a case study of the social and governmental outcome of biblical theism. However, the principles of biblical theism do not belong to any one nation or people; they are universal principles given by God to all people.

Freedom and Judeo-Christian Theism

The American Declaration of Independence framed the terms for a new nation and shook the political philosophies of the world. Thomas Jefferson wrote, and the founding fathers ratified, "We hold these truths to be self-evident, that all men are created equal, that they are endowed by their Creator with certain unalienable Rights, that among these are Life, Liberty, and the pursuit of Happiness."[2]

Such language derives from the moral vision that "all men are created equal." The concept of human dignity is not the product of evolution, in which the fittest, most powerful species survive.

Humans are *endowed* by their Creator with rights. These rights are granted by God, built into the fabric of creation. Because they are from God, not the state, they are inalienable. No one has authority to remove or abridge them. Among these are life, liberty, and the pursuit of happiness.

Life is sacred. All human life—from conception, for all human beings, male and female, of every race and tribe—is equally valued and significant. This belief in the sacredness of life refutes the concept of the "quality of life" which suggests that only certain lives—the enjoyable or beautiful—are worth protecting.

Liberty is freedom to *be* good and *do* good, the responsible choice of a morally upright life. This contrasts with the secular humanist definition of liberty as *license*—following one's natural instincts, doing what *feels* good. License is exercising the will without responsibility, letting another pay the cost of one's decisions.

Happiness differs from the secular humanist pursuit of what the late Francis Schaeffer identified as "personal peace and affluence."[3] Many try to equate the founders' concept of happiness with hedonism: "Eat, drink, and be merry for tomorrow we die!" But the founders were not hedonists. They believed in moral law and in personal and national obedience to that law.[4] The founding fathers drew their understanding of happiness from the work of English lawyer and legal scholar, Sir William Blackstone, as expressed in his *Commentaries on the Laws of England,* published shortly before the founding of the United States. "[God] has so intimately connected, so inseparably interwoven the laws of eternal justice with the happiness of each individual, that the latter cannot be attained but by observing the former; and, if the former be punctually obeyed, it cannot but induce the latter . . . ; [God] has graciously reduced the rule of obedience to this one paternal precept, 'that man should pursue his own true and substantial happiness.' This is the foundation of what we call ethics, or natural law."[5]

Human rights and civil liberties are grounded in the Judeo-Christian ethic. Human rights have six basic elements:

1. The inalienability of rights: God alone gives them.
2. The sanctity of all human life: every person is of inestimable value.
3. The dignity of all races and both sexes: racism and sexism offend God.
4. The sinfulness of humankind: government by men must be limited.
5. The personal responsibility entailed in human freedom: the individual must self-govern based on biblical principles.
6. The moral nature of the universe: true justice must prevail in society.

Some of the basic civil liberties are:

1. The right to life (the foundational liberty)
2. Freedom of religion or conscience
3. Freedom of speech and the press
4. Freedom of association and assembly
5. Equal protection under the law and due process

The basis for human rights and civil liberties is the Judeo-Christian view that all people—women and men, young and old, sick and healthy—are made in God's image.

James Reichley, senior fellow at the Public Policy Institute at Georgetown University, helps us see the theistic basis of human rights: "The founding fathers were right: republican government depends for its health on values that over the not-so-long run must come from religion. Through theist-humanism, human rights are rooted in the moral worth with which a loving Creator has endowed each human soul, and social authority is legitimized by making it answerable to transcendent moral law."[6]

As will be discussed in detail in later chapters, God has built a comprehensive physical, metaphysical, moral, and aesthetic order into the universe. This order of reality, the creation order, is a common grace that is the property of *all* human beings. This objective reality is the real world that we all inhabit. Yet not all cultures and certainly not all worldviews allow people to discover, appreciate, and live within the framework of this order. It is Judeo-Christian theism and the testimony of the Old and New Testaments that accurately comports with objective reality. It is the message of Scripture that points humankind to the truth. All human beings, however, have the ability to look at the created order and come to understand that God exists, and discover something of his character and of the nature of the created order.[7] The apostle Paul makes the case for what is known as *natural law*, objective moral standards: "For when Gentiles, who do not have the law, by nature do what the law requires, they are a law to themselves, even though they do not have the law. They show that the work of the law is written on their hearts, while their conscience also bears witness, and their conflicting thoughts accuse or even excuse them on that day when, according to my gospel, God judges the secrets of men by Christ Jesus" (Rom. 2:14–16 ESV). As people and nations discover and apply this order, the result will be more justice and less corruption, more wealth and less poverty, more social peace and fewer disharmonies.

The relationship between Judeo-Christian theism and free societies is attested to by many. The drafter of the Declaration of Independence, Thomas Jefferson, wrote, "God who gave us life gave us liberty. And can the liberties of a nation be thought secure if we have removed their only firm basis; a conviction in the minds of men that these liberties are the gift of God? That they are not to be violated but with His wrath? Indeed, I tremble for my country when I reflect that God is just; that His justice cannot sleep forever."[8]

Two things strike me about this statement. Note first Jefferson's utter conviction that freedom is a God-given right, and that conviction came from a man many say was not a biblical theist. The second is Jefferson's trembling for his country before a just God. What would he say today in view of our moral and spiritual bankruptcy? Wouldn't he tremble even more? Ought we not to tremble as well?

Noah Webster was America's first lexicographer and author of the 1828 *American Dictionary of the English Language*. He is called the father of American scholarship and education. In his *History of the United States* (1831) he wrote that our free nation was founded on a particular ideology: "The Christian religion ought to be received and maintained with firm and cordial support. It is the real source of all genuine republican principles. It teaches the equality of men as to rights and duties; and while it forbids all oppression, it commands due subordination to law and rulers. . . . The religion of Christ and his apostles, in its primitive simplicity and purity, unencumbered with the trappings of power and the pomp of ceremonies, is the surest basis of a republican government."[9]

Consider this more recent word about Judeo-Christianity's contribution to the rise of freedom from Germany's foremost philosopher, Jürgen Habermas: "Egalitarian universalism, from which sprang the ideas of freedom and social solidarity, of an autonomous conduct of life and emancipation, of the individual morality of conscience, human rights, and democracy, is *the direct heir to the Judaic ethic of justice and the Christian ethic of love*. . . . To this day, there is no alternative to it . . . we continue to draw on the substance of this heritage. Everything else is just idle postmodern talk."[10]

The Bible and America's Founding

Reporters Kenneth Woodward and David Gates, in *How the Bible Made America*, make the provocative claim: "Historians are discovering that the Bible, perhaps even more than the Constitution, is our founding document."[11] Is this true?

Donald S. Lutz, professor of political science at the University of Houston, acknowledges that "the Constitution is the product of a constitution-making tradition that can be traced to colonial charter and is modeled on the biblical idea of covenant—a solemn agreement between God and man. . . . [The colonists] didn't come over with John Locke in hand. . . . They came over with the Bible in hand."[12] At least fifty of the fifty-five framers of the US constitution were orthodox Christians.[13]

Lutz and Charles Hyneman, of the University of Indiana, studied fifteen thousand documents that the founders referenced. Of the quotes they used, 34 percent were from Scripture, and a majority of those were from Deuteronomy, which lays the moral and legal foundation for the nation of Israel. Of other authors quoted, 60 percent referred to the Bible.[14]

The Protestant Reformers in Europe also had an influence on America's government. John Calvin (1509–64), the French theologian, pastor, and leader of the Reformation in Geneva, consciously propagated the biblical world and life view. He understood and taught that God is sovereign over all of life. His voluminous *Institutes of the Christian Religion* became the well from which later theologians, pastors, and leaders drank. Calvin's influence spread to Scotland and the Netherlands, to the Puritans in England, and the Huguenots in France. His influence then spread through the English Puritans to New England, through the Dutch to New Amsterdam (New York), and, to a lesser extent, through Huguenots, Dutch, and British Calvinists to the mid-Atlantic region.

America's population at the time of the American Revolution was three million, including nine hundred thousand predominantly Presbyterian Scots or Scotch-Irish, six hundred thousand English Puritans, four hundred thousand German and Dutch Reformed, and a smattering of French Huguenots. Dr. Loraine Boettner, author, theologian, and staff member at the Library of Congress, calculates that "about two-thirds of the colonial population had been trained in the school of Calvin."[15] George Bancroft (1800–1891), American historian and statesman, secretary of the Navy, and founder of the US Naval Academy at Annapolis, calls Calvin "the Father of America" and says, "He that will not honor the memory and respect the influence of Calvin knows but little of the origin of American liberty."[16]

Woodward and Gates are correct: the Bible is the primary document behind America's founding.

Freedom for All Nations

It was the firm belief of early Americans that the Bible would form the basis of freedom for all nations, not just the United States. Noah Webster writes, "The moral principles and precepts contained in the scriptures ought to form the basis of all our civil constitutions and laws. . . . All the miseries and evils which men suffer from vice, crime, ambition, injustice, oppression, slavery and war, proceed from their despising or neglecting the precepts contained in the Bible."[17]

John Adams (1735–1826) states, "Suppose a nation in some distant region should take the Bible for their only law-book, and every member should regulate his conduct by the precepts there exhibited! Every member would be obliged, in conscience, to temperance and frugality and industry; to justice and kindness and charity towards his fellow men; and to piety, love, and reverence, towards Almighty God. . . . What a Utopia; what a Paradise would this region be!"[18]

George Washington (1732–99), the first US president, said on Thanksgiving Day, 1789, "It is the duty of all Nations to acknowledge the providence of Almighty God, to obey his will, to be grateful for his benefits, and humbly to implore his protection and favors."[19]

Robert C. Winthrop (1809–94), speaker of the US House of Representatives, powerfully states the relationship between freedom and tyranny: "All societies of men must be governed in some way or other. The less they may have of stringent State Government, the more they must have individual self-government. The less they rely on public law or physical force, the more they must rely on private moral restraint. Men, in a word, must necessarily be controlled either by a power within them, or by a power without them; either by the Word of God, or by the strong arm of man; either by the Bible or the bayonet."[20]

Pluralism

In the United States and other free countries, one does not have to confess Christianity (or any other religion) to live there. Freedom of religion and conscience is rooted in *social and political pluralism,* "a condition in which numerous distinct ethnic, religious, or cultural groups are present and tolerated within a society."[21] There is an important distinction between this type of pluralism and *ideological pluralism,* "the belief that no single explanatory system or view of reality can account for all the phenomena of life."[22]

What foundation undergirds a pluralistic society? Secularists say that ideological pluralism produces political and social pluralism. They fight not for freedom *of* religion but freedom *from* religion, particularly religion that affirms moral and metaphysical absolutes. However, atheism, or secular materialism, is a religion. Its doctrines include the rejection of God, the sovereignty of nature, the evolution of man from lower life forms, the denial of absolute truth, and the relativity of morals. Their only absolute is the rejection of absolutes. Tolerance is the only virtue, and it extends even to tolerating lies, evil, injustice, and the hideous. D. James Kennedy writes, "Tolerance is the last virtue of a depraved society. When you have an immoral society that has blatantly, proudly violated all of the commandments of God, there is one last virtue they insist upon: tolerance for their immorality."[23] In a similar vein, G. K. Chesterton is attributed with saying, "Tolerance is the virtue of the man without convictions."

The ultimate value of secular materialism is power. English philosopher Herbert Spencer captured the idea in the phrase "survival of the fittest." Richard Dawkins, the prominent British atheist, pairs his evolutionary biology with social Darwinism: "I think 'nature red in tooth and claw' sums up our modern understanding of natural selection admirably."[24]

Contrary to the claims of secularists, ideological pluralism will not produce social and political pluralism. Public policy based on atheism's moral relativism leads to anarchy, where everyone does what is right in their own eyes.[25] An example is the rioting and looting in England during August 2011. The British government estimated that 120,000 families across England were involved in the wanton violence and rampage. On August 15, Prime Minister David Cameron said:

> Do we have the determination to confront the slow-motion moral collapse that has taken place in parts of our country these past few generations?
>
> Irresponsibility. Selfishness. Behaving as if your choices have no consequences. Children without fathers. Schools without discipline. Reward without effort.
>
> Crime without punishment. Rights without responsibilities. Communities without control. Some of the worst aspects of human nature tolerated, indulged—sometimes even incentivized—by a state and its agencies that in parts have become literally de-moralised.
>
> So do we have the determination to confront all this and turn it around?[26]

Nations cannot long tolerate anarchy, so eventually the state will establish what Francis Schaeffer has called "arbitrary absolutes" and will begin to rule with an iron fist.[27]

James Reichley of Georgetown University states the case very clearly: "Yet the classical version of civil humanism [secularism] by itself hardly provides an adequate value base for a democratic society. . . . Classical humanism has serious functional shortcomings from the more limited perspective of providing moral support for democracy."[28]

Atheistic assumptions would not have founded America; they cannot build free societies. Tyranny is their only legacy, as evidenced by Freedom House's *Freedom in the World* reports. Many countries rated "not free" are atheistic. Examples are Belarus, China, Cuba, North Korea, Russia, and Vietnam. Most countries rated "free" were birthed in Judeo-Christian theism. Examples are Austria, Canada, Poland, Switzerland, and the United States.[29]

Only Judeo-Christian theism (non-ideological pluralism) produces truly free societies. America's founding fathers understood that *one* belief system creates the conditions for freedom. Public policy based on Judeo-Christian theism leads to freedom of religion and civil rights. Was this applied perfectly? No. Our treatment of Native Americans and black Africans mark some of our darkest moments, when this ideal was suspended. Racism and slavery were blights on the American experience. But the principle of freedom was enshrined in our founding documents; it became the standard to strive for. The abolition of slavery and the civil rights movement show that the nation continues to push toward its ideal.

Conclusion

The United States, our case study in this chapter, was formed as a nation of refugees seeking freedom, as expressed in Emma Lazarus's stirring poem "The New Colossus" on a bronze plaque inside the Statue of Liberty at the entry of New York harbor:

> Give me your tired, your poor,
> Your huddled masses yearning to breathe free,
> The wretched refuse of your teeming shore.
> Send these, the homeless, tempest-tost to me,
> I lift my lamp beside the golden door!

This ideal—the equality, dignity, and freedom of all people—has guided America from its beginning even though it has never been achieved perfectly.

The roots of freedom—for America and every nation—are found in the distinctive ideology of Judeo-Christian theism. With this understanding, we now turn to an alternative ideology and the combatant for the soul of the West: atheism.

CHAPTER 6

The Tyranny of Fundamentalist Atheism

If you were to destroy in mankind the belief in immortality, not only love but every living force maintaining the life of the world would at once be dried up. Moreover, nothing then would be immoral, everything would be lawful, even cannibalism.
— DOSTOYEVSKY, *The Brothers Karamazov*

An atheist, by definition, denies God's existence. For generations atheists acknowledged freedom of religion. They welcomed a level playing field on which to reason with theists over the basic questions of life. They believed that the best ideas would win.

But today's atheists are *anti*-theists. They regard theists, with their belief in absolutes, as the enemy. Today's atheists are not content to outthink theists; their mission is to free society from religion. Naturalism, the philosophy of atheists, asserts that nature is all that exists: there is no God, no supernatural, no revelation.

The "death of God" leads to the death of all things grounded in his existence. Truth, justice, beauty, the significance of human life, and love all disappear. Proverbs 8:35–36 says, "For those who find me [wisdom] find life and receive favor from the LORD. But those who fail to find me harm themselves; all who hate me love death." Echoing the words of Dostoyevsky, Italian novelist Umberto Eco says, "When men stop believing in God, it isn't that they then believe in nothing: they believe in everything."[1]

The West is in the midst of a war—a battle of ideas—between anti-theists, who seek to determine for themselves what is right and wrong, and theists, who value truth and freedom grounded in moral absolutes. In this chapter we will focus on the beliefs, motives, and consequences of the new atheism.

The New Atheism

The new atheists are people of faith, the faith of secular humanism. *A World Religious Reader* lists secular humanism alongside Christianity, Hinduism, Buddhism, Islam, and other religions. The atheist's bible is the *Humanist Manifesto*, first published in 1933 and revised in 1973 and again in 2003. In the original version, humanists asserted a "widespread recognition of the radical changes in religious beliefs throughout the modern world."[2] They acknowledged that theirs is a belief system and identified themselves as *religious* humanists.

Secular humanists subscribe to a series of atheistic religious positions. The original *Manifesto* defined their views on theology ("religious humanists regard the universe as self-existing and not created"); anthropology ("man is a part of nature"); biology ("[man] has emerged as a result of a continuous process"); and social philosophy ("the complete realization of human personality [is] the end of man's life," and "its development and fulfillment [is] in the here and now").[3] The 1973 *Manifesto* identified their soteriology: "Humans are responsible for what we are or will become. No deity will save us; we must save ourselves."[4]

Secular humanists are not only religious; they are also dogmatic. While they take pride in being tolerant of many lifestyles and behaviors, they categorically reject transcendence, thus profoundly changing the concept of tolerance. The Judeo-Christian concept of tolerance is "accepting those with whom we disagree." Tolerance in today's atheistic framework affirms that "all ideas are equally valid *except* ideas rooted in objective truth." Anti-theists preach tolerance but practice intolerance toward those who acknowledge transcendent revelation and absolute morals.

Dr. Daniel O. Conkle, professor of law and adjunct professor of religion at Indiana University, speaks of *secular fundamentalism*: "Those who adhere to comprehensive secular fundamentalism, however, are absolutists in at least one respect: they are not open to the possibility of religious truth and therefore are not willing to consider arguments that depend upon religious perspectives. . . . [They] actually ignore the cardinal value that they claim to prefer, the value of reason itself."[5]

The old atheists sought dialogue with those of other persuasions; the new atheists are aggressively anti-theistic. They propagate absolutism through books, movies, language, education, and more. Their more popular books include Richard Dawkins's *The God Delusion* (2006), Christopher Hitchens's *God Is Not Great: How Religion Poisons Everything* (2007), and Sam Harris's *Letter to a Christian Nation* (2006).

Al Gore's award-winning movie *An Inconvenient Truth* (2006) attempted to silence global warming critics. In an interview Gore stated, "The debate in the scientific community is over," when in fact there is no scientific consensus on climate change.[6] Ben Stein's movie *Expelled: No Intelligence Allowed* (2008) exposed the intolerance and lack of academic freedom in mainstream science when it comes to alternatives to Darwinian science.

Language is manipulated to shape the mindset of a nation. Abortion has morphed from "killing an unborn child" to "a woman's right to choose"; euthanasia from "killing the infirm" to "death with dignity"; morals from "sexual immorality" to "lifestyle choices"; marriage from "one man and one woman for life" to "any consenting adults."

Regarding education, secular activist John J. Dunphy argues that public school teachers should propagate atheistic humanism in the classroom:

> The battle for humankind's future must be waged and won in the public school classroom by teachers who correctly perceive their role as the proselytizers of a new faith. . . . These teachers must embody the same selfless dedication as the most rabid fundamentalist preachers, for they will be ministers of another sort, utilizing a classroom instead of a pulpit to convey humanist values in whatever subject they teach, regardless of the educational level—preschool day care or large state university. The classroom must and will become an arena of conflict between the old and the new—the rotting corpse of Christianity, together with all its adjacent evils and misery, and the new faith of humanism.[7]

Richard Dawkins suggests that parents should be replaced by the state: "How much do we regard children as being the property of their parents? It's one thing to say people should be free to believe whatever they like, but should they be free to impose their beliefs on their children? Is there something to be said for society stepping in? What about bringing up children to believe manifest falsehoods?"[8]

How do secular humanists' ideas affect society? Historian Donald Kagan of Yale University describes the ultimate end of secularism: "[A] vulgar form of Nihilism has a remarkable influence in our educational system through our universities. The consequences of the victory of such ideas would be enormous. If both religion and reason are removed, all that remains is will and power, where the only law is that of tooth and claw."[9] National examples include Nazism in Germany, fascism in Italy and Japan, and communism in the USSR and China.[10]

License vs. Liberty

Metaphysical atheists believe that nature is all that exists. *Moral* atheists disbelieve in God for pragmatic reasons: God's existence entails moral restraints, and they want freedom from restraints. This is especially true of sexual restraint: if there is no God, a person may have sex with as many partners, of any kind, as they like. License replaces condemnation.

It is important to distinguish between license and liberty. Roman Catholic economics professor Taketoshi Nojiri explains: "License is the freedom to follow one's instincts and do as one desires, as naturally as cats and dogs do. Liberty is the duty to do what . . . one knows that one ought to do."[11]

In other words, license is freedom to do wrong, without moral responsibility. License is self-indulgent and narcissistic. On the other hand, liberty is freedom to do good and is grounded in a moral framework. Former American diplomat and author Dr. Alan Keyes presses the case for this type of freedom:

> We're going to have to find the courage one of these days to tell people that freedom is not an easy discipline. Freedom is not a choice for those who are lazy in their heart and in their respect for their own moral capacities. Freedom requires that, at the end of the day, you accept the constraint that is required, the respect for the laws of nature and nature's God that says unequivocally that your daughters do not have the right to do what is wrong, that our sons do not have the right to do what is wrong. They do not have the right to steal bread from the mouths of the innocent; they do not have the right to steal life from the womb of the unborn.[12]

Theodore Roosevelt, twenty-sixth president of the United States, witnessed firsthand the slide from Christian liberty to atheistic license: "There are those who believe that a new modernity demands a new morality. What they fail to consider is the harsh reality that there is no such thing as a new morality. There is only one morality. All else is immorality. There is only true Christian ethics over against which stands the whole of paganism."[13]

License switches the labels on truth, goodness, and beauty. If people believe your lie, it actually becomes true. In secular humanist ethics, tolerance of immorality is virtue, and defending morality is vice; darkness becomes light; the vulgar becomes beautiful. License unleashes a person to do what feels good without any constraints.

English humanist and novelist Aldous Huxley states clearly and honestly, "I had motives for not wanting the world to have meaning; consequently assumed it had none, and was able to find satisfactory reasons for this assumption. . . . For myself, as no doubt for most of my contemporaries, the philosophy of meaninglessness was essentially an instrument of liberation. We objected to the morality because it interfered with our sexual freedom."[14] Modern libertines, like Huxley, want to free humankind from moral absolutes and from traditional institutions like the family and the church. They want to revert to a "natural" state in which people follow their animal instincts.

The deconstruction of Western values churns in high gear. Writer-editor David Kupelian calls this turning evil into good and good into evil the "marketing of evil."[15]

Hollywood promotes moral license through the nonstop broadcast of movies and television with ever-increasing themes of sexual fantasy and violence. Marriage, designed by the Creator as a covenant relationship, has devolved into a civil contract, and from there to a common-law relationship. This descent has been followed by sexual perversions. *Sex and the City* promoted fornication and adultery. Homosexuality was idolized in the 2005 award-winning movie *Brokeback Mountain.* The TV sitcom *All My Children* used its portrayal of the character Zoe to open the curtain on transgender sexuality. The movie *Birth* shifts the boundaries of acceptability on pedophilia.

As if the above perversions were not enough, consider the following excerpt from an article by radio talk-show personality and psychologist Dr. Laura Schlessinger entitled "As Predicted, Bestiality Goes Mainstream": "Showing up in two leading fashion magazines this winter is a multi-page advertising spread for a couturier that pairs the obligatorily skinny woman in provocative poses with an enormous dog in a studded leather collar. Lest the not-so-subliminal message in this advertising campaign be lost, there are pages of 'playful' encounters between them."[16]

The West's debasement of God's gift of sexuality evokes God's words to Ezekiel: "You will see things that are even more detestable than this" (Ezek. 8:15).

People who embrace atheism for moral reasons cannot bear the gaze of a moral God.[17] They challenge the concept of freedom within a moral order, promoting instead the license to live as if there were no moral demands. They foolishly pursue immoral lifestyles to their own enslavement and self-destruction.

The Death of Civilizations

Great civilizations do not endure forever. They live for a time and then die. Sometimes nations are conquered from outside, but often they rot from within. This was the thesis of historian Edward Gibbon in his classic *The Decline and Fall of the Roman Empire.*[18]

Historian and theologian Dr. Jack L. Arnold helpfully summarizes the moral failure that led to the decline of Rome. He points to the development of huge armaments while neglecting the enemy within: the undermining of the sanctity of the home; the rapid increase in divorce; the moral degeneracy of the whole society by sexual perversion, including homosexuality; and the decline of religious vitality, with formalism supplanting faith and impotence replacing power. He adds that Rome exhibited "(1) political chaos and distrust of political leaders; (2) a breakdown of justice; (3) a failure to maintain law and order; (4) increasing taxes; and (5) a mass movement from the rural areas to the cities."[19] The familiar ring of all this is chilling.

One of the most powerful essays to shape my life is Malcolm Muggeridge's "The Great Liberal Death Wish." Muggeridge (1903–90) was born into a British Marxist family and became a journalist, author, satirist, and communist before ultimately converting to Christianity. He traveled to Russia in 1932 and witnessed firsthand the *Holodomor* ("murder by starvation"), Stalin's planned famine of 1932–33 that killed as many as ten million Ukrainians. The Holodomor staggered Muggeridge.

Muggeridge was dumbfounded when Western liberals converged on Russia and, in the face of such horror, praised this atheistic state. He describes Western clergy admiring the anti-god museum, politicians from free nations proclaiming that there was never a more just and free political system, Western attorneys testifying to the impartial justice of the Soviet Union, Western businessmen speaking of the superiority of the Soviet economy. Muggeridge wondered how such paragons of Western liberalism could promote such distortions.

> How could this be? . . . It was from that moment that I began to get the feeling that a liberal view of life was not what I'd supposed it to be—a creative movement which would shape the future—but rather a sort of death wish. How otherwise could you explain how people, in their own country ardent for equality . . . should in the USSR prostrate themselves before a regime ruled over brutally and oppressively and arbitrarily by a privileged party oligarchy?[20]

Muggeridge came to recognize the fallacy and danger of secular humanism:

> On a basis of liberal-humanism, there is no creature in the universe greater than man, and the future of the human race rests only with human beings themselves, which leads infallibly to some sort of suicidal situation. . . . The efforts that men make to bring about their own happiness, their own ease of life, their

own self-indulgence, will in due course produce the opposite.
. . . Once you eliminate the notion of a God, a creator, once you
eliminate the notion that the creator has a purpose for us, and
that life consists essentially in fulfilling that purpose, then you
are bound . . . to induce the megalomania of which we've seen
so many manifestations in our time—in the crazy dictators. . . .
Alternatively, human beings relapse into mere carnality, into
being animals.[21]

Communism in the Soviet Union and Eastern Europe collapsed
because its atheism did not comport with truth or reality. Human
beings are not animals or machines. Atheists will watch their nation
and civilizations die rather than admit their assumptions are wrong
or their grand vision is only an illusion.

Today atheism is hastening the death of the West. An atheistic
foundation will not sustain life or freedom. Many in the West live on
borrowed capital from the biblical worldview. Atheist and secularist
academics—the intellectual elites—want to enjoy the blessings of
Judeo-Christian roots. Yet they despise the tree and hack at its roots,
seeking to overthrow the biblical moral and metaphysical order.

When atheism informs popular culture, life becomes trivial-
ized, focused on material consumption. American media theorist
and cultural critic Neil Postman (1931–2003) projected: "When a
population becomes distracted by trivia, when a cultural life is rede-
fined as a perpetual round of entertainments, when serious public
conversation becomes a form of baby-talk, when, in short, a people
become an audience and their public business a vaudeville act, then
a nation finds itself at risk; culture-death is a clear possibility."[22]

The atheistic West has become self-absorbed. Our hedonistic
cultures have abandoned history and ignored the future, living only
for the present. The modern mantra is the ancient hedonist motto
"Eat, drink, and be merry, for tomorrow we die!" Personal pleasure
is the greatest good in life: "If it feels good, do it!" We confuse the
pursuit of happiness with license to do evil. The West is on a path
of cultural suicide.

The death of God, we have seen, also means the death of truth—any concept of moral or metaphysical absolutes. In the end, a godless world has no future. The death of a culture leads inevitably to the death of a nation. The only variables are the speed of the death and the route it will take.

Before we explore God's call to his church to respond to these twin conflicts, we must see how the war from the East and the war in the West connect.

CHAPTER 7

The Connection between
the Twin Wars

*A great civilization is not conquered from without until it has
destroyed itself from within.*
          —WILL DURANT

Between the death of culture and the corresponding death of a
nation or civilization lies a phenomenon that could be called
pathological self-loathing. This entails individuals and societies
hating their heritage and wanting to distance themselves from their
past. Let's look at several examples of this self-loathing.

In a story entitled "Hostage Drill Prepares School for Crises,"
journalist David Levinsky reported:

The mock terror attack involved two irate men armed with
handguns who invaded the high school through the front door.
They pretended to shoot several students in the hallway and
then barricaded themselves in the media center with 10 student
hostages.

Two Burlington Township police detectives portrayed the gunmen. Investigators described them as members of a right-wing fundamentalist group called the "New Crusaders" who don't believe in separation of church and state. The mock gunmen went to the school seeking justice because the daughter of one had been expelled for praying before class.[1]

Jihadists are attacking daily around the world. Their attacks in the United States are increasing. So why would a simulated hostage attack in a public school in America cast Christians as the terrorists? And how is it that the term "Islamic terrorists" has been stripped from our political vocabulary?[2]

Another example of Western self-loathing is pictured in the lack of any Western feminist response to the recent liberation of Afghanistan from the Taliban. Under Taliban rule, women were prisoners in their own homes. They could not venture out without a burka and a male escort. Girls could not attend school; women could not serve as medical doctors or educators. Feminists rail against such treatment in the West, but their rage against the Taliban and their celebration at the liberation of Afghan women by Western armies were conspicuous by their absence. Feminists did not consider the merits of the war. The joy of seeing a nation of women freed from barbaric Islamic law failed to overcome their loathing of the US military and commander-in-chief George W. Bush, by whose actions those women had been liberated.

Self-loathing is rooted in cultural relativism, which undermines the importance of a given culture's unique identity and strengths and maximizes that culture's weaknesses. Cultural relativism denies an objective moral and metaphysical order that leads to freedom, economic sufficiency, social health, and public justice. Cultural relativists seem embarrassed by their national identity. Somali political refugee Ayaan Hirsi Ali noted this tendency in her adoptive homeland of Holland: "[The Dutch] saw nationalism almost the same as racism. Nobody seemed *proud* to be Dutch."[3] A logical consequence of cultural relativism is the denial of the uniqueness of one's own culture. Thus, cultural relativists do not recognize the problem of Islamic terrorism and instead lay the world's problems at the feet of freedom-seeking theists who believe in absolutes. An example comes from Robert Reich, secretary of labor in President Clinton's administration:

> The great conflict of the 21st century will not be between the West and terrorism. . . . The true battle will be between modern civilization and anti-modernists; between those who believe in the primacy of the individual and *those who believe that human beings owe their allegiance and identity to a higher authority*; between those who give priority to life in this world and those who believe that human life is mere preparation for an existence beyond life; between those who believe in science, reason, and logic and *those who believe that truth is revealed through Scripture* and religious dogma. Terrorism will disrupt and destroy lives. But terrorism itself is not the greatest danger we face.[4]

While much of Reich's offering is spurious, his main point is clear: the battle is not between Jihadists and the West; it is between atheists and theists. Not only do those who deny God and moral absolutes promote freedom to do anything without moral restraint; they also open the door to the enemy who is seeking to destroy them for that very reason.

Perhaps a mental picture would be helpful. Political cartoonist D. T. Devareaux drew a cartoon titled "Suicide of the West." In it, Uncle Sam, the national personification of the United States government, is holding a pillar labeled "Western civilization" in one hand and a gun marked "Liberalism" in the other hand. The gun is aimed in the mouth of the morally and spiritually exhausted Uncle Sam, whose finger is on the trigger. Another person's finger, labeled "Islam," reaches in from outside the frame of the picture to cock the weapon for firing. The message is clear: the United States, the upholder of Western civilization, is in the process of committing national suicide and thus ending the hope of the West's recovery;

and Islamists are all too eager to speed up the demise of both America and the ideal of liberty.

Surrender and Appeasement

On July 6, 2008, in Jonesboro, Georgia, Chaudhry Rashid, a fifty-four-year-old Pakistani immigrant, strangled his twenty-five-year-old daughter, Sandeela Kanwal. Ms. Kanwal had refused an arranged marriage. This horrible murder, an Islamic honor killing in America, received scant news coverage. Contrast that with months of sensational news coverage of the disappearance and suspected murder of American blond beauty Natalee Ann Holloway, last seen in Aruba. Two stories of young American women murdered, one story repeatedly broadcast for months, the other buried.

Why the different treatment? Why were women's rights advocates silent about the Muslim death? Did the media intentionally bury coverage of a cruel honor killing because it would cast Islamic culture in a negative light? Was the life of a young Muslim woman less valuable than that of a beautiful blonde?[5]

The church has surrendered as well. Dr. Rowan Williams, Archbishop of Canterbury, told BBC Radio 4's *World at One* that the "UK has to 'face up to the fact' that some of its citizens do not relate to the British legal system. Dr. Williams argues that adopting parts of Islamic Sharia law would help maintain social cohesion."[6] Sharia undergirds honor killings, among other unspeakable practices. Western accommodation to such a system would undermine the dignity of women and jeopardize their right to life and protection. At his trial for the murder of his daughter, Chaudhry Rashid stated that he had done nothing wrong. Indeed, failure to restore the honor of his family by murdering his daughter would have violated the Islamic code.

Why this surrender? Mathias Döpfner, chief executive of the German media company Axel Springer, wrote an explosive piece in the daily newspaper *Die Welt* titled "Europe—Thy Name Is

Cowardice." He states the cause of the surrender as the absence of a moral compass:

> Appeasement cost millions of Jews and Gentiles their lives.
> . . . Appeasement stabilized the Communist Soviet Union. . . .
> Appeasement crippled Europe when genocide ran rampant
> in Kosovo. . . . Appeasement generates a mentality that allows
> Europe to condone the 300,000 victims of Saddam's torture
> and murder. . . . [We Europeans] present ourselves as the world
> champions of tolerance against the intolerants. . . . And why,
> actually? Because we're so moral? I fear it's more because we're
> so materialistic. . . . These days, it sometimes seems that Europe
> is like a little old lady who cups her shaking hands around her
> last pieces of jewelry as a thief breaks in right next door. Europe,
> thy name is Cowardice.[7]

Self-loathing eventually dissolves the will to survive. As a nation increasingly embraces cultural relativism, it loses interest in its history or cultural heritage. It feels guilty for its very existence, lacking the ambition or the will to defend or even perpetuate itself. A self-loathing culture has no reason to reproduce.

Nineteen of the twenty lowest national birthrates in the world are in Europe. Not one European country has a replacement level birth rate.[8] A similar anti-natal pattern characterizes the United States, especially politically liberal states. In the 2004 US presidential elections, John Kerry won the sixteen states with the lowest birthrates, those most like Europe, home to social liberals, averaging 1.47 children per woman. In the same race, George W. Bush won twenty-five of twenty-six states where social conservatives live, with the highest birthrates, averaging 2.08 children per woman.[9]

These statistics reveal the powerful impact of cultural narrative, the implications of the culture wars. They are an ominous portent for the survival of Western civilization. Malcolm Muggeridge's reflections are instructive:

The final conclusion would seem to be that whereas other civilizations have been brought down by attacks of barbarians from without, ours had the *unique distinction of training its own destroyers* at its own educational institutions and providing them with facilities for propagating their destructive ideology far and wide, all at the public expense. Thus did Western man decide to *abolish himself,* creating his own boredom out of his own affluence, his own vulnerability out of his own strength, his own impotence out of his own erotomania, himself blowing the trumpet that brought the walls of his own city tumbling down. And, having convinced himself that he is too numerous, labors with pill and scalpel and syringe to make himself fewer, until at last, having educated himself into imbecility and polluted and drugged himself into stupefaction, he keels over, a weary, battered old brontosaurus, and becomes extinct.[10]

Europe has marched into death; America is the dead man walking.

Tolerating the Intolerant

The absence of moral or metaphysical absolutes erases the concepts of falsehood, moral evil, or the artistically abhorrent. No moral judgment can be brought to an individual's or culture's behavior. The result is tolerating the intolerant, accepting conduct that once was morally and aesthetically incomprehensible.

Many Islamic societies practice honor killings, deny personal freedom, practice severe discrimination, shun non-Muslims, and fight from behind children and the elderly. How can so many Western academics, media personalities, bureaucrats, and feminist leaders ignore such injustices? As we have seen, Malcolm Muggeridge called it "The Great Liberal Death Wish." Ayaan Hirsi Ali's phrase is the "seduction of totalitarianism."[11]

In the United States terms like "jihadists" or "Islamic militants" are politically incorrect. Such folly masquerading as sophistication could be simply dismissed were it not so dangerous. Atheists (by confession or lifestyle) reject jihadists' explanations for their behavior. They cling to a Western account of the jihadists' attacks on the West: Muslims attack us because "America is bad" and we support Israel; Arabs are poor because Americans are rich. Such economic and political analysis, no matter how erroneous, appeals to the secular humanist; a reasoned critique of Muslim religious ideology does not. In *Terror and Liberalism,* author and political writer Paul Berman describes how jihadist violence "produced a philosophical crisis among everyone around the world who wanted to believe that a rational logic governs the world."[12]

Walid Phares writes, "Between the mosaic of democracies and the panoply of Jihadism, the disagreement is philosophical, historical, and doctrinal: it is about how the world has functioned for centuries and how it should evolve."[13] Democracies by nature are transparent; they offer freedom of religion and of speech. Arab nations are opaque and restrict or deny freedom of religion or speech. A huge dilemma results when a democracy welcomes people who reject democratic values, who refuse to assimilate, who want to dominate. The plan by New York Muslims to build a mosque two blocks from Ground Zero illustrates this dilemma.

The year 2005 witnessed another example of the dilemma of democracy confronted by totalitarianism when the Danish *Jyllands-Posten* newspaper published twelve editorial cartoons depicting Muhammad. The newspaper ran the cartoons as part of the debate about freedom of the press and freedom of speech versus the limits of irreverence toward religious figures. As word about these cartoons circulated in the Muslim world, riots broke out in Arab and European capitals. Newspapers that think nothing of portraying Christ irreverently suddenly began to self-censor the *Jyllands-Posten* cartoons. Political correctness and fear of jihadist wrath trumped the traditional Western value of freedom of the press.

Mark Steyn, Canadian author and cultural critic, challenges cultural relativism: "It's easy to be sensitive, tolerant, and multicultural—it's the default mode of the age—yet, when you persist in being sensitive to the insensitive, tolerant of the intolerant, and impeccably multicultural about the avowedly unicultural, don't be surprised if they take it for weakness."[14] French writer Jean-François Revel famously said, "Clearly, a civilization that feels guilty for everything it is and does will lack the energy and conviction to defend itself."

The Great Satan

Jihadists label the United States, with its moral and cultural relativism, "the Great Satan." What does this mean?

The apostle John reveals that Satan is the father of lies and the author of death: "You belong to your father, the devil, and you want to carry out your father's desires. He was a murderer from the beginning, not holding to the truth, for there is no truth in him. When he lies, he speaks his native language, for he is a liar and the father of lies" (John 8:44). In Revelation, Satan not only lies; he deceives entire *nations* (Rev. 20:3, 7–8). Satan is the personification of evil. And beyond this, Satan's nature is to deceive and, through that deception, to destroy nations.

When Islamists call America the Great Satan, they do so in this sense of deception. Islam scholar Bernard Lewis describes the Muslim concept of the demonic: "Satan as depicted in the Qur'an is neither an imperialist nor an exploiter. He is a seducer, 'the insidious tempter who whispers in the hearts of men' (Qur'an CXIV, 4, 5)."[15] The fundamentalist Muslim regards the United States as the great seducer. Not content with our own spiritual bankruptcy, we spew our vileness to the world. Through the media and Internet, we draw people in Muslim nations away from Allah and from their traditional values into godless materialism and immorality.

Professor Samuel Huntington explains how Muslims view the West: "They see Western culture as *materialistic, corrupt, decadent, and immoral.* They also see it as seductive, and hence stress all the more the need to resist its impact on their way of life. Increasingly, Muslims attack the West not for adhering to an imperfect, erroneous religion, which is nonetheless a 'religion of the book,' but for not adhering to any religion at all. *In Muslim eyes Western secularism, irreligiosity, and hence immorality are worse evils than the Western Christianity that produced them.* . . . Muslims see their opponent as 'the godless West.'"[16]

In his "Letter to the American People" dated November 24, 2002, Osama bin Laden raised two questions: "Why are we fighting and opposing you?" and "What are we calling you to, and what do we want from you?" One would think that the 9/11 attacks would provoke the West, particularly the United States, to seek the answers. Apparently our desire for personal peace and affluence outstrips our interest in such questions. Nevertheless, we would be foolish not to listen to the mastermind behind the war from the East.

In answer to his question "What are we calling you to, and what do we want from you?" bin Laden writes:

(1) The first thing that we are *calling you to is Islam.* . . .

(2) The second thing we call you to, is *to stop your oppression, lies, immorality and debauchery* that has spread among you. . . .

(3) What we call you to thirdly is to . . . *discover that you are a nation without principles or manners.* . . .

(4) We also advise you to stop supporting Israel. . . .

(5) We also advise you to pack your luggage and get out of our lands. . . .

(6) Sixthly, we call upon you to *end your support of the corrupt leaders* in our countries. . . .

(7) We also call you to *deal with us* and interact with us on the *basis of mutual interests* and benefits. . . .

Bin Laden continues:

> (a) We call you to be a people of manners, principles, honour, and purity; to reject the immoral acts of *fornication, homosexuality, intoxicants, gambling's* [*sic*], and trading with interest....
>
> (b) It is saddening to tell you that you are *the worst civilization* witnessed by the history of mankind....
>
> (iv) *You are a nation that permits acts of immorality, and you consider them to be pillars of personal freedom.* You have continued to sink down this abyss from level to level until incest has spread amongst you, in the face of which *neither your sense of honour nor your laws object.*[17]
>
> Who can forget your President Clinton's immoral acts committed in the official Oval office? ...
>
> (vi) You are a nation that exploits women like consumer products or advertising tools calling upon customers to purchase them. *You use women* to serve passengers, visitors, and strangers *to increase your profit margins.* You then rant that you support the liberation of women.
>
> (vii) You are a nation that *practices the trade of sex in all its forms,* directly and indirectly. Giant corporations and establishments are established on this, *under the name of art, entertainment, tourism and freedom,* and other deceptive names you attribute to it.[18]

Moral atheists, whose goal is sexual freedom, dismiss bin Laden's words as moral ranting. Moral relativists challenge his right to judge others' behavior. Those who seek to live within a moral framework see some truth in his accusations.

Bin Laden's statement that the United States is "*the worst civilization* witnessed by the history of mankind" is patently false. No nation is perfect. But America has set a standard of civilization that has been the envy of many in the world. Furthermore, bin Laden's life and immoral behavior, including his treatment of women, has often reflected his very critique of the United States. Nor can his heinous attacks on the United States and innocent civilians be justified on any grounds.

Parts of bin Laden's critique, however, have the sad ring of truth. In many ways we have become a culture that encourages "acts of immorality," substance abuse, adultery, and premarital sex. Women have become objects, not subjects; they become the "sex toys" of men. Too often women are exploited for commercial purposes to sell all variety of material things. Many thousands of women and girls are trafficked each year into the United States for sex slavery. There is no denying that pornography has become a multibillion-dollar industry. Things that would have been unthinkable in the United States fifty years ago, such as redefining "marriage" to be between two men or two women, are becoming mainstream. A movement to make pedophilia legal in the United States is now under way.[19] We have indeed become a culture that "practices the trade of sex in all its forms."

So, while we must condemn bin Laden's actions and hateful rhetoric, we must also see the painful truth of his moral critique. The United States is spiraling into a moral and spiritual abyss. Too often the American church stands uncritical of the decadent lifestyles of the modern atheistic and materialistic culture; and more tragically, Christians often practice the same lifestyles. The American patterns of adultery and divorce, pornography, abortion, and support of same-sex marriage are found in the church in growing numbers.[20] Instead of being radically countercultural, too many Christians have been caught up in the increasingly depraved culture of modern America.

A Battle of Ideas

Ultimately we face a conflict of ideas, ideals, and vision—a battle of worldviews and religious narratives. As Proverbs reminds us: "For as he thinketh in his heart, so is he" (Prov. 23:7 KJV). As we have seen, our religious worldview not only tells us how to see the world but also determines the kind of nations we will build.

Each narrative has a symbol, a driving vision, and a focus. Atheistic materialism's symbol is the *condom*. The vision is "Eat, drink, and be merry, for tomorrow we die!" Its focus is the self and the immediate satisfaction of one's natural instincts (hedonism).

The symbol of militant Islam is the *sword*. Would-be martyr Ijaz Khan Hussein expresses its vision: "We went to the Jihad filled with joy, and I would go again tomorrow. If Allah had chosen me to die I would have been in paradise, eating honey and watermelons and grapes and resting with beautiful virgins."[21] The focus is obedience to Allah by murdering innocents through jihad.

Biblical theism's symbol is the *cross*. The driving vision was stated by the apostle Paul: "It is for freedom that Christ has set us free. . . . You, my brothers and sisters, were called to be free . . . use your freedom to . . . serve one another humbly in love" (Gal. 5:1, 13). The focus is personal and national liberty through obedience to God's order.

These radically diverse narratives lead to drastically different ends. The first ends in disorder (moral anarchy), the second in tyranny, the third in freedom.

This battle of ideas must be fought on two levels. First, the license of secular atheism and the freedom of biblical theism must face off. The winner—license or freedom—will confront the tyranny of jihadist Islam. The outcome will determine the future of Europe and America, the future of the Middle East, the future of the world.

To engage in this battle fully, we must see it from its deepest level—the spiritual level.

CHAPTER 8

Captivating Culture

A faith that does not become culture is a faith not fully accepted, not entirely thought out, not faithfully lived.
—JOHN PAUL II

The war from the East and the war in the West intersect in the realm of the moral and spiritual bankruptcy of the West. Thoughtful Christians must engage both fronts. Blind loyalty to the West ignores our nations' moral poverty. This we must not do. We must honestly face and address the moral and spiritual poverty of Western nations while we simultaneously confront jihadist ideology from the East.

At their root these are wars of vision and ideology. We are to take the offensive, captivating the imagination of our ideological enemies and emancipating them from the lifestyles that enslave them. We do this, as Paul put it, in the hope "that they will come to their senses and escape from the trap of the devil, who has taken them captive to do his will" (2 Tim. 2:26). For at its deepest level this is a spiritual battle.

Captivation and Emancipation

James Davison Hunter, professor of religion, culture, and social theory at the University of Virginia, popularized the term "culture war" in his 1992 groundbreaking book *Culture Wars: The Struggle to Define America*.[1] The term became a handy label to describe the conflict for the soul of the West.

I have used this phrase for years and have found it very helpful. But now I am wondering if we need a new metaphor, because "war" connotes physical struggle and violence. The culture war is a battle, not for physical territory, but for the hearts and minds of individuals and the souls of nations.

Perhaps a new image can be found in the words of the apostle Paul in 2 Corinthians 10:3–5: "For though we live in the world, we do not wage war as the world does. The weapons we fight with are not the weapons of the world. On the contrary, they have divine power to demolish strongholds. We demolish arguments and every pretension that sets itself up against the knowledge of God, and we take captive every thought to make it obedient to Christ."

We're in a war, but "we do not wage war as the world does." Physical conflict is rooted in the moral and metaphysical vision of a people. In contrast to the world's methods of war, Christians are to "demolish strongholds" and "take captive every thought."

What are we to destroy? In verse 4 Paul uses the Greek word *ochurōma*, which means "castle, stronghold, or fortress" and can also mean "anything on which one relies."[2] In the next sentence (v. 5), he switches words to *logismos*, "thought" and "imagination," "a reasoning: such as is hostile to the Christian faith."[3] These arguments are the strongholds of the mind. Our battle is for the minds of people and cultures—their moral vision and metaphysical infrastructure. We are to pull down these mental strongholds.

Paul continues by calling us to "take captive every thought." The Greek word translated "take captive" literally means "to lead away captive" and metaphorically means "to capture one's mind, captivate."[4] Here we find a beautiful contrast to the ravages of war.

In English, *captivate* means "to overpower and gain with excellence or beauty; to charm; to engage the affections; to bind in love."[5]

Perhaps the new metaphor for *culture wars* should be *captivating culture*. The war in the West and the war from the East are both battles for the soul of culture. It is not fought with guns and bombs but with love and ideas. We are to overpower with the excellence of our ideas and the beauty of our love, to captivate the culture by speaking the truth to lies, by living just and merciful lives in the midst of unjust and cruel societies, and by promoting beauty instead of the mundane and hideous. This is not only a work of persuasion; it is also a labor of *emancipation* from lies, injustice, and the hideous. It is a struggle to set people free, free in mind and heart, free in life. Ultimately it is to bring freedom to the community and nation.

We need a renewed vision: "All the nations you have made will come and worship before you, Lord; they will bring glory to your name" (Ps. 86:9). We need to aggressively assail the strongholds of the mind of the West to restore her soul. Likewise, we need to challenge the stronghold of the jihadist mind to bring true peace. Muslims recognize Europe and America as Christian lands. Since Europe and America are self-indulgent and immoral, Muslims regard Western immorality as a product of Christianity. How are Christians to respond?

The Kingdom Offensive

All earthly wars, whether of ideas or of bullets, are rooted in the spiritual struggle between God and the demonic: "For our struggle is not against flesh and blood, but against the rulers, against the authorities, against the powers of this dark world and against the spiritual forces of evil in the heavenly realms" (Eph. 6:12). Every war at its heart is a *spiritual war*.

In December 2001, in an Al-Jazeera television interview, Sheikh Ahmad al-Qataani made the startling claim, "Every day, 16,000 Muslims convert to Christianity. Every year, 6 million Muslims convert."[6] Even if this number is exaggerated, the claim of widespread conversion is supported by others.[7]

What is driving this astonishing move to Christ? Just this: as people made in God's image, Muslims are repelled by jihadist hatred and violence. They are in fact hardwired for love. They are responding to the demonstrated love of Christ.

Governments rightfully bear arms to defend their citizens, but the church's battle is different. When a contingent of armed Roman guards came to arrest Christ in Gethsemane and some of his disciples responded with force, Christ forbade them, and in so doing he disarmed the church.[8]

The Lord Jesus Christ declares of his people, "You are the salt of the earth. But if the salt loses its saltiness, how can it be made salty again? It is no longer good for anything, except to be thrown out and trampled underfoot. You are the light of the world. A town built on a hill cannot be hidden" (Matt. 5:13–14). Like salt, Christians are to season, heal, and preserve society. Like light, they are to reveal truth, goodness, and beauty in the midst of a dark world.

The kingdom offensive begins with recognizing "Christ and him crucified" (1 Cor. 2:2). It commences with people putting their faith in Christ for their salvation. Christ died to save the whole of each person and all of their relationships. But this is not the end; it is the beginning. The kingdom offensive puts feet to the prayer, "Thy kingdom come, thy will be done on earth as it is in heaven." We are conduits of truth, goodness, and beauty to our atheistic and Muslim neighbors. We are to engage in a love-and-service offensive (see chapter 13). Our message?

> Life is better than death.
> Health is better than sickness.
> Liberty is better than slavery.
> Prosperity is better than poverty.
> Education is better than ignorance.
> Justice is better than injustice.[9]

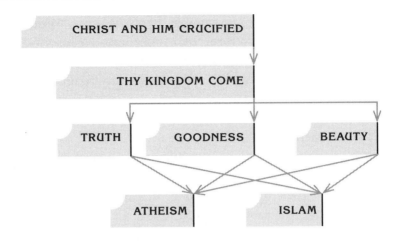

Figure 2. The kingdom offensive

Is There Hope?

In Europe the fire of Western civilization has almost burned out. Only a few embers remain. But anyone who has tended a fire knows that one small ember can rekindle a flame. A fire still burns in the United States, but today's atheists are trying to douse it. If the American church abandons Christ, his kingdom, and the Judeo-Christian worldview, the fire will die. While Europe and the United States may continue to exist as geographic and political entities, Western civilization as we have known it will cease. Anarchy, expressed in the riots in major European and American cities, will eventually lead to tyranny. The civilization born out of the gospel and framed by a biblical worldview will die, and the sun will set on the West.[10]

Because God is active in history, the death of the West is not inevitable. Revival in the West does not depend on government or academia. It rests on God's people. In 2 Chronicles 7:14 God reminds us: "If my people, who are called by my name, will humble themselves and pray and seek my face and turn from their wicked ways, then I will hear from heaven, and I will forgive their sin and will heal their land." God is waiting for four acts of obedience from those who profess his name: humble themselves, pray, seek anew the face of God, and turn from their wickedness. Whose wickedness? Not the wickedness of atheists or jihadists, but that of God's people! It is the believers—us—who are to turn from our wicked ways. What will God do upon our repentance? He will hear our humble hearts and prayers of repentance, he will forgive our sins, and *he will heal the land!*

With this attitude and goal in mind, we are now ready to move on to the second part of this book and discuss the church's response to the twin wars. Our response is rooted in the mission of the church through the centuries—the Great Commission—which the church must once again fervently undertake in the context of our age.

PART 2

The Great Commission

CHAPTER 9

Christ and the Kingdom

*You lead people to become disciples of Jesus by ravishing them with
a vision of life in the kingdom of the heavens in the fellowship of
Jesus. And you do this by proclaiming, manifesting, and teaching
the kingdom to them in the manner learned from Jesus himself. You
thereby change the belief system that governs their lives.*
—DALLAS WILLARD

In the epic movie *The Lord of the Rings: The Two Towers,* the
kingdom of Rohan has shriveled from its glory days. Watching
the forces of darkness advance against his once proud city, King
Théoden laments, "The days have gone down in the West behind
the hills into shadow. How did it come to this?"[1] This question
applies to the West today. In "A Pastoral Letter on Mission," a group
of pastors of the Reformed Episcopal Church give an answer to this
question: "It came to this because the Great Commission of Jesus
Christ has been all but neutralized by a return of paganism to North
America and Europe."[2] In other words, the *Great* Commission has
been reduced to the *Greek* Commission. In the second half of this
book, my aim is to "deneutralize"—that is, to restore, revalidate,

and recharge—the Great Commission. My desire is to put the *great* back in the church's mission.

As we begin our study of the Great Commission, we must first look at the person of Jesus Christ, whose *great claim* of authority is foundational to the assignment he has for his people. We will then discuss the nature of the kingdom of God and, in the next chapter, its relation to the Great Commission.

Christus Victor

The Great Commission has two settings, the earthly and the cosmic. The earthly setting overlooked the Sea of Galilee on a physical mountain. After the resurrection, Jesus instructed the disciples to meet him in the north of Israel: "Then the eleven disciples went to Galilee, to the mountain where Jesus had told them to go. When they saw him, they worshiped him; but some doubted" (Matt. 28:16–17). They had encountered the resurrected Jesus in various ways near Jerusalem, yet they did not all react alike. Some prostrated themselves before him as an act of reverence. Others wavered, unsure of what to think or how to respond.

Who can blame them? They had left everything to follow Jesus, expecting him to ride victoriously into Jerusalem as the Messiah who would overthrow the Roman army and set up a political kingdom. Instead, after three years of building anticipation, the inconceivable unfolded before their eyes: Jesus was arrested, tried, and crucified! Their dreams had been shattered; their lives seemed over.

But then there was a miraculous event. Jesus rose from the dead and appeared to his disciples. He instructed his disciples to meet him in Galilee.[3] In obedience and, no doubt, in wonder, they went to Galilee. There, in the beautiful Galilean hills, Christ made his profound announcement—his great claim: "Jesus came to them and said, 'All authority in heaven and on earth has been given to me'" (Matt. 28:18). Then he gave his disciples the task that we call the Great Commission: "Therefore go and make disciples of all nations, baptizing them in the name of the Father and of the Son and of the Holy Spirit, and teaching them to obey everything I have commanded you. And surely I am with you always, to the very end of the age'" (Matt. 28:19–20).

The cosmic setting of the Great Commission is in the heavens, framed by a battle between God and Satan, a conflict over the old order of death and the new order of life. Whoever won this epic battle would rule the world and determine the outcome of history.

The first of two skirmishes took place in the Garden of Gethsemane, where Jesus had to overcome the *fear of death*.[4] He prayed, "Father, if you are willing, take this cup from me; yet not my will, but yours be done" (Luke 22:42).[5] Facing the cross, Jesus experienced a fierce struggle of the inner man. Three times he prayed, asking the Father to let the cup pass. But he wanted the Father's will more than he wanted the cup's removal.[6] Thus the Father's will became the Son's will, and the means to redemption for man was secured. Christ portrays his work as binding Satan,[7] and Paul describes the nature of the victory of the cross: "Having disarmed the powers and authorities, he made a public spectacle of them, triumphing over them by the cross" (Col. 2:15).

The second skirmish was in the tomb of Joseph of Arimathea; it was the battle to overcome *death itself*.[8] Until Christ came, death had always won. Even in the isolated cases of people being raised from the grave, death won in the end. Lazarus, for example, died a second time. But death could not hold Christ, who was irreversibly raised from the dead.[9] He conquered death, overcame the forces of evil, and began the process of reconciling all things to himself,[10] introducing a new era in human history. Now we need no longer live in the fear of death.[11] The creation order is being restored; the kingdom of God is coming.

Every war has its turning-point battle, even if it is not obvious until later. The turning point in the cosmic spiritual war was the cross. On the cross, Christ won. He is *Christus Victor*. Satan is the defeated enemy. He has been dethroned; his counterfeit reign and order are drawing to an end. Christ will now restore the creation order as he restores life over death. In the cosmic conflict, mop-up operations continue, but the outcome is certain.

The late balladeer for Christ, Keith Green, captured Christ's conquest in his song "The Victor":[12]

> Swallowed into earth's dark womb
> Death has triumphed
> That's what they say
> But try to hold Him in the tomb
> The Son of Life
> Rose on the third day . . .
>
> It is finished
> He has done it
> Life conquered death
> Jesus Christ
> Has won it . . .
>
> Just listen to those demons screaming
> See Him bruise the serpent's head
> The prisoners of Hell
> He's redeeming (Oh!)
> All the power of death is dead

English writer, journalist, and culture critic G. K. Chesterton (1874–1936) captured the wonder of the new era that dawned with the resurrection: "On the third day the friends of Christ coming at daybreak to the place found the grave empty and the stone rolled away. In varying ways they realized the new wonder; but even they hardly realized that the world had died in the night. What they were looking at was the first day of a new creation, with a new heaven and a new earth; and in a semblance of the gardener God walked again in the garden, in the cool not of the evening but the dawn."[13]

In the new era that has dawned with his resurrection, Christ is establishing his kingdom on earth.[14] Christus Victor calls us to live in the framework of his ordinances and extend his rule from heaven to earth.

Too often the church functions as if Satan were the victor and Christ the vanquished. We give too much credit to the demonic, living defensively in our world and communities. Although the Bible acknowledges that Satan is the "prince of this world" (John 12:31) "who leads the whole world astray" (Rev. 12:9), Satan's power extends only to those areas where people willfully live in darkness and do evil. First John 3:8 states, "The one who does what is sinful is of the devil, because the devil has been sinning from the beginning." But the verse continues, "The reason the Son of God appeared was to destroy the devil's work." The Bible is clear that Satan has been ultimately defeated by Christ's death and resurrection. The language that Paul uses is unambiguous: "And having disarmed the powers and authorities, he made a public spectacle of them, triumphing over them by the cross" (Col. 2:15). In this passage we see the language of war, where one side wins and one side loses a critical battle. Christ's death on the cross was the turning point of the great spiritual war between God and Satan. Satan is a defeated enemy; he is in retreat, and his final judgment is certain.[15] The unconquerable Christ calls us to follow him to storm the very gates of hell and assures us they will not prevail against us.[16] Of all people on earth, Christians should be most optimistic, because Christ has won the decisive battle of the great cosmic conflict, and we know the end of history!

The Rule of God on Earth

As I have had the privilege of traveling around the world, I have asked pastors and church leaders, "Of what is Jesus king today?" The almost uniform answer is, "He is king of heaven today and will be king of earth when he comes back!" But what does the Bible say?

Paul delineates Christ's supremacy over all things now, not merely over the heavenly realm. Notice how many times Paul says "all creation," "all things," and "everything":

The Son is the image of the invisible God, the firstborn over *all creation*. For in him *all things* were created: things in heaven and on earth, visible and invisible, whether thrones or powers or rulers or authorities; *all things* have been created through him and for him. He is before *all things*, and in him *all things* hold together. And he is the head of the body, the church; he is the beginning and the firstborn from among the dead, so that in *everything* he might have the supremacy. For God was pleased to have all his fullness dwell in him, and through him to reconcile to himself *all things*, whether things on earth or things in heaven, by making peace through his blood, shed on the cross. (Col. 1:15–20)

Jesus confirms his earthly rule in his dialogue with the Roman governor of Judea, Pontius Pilate:

Pilate then went back inside the palace, summoned Jesus and asked him, "Are you the king of the Jews?"

"Is that your own idea," Jesus asked, "or did others talk to you about me?"

"Am I a Jew?" Pilate replied. "Your own people and chief priests handed you over to me. What is it you have done?"

Jesus said, "My kingdom is not *of* this world. If it were, my servants would fight to prevent my arrest by the Jewish leaders. But now my kingdom is *from* another place."

"You are a king, then!" said Pilate.

Jesus answered, "You say that I am a king. In fact, the reason I was born and came into the world is to testify to the truth." (John 18:33–37)

N. T. Wright, Bible scholar and former bishop of Durham, England, helps us understand the nuance of Christ's words concerning his kingdom: "It's quite clear in the text that Jesus' kingdom doesn't start with this world. It isn't a worldly kingdom, but it is *for* this world. It's from somewhere else, but it's for this world."[17] Christ's kingdom is not of this world; it is not founded on the pagan world-views or values of humanism or animism.[18] His kingdom is from heaven, where it is already established comprehensively and perfectly. When Christ came incarnate, he began to establish his kingdom on earth.

We see this reflected in the prayer the Lord taught his disciples to pray: "Our Father in heaven, hallowed be your name, your kingdom come, your will be done, on earth as it is in heaven" (Matt. 6:9–10). Too often we unthinkingly pray the Lord's Prayer, not recognizing God's intentions. He wants his kingdom to come and his will to be done *on earth* as it is in heaven.

God has a big agenda for the world. It includes, among other things, the stewarding of creation, the blessing of all nations, the discipling of nations, and the reconciliation of all things to Christ.[19] He also intends to make one kingdom out of many nations—*E pluribus unum* (out of many, one).[20]

Every kingdom, including the kingdom of God, has five essentials:

- A king who rules: Jesus is the King
- The king's subjects. Today, all who put their trust in Christ are his subjects. At the end of time, every knee will bow and every tongue will confess that Jesus Christ is Lord.[21]
- The king's realm: heaven and earth
- Laws and ordinances that comprise the order of the kingdom. These are the laws of creation, which we will look at later.[22]
- The king's embassy with its envoys who represent the kingdom. The church is the embassy, and Christians are the king's envoys or ambassadors.

How does a church serve as God's embassy? One example comes from Ayacucho, Peru, during the period of the Maoist terrorist movement, the Shining Path, in the 1990s. Pastor Samuel Alcarraz Curi recalls that "when the guerillas were really active in

Peru, they were preaching death but my church was preaching life. We gained the reputation as a church that loved the people; the guerillas were calling to kill and be killed. And so our church grew greatly because we offered health, security, nutrition, clothing, love and peace, the practical kingdom of God."[23]

God's kingdom order builds free and prosperous societies. Satan's counterfeit order brings bondage and poverty.[24]

Concurrently Growing Kingdoms

Many Christians believe that things on earth will get worse and worse, and when they get bad enough, Jesus will come back. Several years ago, the Bolivia country director of Food for the Hungry told me that his staff, mostly evangelical and charismatic Christians, believed that because things were getting worse, Christ's return must be imminent. The irony was that they worked for a development organization to bring improvement and reduce poverty in Bolivian communities. They lived in tension: would their community development work delay Christ's return?

The kingdom of darkness is growing.[25] If one thinks sequentially (as in the great Hindu cycles of life: birth-life-death-rebirth), things indeed appear desperate. But if one thinks concurrently, we see a more hopeful future and abundant reason to work against moral, natural, and institutional evil.

The Bible speaks of concurrently growing kingdoms: the kingdom of darkness and the kingdom of light. We see this in the words of Jesus: "The kingdom of heaven is like a man who sowed good seed in his field. But while everyone was sleeping, his enemy came and sowed weeds among the wheat, and went away. When the wheat sprouted and formed heads, then the weeds also appeared. . . . Let both grow together until the harvest. At that time I will tell the harvesters: 'First collect the weeds and tie them in bundles to be burned; then gather the wheat and bring it into my barn'" (Matt. 13:24–26, 30).

We also see this in the images of the refiner's fire and the fuller's soap[26] and in the great shaking to separate the permanent from the transient.[27] The city God has built will stand; what Satan has built will be destroyed. St. Augustine, reflecting on the sack of Rome in AD 410, said, "All earthly cities are vulnerable. Men build them and men destroy them. At the same time there is the City of God which men did not build and cannot destroy and which is everlasting."[28]

Christ's kingdom is not static; it is expanding. It is overwhelming,[29] progressing,[30] and growing.[31] The old order is passing away; the new order is coming.[32] Jesus announces, "I am making everything new!" (Rev. 21:5). He is transforming culture from within, and he calls us to play a part in the spread of his kingdom on earth.

CHAPTER 10

Reawakening the Cultural Commission

Culture in the broadest sense is the purpose for which God created man after His image.
—HERMAN BAVINCK

Several years ago I had the privilege of visiting the South African town of Stellenbosch. Undeveloped, it would resemble a barren moonscape. Yet this area is the wine-making capital of South Africa. The hills around Stellenbosch are filled with some of the most beautiful vineyards I have ever seen. What force tapped into this potential? What transformed the stark, barren landscape into some of the most beautiful, productive vineyards in the world? The answer lies in the nature of human beings and in the cultural narrative held by those who developed the land.

Stories are powerful! They shape how we see and understand the world and determine the kind of nations we build. On a personal level, stories shape our values, behaviors, and lifestyles. On a national level, stories mold our culture, which in turn founds the laws, institutions, and structures of society. As we have observed, we are in a battle between stories, a conflict of moral vision and worldview. Every nation is born from a cultural story. To the extent that nations consciously worship the living God, their culture will build economically prosperous societies of beauty, justice, and peace. To the extent that cultures worship false gods, their nations will suffer, reaping poverty instead of prosperity, tyranny instead of justice, anarchy instead of peace, depravity instead of beauty. But as mentioned before, even if people do not worship the living God, they still inhabit the reality that he created. God governs the universe through natural law, which is a common grace available to all human beings. As we apply the law written in creation and in our hearts, life will follow. If we deny God's laws or fail to obey them, death will follow.

Only one story reflects reality; there is only one Lord. Our task is to live out the true story in the world. God has revealed his truth through the Word of God—the historical narrative of his work in the world. The biblical narrative reveals humankind's purpose on earth in four major stages: creation, fall, redemption, and consummation.[1] In this flow of history, God has given human beings two mandates, or commissions. The first is the Cultural Commission; the second is the Great Commission. To be truly effective in its mission, the church must understand and embrace both of these. We must reconnect the Cultural Commission and the Great Commission.

Creation and the Cultural Commission

Genesis 1 records the first Artist critiquing his creation. He says, "it was good"[2] (precious, beautiful) and "it was so"[3] (right, correct, as the Creator intended). He declares the creation of Adam and Eve "very good," exceedingly good.[4] When God finishes, his creation is perfect and filled with potential, but it is not complete! God has done his part; now it is mankind's turn to be his co-creators. Creation is waiting for God's vice-regents to steward the house, to discover and develop its potential. Being made in God's image, Adam and Eve and their descendants used their creativity and intelligence to name and rule over the animals, fill the earth with more image bearers, work the garden, plant vineyards and orchards, and create music, art, poetry, and dance. In short, human beings *filled the earth* with the knowledge, glory, and beauty of God—in essence, they created culture. This is the first mandate given to humans by God—the Cultural Commission.

The New Testament picks up this stewardship theme, using the Greek word *oikonomia,* which is sometimes translated "management," "administration," or "stewardship."[5] Our English word *economics* derives from this Greek word. The fact that the Holy Spirit inspired biblical writers to use this word indicates it should not be restricted to a materialist framework (as Christians often do). Economics is part of God's truth; stewardship of the earth is part of his mandate to humankind.

The atheist regards man and the earth as a speck of dust in a limitless universe. But the psalmist says:

> When I consider your heavens,
>   the work of your fingers,
> the moon and the stars,
>   which you have set in place,
> what is mankind that you are mindful of them,
>   human beings that you care for them?
> You made them a little lower than the angels
>   and crowned them with glory and honor.
> You made them rulers over the works of your hands;
>   you put everything under their feet.
> (Ps. 8:3–6)

The measure of human significance is not physical size but our nature as God's image bearers. We are just a little lower than the angels, made to rule the earth in God's name, crowned with "glory and honor."

Human beings are royal vice-regents, acting for God as stewards of his creation. When God made human beings, he made them like himself: "Let us make mankind in our image, in our likeness, so that they may rule" (Gen. 1:26).[6] *Imago Dei*—the image of God— has three facets: structural (what we have), relational (what we are), and functional (what we do).

First, human beings are created with structure. Though creatures, we are "like God" and thus distinct from the rest of creation. While God is infinite, we share his attributes in a finite way. We are endowed with mind, heart, and will, corresponding to attributes of intellect (knowledge, truth, wisdom); moral attributes (love, goodness, mercy, patience, righteousness); and attributes of purpose (freedom to make choices, moral responsibility). The attributes we share with God enable us to function as stewards. Internal self-government of the mind, heart, and will is required for the external stewardship of creation.

Second, human beings are relational, desiring community. God exists in relationship and made us for relationship. This relational or social view is connected to the first part of the Cultural Commission, "Be fruitful and increase in number; fill the earth" (Gen. 1:28). We procreate eternal beings who walk the bounds between heaven and earth, time and eternity. (Note the contrast with the materialist view of children as mere mouths to feed.)

Third, human beings, female and male, were made for a purpose or function on earth. This developmental view relates to the second part of the Cultural Commission to "rule over" and "take care of" the earth (Gen. 1:28; 2:15).

In summary, we have been made "like God" (structural aspect) to fulfill the Cultural Commission by filling the earth with community (relational aspect) in order to fulfill God's purpose to develop the earth (functional aspect). As my good friend Dr. Bob Moffitt so frequently says, "God created us to write our signature on the universe." We have been designed to make decisions that will have an impact in eternity.

The Fall and the Distortion of Culture

Genesis 1 shows us that God's creation was good and humans were given all the necessary faculties to exercise the Cultural Commission. Genesis 3 shows us that humanity's rebellion against God, the fall, brought a new reality and the distortion of culture. Evil entered the world in three forms: personal evil, such as murder and adultery;[7] natural evil, such as earthquakes, floods, and droughts;[8] and institutional evil, such as slavery, corporate corruption, and caste systems.[9]

I use the word *form* above intentionally. The fall did not bring an end to God's original *plan* for humans to rule creation and create culture, but it changed the *form* of creation. Variations of this word trace the history of the creation:

- The world is form*less* (Gen. 1:2).
- The Spirit of God *forms* creation (Gen. 1:3–31).
- Humanity's rebellion *de*forms creation (Gen. 3:14–19; Rom. 1:18–31).
- God *re*forms what is wrong, restoring what is good (Joel 2:12–32; Acts 3:17–26; 1 Pet. 3:18).
- God's people *con*form to Christ (Rom. 8:29; Phil. 2:1–8).
- *Trans*formation of mind and life leads to reforming of the nation (Gen. 17:1–7; Rom. 12:1–2).

Al Wolters says that the Cultural Commission "stands as the first and fundamental law of history." It has never been rescinded. After the fall, God reiterated the mandate to Adam and Eve to "cultivate the ground" (Gen. 3:23). Following the flood, God instructed Noah to "be fruitful and increase in number and fill the earth" (9:1). The entire book of Genesis traces the ever-widening history of successive generations striving to "cultivate the earth" and establish cities (one aspect of culture).

Redemption and the Great Commission

After the fall, human behavior became wildly destructive. The Bible recounts story after story of human sinfulness and the devastation and death it causes on earth. Paul writes, "Sin entered the world through one man, and death through sin, and in this way death came to all men, because all sinned" (Rom. 5:12). To renew the world, to renew culture, people needed personal renewal. Humanists believe that the evils of the world can be overcome by human virtue and goodness, that humans have the power to bring about good and just societies. Christians, however, acknowledge that human depravity must be addressed at a deeper level, which only God can do.

Centuries before the coming of Christ, the prophet Isaiah spoke of God's redemptive work in Christ and the renewal of humanity: "He poured out his life unto death, and was numbered with the transgressors. For he bore the sin of many, and made intercession for the transgressors" (Isa. 53:12). Christ gave the disciples the Great Commission in light of his death and resurrection and the sending of the Holy Spirit after Christ's ascension. Christ and the Spirit empower Christians to partner in God's mission on earth. Paul speaks of the new reality brought about by Christ's death and resurrection: "For we know that since Christ was raised from the dead, he cannot die again; death no longer has mastery over him. The death he died, he died to sin once for all; but the life he lives, he lives to God. In the same way, count yourselves dead to sin but alive to God in Christ Jesus" (Rom. 6:9–11).

The Great Commission specifically takes into account and exists because of the fall and the redemption provided by Christ. Its purpose leads to the final stage of history.

Consummation and the Kingdom of God

In Genesis 12:1–4 God called Abram to leave everything familiar and go to a place God would show him. So he did! He left fatalistic, pagan animism to enter a *new world* where growth and significance were possibilities. The book of Hebrews reveals what Abram was looking for: the City of God.[10] Just as there was both a physical and cosmic setting for the announcement of Christ's claim, so it was with Abram. He traveled in a desert in space and time. But he was also looking for something cosmic, the glorious kingdom of God.

All of history is moving toward the coming of the kingdom of God and the consummation of all things.[11] Christ died to reconcile *all things* to himself, including *all creation*, which Paul says is eagerly awaiting redemption.[12] The church's favorite verse, John 3:16, states, "For God so loved the world"—the cosmos, the universe—"that he gave his one and only Son." God has a big agenda: to renew every human being, the whole of human relationships, and all of creation.

This renewing can be understood by exploring a family of Greek words derived from the root *tellō*, "to set out for a definite point or goal."[13] First, *telos* refers to the end or end purpose and can refer to the final events of history, the eschatological end. The Bible gives us images of the *telos* of history: (1) the blessing of all nations; (2) the filling of the earth with the knowledge of the Lord; (3) the wedding of the Lamb (Christ) and his bride (the church); (4) the City of God, the New Jerusalem; (5) the glory and honor of the nations; and (6) the absence of death and sorrow.[14] In Matthew 28:20, this is called the *sunteleia*, "the consummation of the age."[15]

Another word in this family is *teleios*, which refers to the anthropological end of every redeemed person. Each Christian will be perfect and complete, lacking in nothing.[16] They will become all that God intends, conformed perfectly to the image of Christ.

A third word, *entellomai*, "to order, command to be done," is the means by which the eschatological and anthropological outcomes will be achieved. We are to obey all that Christ has commanded. (We will explore this word and theme in chapter 14.)

The end of history will be marked by the *ingathering of the nations*. God's royal vice-regents are to create culture and ultimately bring the godly fruit of their nation's culture into the consummated kingdom.[17] Abraham's pursuit is to be ours. We are to live with the end in mind, the coming of Christ and his kingdom. This incredible scene is to frame my life and yours.

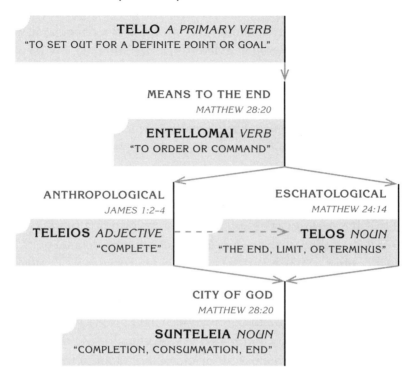

Figure 3. Word family: *telos*

The Connection between the Two Commissions

Now we can connect the first and second commissions, the Cultural Commission and Great Commission. The Great Commission is the task to create *kingdom* culture, and it is to be lived out by the church in each generation with the end—the *telos*—of history in mind. Here we catch a glimpse of what kingdom culture looks like (we will explore this in more detail in chapters 15–17). Kingdom culture includes three fundamental elements: truth (reflecting God's physical and metaphysical laws), goodness (reflecting God's moral laws), and beauty (reflecting God's aesthetic laws).

The three elements of kingdom culture connect with the three dimensions of the Great Commission. For many years I viewed the Great Commission as one-dimensional: "Go into all the world, preach the gospel, and save souls for heaven." Then I began to study the three main Great Commission passages and found that it is actually multidimensional, like a three-sided prism that refracts differently as the light shines on it from varying directions.

The first dimension, found in Acts 1:8, presents the *geographic* commission. The gospel will go around the world from Jerusalem to Judea to Samaria to the ends of earth. This represents the breadth of the mission and reflects a horizontal movement. The second dimension, in Matthew 28:19, presents the *demographic* commission. Here the gospel is to penetrate culture, pointing to the depth of the mission to all *ethnē* (peoples) and to every sector of society. This is the vertical dimension. The third dimension, in Mark 16:15, presents what I call the *ktizographic* commission (*ktizō* in Greek relates to creating and creation): "He said to them, 'Go into all the world and preach the gospel to all creation.'"[18] The gospel has implications for the creation that is awaiting redemption.[19] This represents the length of the commission—to all creation.

The demographic dimension of the Great Commission must be understood in light of the Cultural Commission of Genesis 1. At this intersection we find the reawakening of the Cultural Commission in the Great Commission.[20] The church can positively influence the building of healthy, prosperous, and free societies only by recovering her grasp of the Cultural Commission.

By focusing on the geographic dimension of the Great Commission as found in Acts 1:8, the evangelical church has lost sight of the Cultural Commission. As a result, we have more Christians, churches, and Christian organizations than ever before, but less impact than ever on shaping and transforming culture. Our societies are terribly broken, and we are rapidly damaging our earthly home. When God's people disconnect the Great Commission from the Cultural Commission, they abbreviate the task to evangelism, personal spiritual discipleship, and church planting. These are essential but not sufficient to the fulfillment of either commission. As Notre Dame sociologist Christian Smith warns, "Worthy as these projects may be, none of them attempt to transform social or cultural systems, but merely to alleviate some of the harm caused by the existing system."[21] Such solutions fall short of making a lasting difference.

The Great Commission does not replace the Cultural Commission—it reestablishes it. Both are part of God's comprehensive redemptive plan for creation. The Great Commission calls us to announce the lordship of the risen and sovereign Christ over all creation and to teach nations to obey all that Christ commanded. It highlights the power and presence of God necessary to clarify our view of the world and rectify the evils we see and do. The Cultural Commission explains what every human is hardwired to do every day. It is the "human job description." God's children, empowered by Christ's resurrection life and indwelt by the Holy Spirit, can now fulfill the Cultural Commission as God originally intended.

We must recognize the power we have been given to carry out God's mission on earth. Every Christian has a role to play in creating culture and discipling nations, which is the primary task of the Great Commission.

The Primary Task: Making Disciples of All Nations

The Church is only the Church when it exists for others.
—DIETRICH BONHOEFFER

The Dutch prime minister Abraham Kuyper, at the inauguration of the Free University in Amsterdam, famously said, "There is not a square inch in the whole domain of our human existence over which Christ, who is Sovereign over *all,* does not cry: 'Mine!'"[1] Christ is sovereign over the university, the hospital, the business, the factory, the auto shop, the farm, and the artist's studio. He wants his people to represent his kingdom, whatever their occupation, wherever they are deployed.

As we saw in chapter 11, Paul speaks of Christ's supremacy over all things: "For in him all things were created: things in heaven and on earth, visible and invisible, whether thrones or powers or rulers or authorities; . . . he is the beginning and the firstborn from among the dead, so that in everything he might have the supremacy. For God was pleased to have all his fullness dwell in him, and through him to reconcile to himself all things, whether things on earth or things in heaven" (Col. 1:16–20). With this background, we can understand Christ's words as he commissions his disciples: "Therefore go and make disciples of all nations" (Matt. 28:19). Because Christ has conquered the fear of death and death itself, because "all authority in heaven and earth" has been given to him (28:18)— *therefore go!*

In this chapter we will examine the primary task of the Great Commission, Jesus' command to "make disciples of all nations."

The Task of the Church

This task is not an option; it is a command from Christ, central to the existence of the church in each generation. Why? Because there is no neutrality in this matter: if the church does not disciple a nation, that nation will disciple the church. Ideas have consequences, and someone's ideas will shape society. Social networks that turn ideas into lifestyle will inevitably shape the institutions and life of a nation. If the church is not consciously incarnating the word of God, and thus impacting the world, then the ideas that dominate the nation will govern the church.

In the Gospel of John, Christ prays for his disciples and the church: "My prayer is *not* that you take them out of the world" (17:15). He went out of his way to articulate what he was *not* praying. Why? Why did he not pray to have his disciples taken out of the world? Because he wants his people *in* the world! Christ left heaven to come to the earth as the incarnate Word of God.[2] Now he wants the church, the body of Christ, to manifest the Word of God in their communities (see chapter 12).

Sadly, many Christians instead become *like* the world. Others, wanting to be distinct from the world, virtually take themselves *out* of the world and *into* a building. Christ wants the church to be *in* the world but not *of* the world. His people are to influence the world in all areas of life and every sphere of society.

It's common to assume that the church is a building. It is not. A mosque is a building, a synagogue is a building, but the church as taught in the Scriptures is a people, a community of believers. The church *gathers* on Sunday for corporate worship and equipping. The church may gather in a rice field in Thailand, under a tree in rural Kenya, in a soccer stadium, or on a large urban campus. The same church *scatters* on Monday all over the city to minister to and influence society.

The church does not exist for itself as a kind of social club, nor does it exist for the pastor as a kind of fiefdom. No, the church is a people established by God for the sake of others. William Temple, archbishop of Canterbury from 1942 to 1944, understood this when he said that the church is "the only cooperative society in the world that exists for the benefit of its non-members."[3]

The church is not merely a base for activities and programs that benefit the congregation, but is an outpost of the kingdom of God for the community. My good friend Dr. Bob Moffitt, founder of the Harvest Foundation, is fond of asking the provocative question, "If your church suddenly disappeared overnight, would anyone notice?" A church that exists for itself could disappear unnoticed, but one that exists for others would be missed.

This way of thinking must influence the way we view our communities. Gary Skinner, founding pastor of the outwardly focused Watoto Church in Kampala, Uganda, instructs his church's leaders and members to identify and address the needs and problems in their communities. He states, "The problems are not the communities' problems—they're our problems!"[4]

Discipling Nations

The West has always recognized the significance of the individual, as it should. More recently, however, we have drifted from a Judeo-Christian concept of the uniqueness and value of every human to a mere shadow of this ideal in the modern concept of individual*ism*.

In the past, Western culture honored God, and the individual found his or her unique place as a free and responsible agent within God's glorious order. Now, Western culture no longer honors God, but makes man the center of the universe. Now we worship man, which is the essence of individualism.

We see this individualism everywhere: Frank Sinatra's song "My Way," the rugged Marlboro Man, Burger King's invitation to have a burger "your way." Shaped by today's values, the church has focused its evangelism and discipleship on individuals, blinded to the communal component of the Great Commission. Individuals must come to a saving knowledge of Christ, but this truth must not blind us to the biblical concept of community. Paul and Silas told the Philippian jailer, "Believe in the Lord Jesus, and you will be saved—*you and your household.*"[5]

Jesus commands us to make disciples of all nations. The word translated "nations" in Matthew 28:19 comes from the Greek word *ethnos*, meaning "a people, a large group based on various cultural, physical or geographic ties."[6] *Ethnos* is related to *ethos*, "the distinctive character, spirit, and attitudes of a people."[7] A culture's ethos includes its sacred belief system, its values system, its first principles, and the virtues of its people.

We must not confuse "nation" (*ethnos*) with the modern concept of a geopolitical state. For instance, Ethiopia, a geopolitical state, is home to dozens of ethnic groups, or *ethnē* (the plural of *ethnos*). Throughout history, nations have been identified in other than geopolitical terms, such as by descent, tribe or clan, language, cultural heritage, religion, or ideals. Today some occupational groups—medical personnel, for example—have aspects of a distinctive culture and language and thus may be considered *ethnē*. In addition, the concept of transnationalism finds growing expression in global organizations. These "transnationals" transcend national borders and often carry greater economic and political clout than the nations where they engage. Transnationals fall into several categories: multinational corporations like Toyota, Airbus, Google, and Conoco-Phillips; nongovernmental organizations like the International Red Cross, Catholic Social Services, and World Vision International; and quasi-governmental organizations like the United Nations, World Bank, and the International Monetary Fund. Today all of these groups can be considered *ethnē*, "nations," to be discipled.

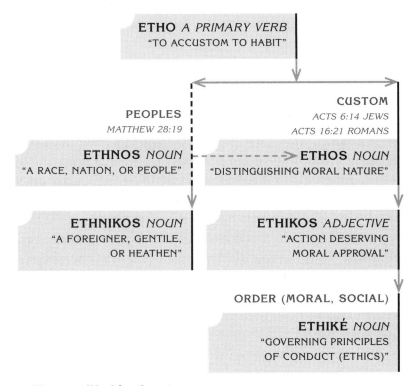

Figure 4. Word family: *ethnos*

Matthew Henry (1662–1714) was an English Presbyterian Puritan perhaps best known for his commentaries on the whole Bible, works bound not by modern sensibilities of individualism but by the biblical frame of community. In his commentary on our text, he wrote:

"Do your utmost to make the nations Christian nations;" not, "Go to the nations, and denounce the judgments of God against them, as Jonah against Nineveh, and as the other Old-Testament prophets" (though they had reason enough to expect it for their wickedness), "but go, and *disciple them.*" Christ the Mediator is setting up a kingdom in the world, bring the nations to be his subjects; setting up a school, bring the nations to be his scholars; raising an army for the carrying on of the war against the powers of darkness, enlist the nations of the earth under his banner.[8]

Discipleship is an inside-out process, beginning in an individual, moving into the family, the vocational sectors or other *ethnē*, and from there to the larger society. The gospel penetrates culture.

Jesus taught that his people are salt and light. Salt must come out of the shaker to flavor and preserve. Light cannot bring life, illuminate, or heal unless it comes out from under the bushel basket.[9] Christians are salt and light, not theocrats; influencers, not autocrats; organic, not hierarchal; bottom up, not top down. We are to be people of light in a world of darkness, people of compassion in a world of cruelty, people of justice in a world of wrong, people of beauty in a world of the mundane. Christians are to be *radicals* in the traditional sense of the word: having roots, going to the origin. We are to call societies back to the *root*, back to first principles. Cultures are not to be Westernized nor destroyed; they are to be thoroughly redeemed. Nations are to be discipled at the level of culture. We call nations into the life of the kingdom under the authority of the King.

Every Christian

As a young Christian, I was taught that the Great Commission was for the professional missionary going overseas. It had nothing to do with the Christian in the pew. Those Christians who were more spiritual went overseas; the less spiritual stayed home and worked "secular" jobs, giving money to support missions.

The problem with this teaching, which many Christians hold, is that it is a dualistic understanding of the world that comes from Greek philosophy. The Bible does not recognize any concept of merely secular work for the Christian. Every calling is sacred because every calling is assigned by Jesus Christ. Nor does the Bible give special status to one's place of deployment. A Christian who goes abroad is not somehow more spiritual or important than one who remains at home; both are essential to the work of the kingdom. The task of discipling nations is shared by every Christian, wherever he or she is.

When Christ says, "Therefore go and make disciples of all nations," the Greek word translated "go" means "to pursue the journey on which one has entered, to continue on one's journey."[10] Christ commands his followers to make disciples as they continue on their journey. The task is not just for professional missionaries overseas but for all Christians wherever God deploys them and in whatever vocation they are called.

Several years ago at a leadership school for 150 young Christian leaders from fifty nations, I taught on Christ's universal sovereignty and exposed the false dichotomy of the sacred versus the secular. As I finished, a young woman came up to me and said that I had "ruined her life." When I asked how, she told me she had studied and practiced law. When she became a Christian, her new Christian friends said her work was secular and thus inferior. They told her she needed to leave law and become an overseas missionary, a "spiritual" and thus superior occupation. So she quit her job, undertook missions training, and went to West Africa as a missionary. Now, years later, having heard teaching on the kingdom of God, this woman realized that God in fact wanted her to be a lawyer. She decided to return to West Africa, her place of deployment, and work as a lawyer, seeking to bring more justice to a corrupt society.

This woman embraced the primary task of the Great Commission. In the following chapters we will see how making disciples takes place through two supporting tasks: baptizing and teaching.

CHAPTER 12

Baptizing the Nations: Union and Transformation

Negating one group of names and establishing another group of names in effect calls for a new order, a transformation. . . . The religious transformation would entail enormous social, economic and political changes as well.

—CHRISTOPHER WRIGHT

Discipling is a life-on-life process. It is to invite someone to walk with you through life, in the circle of your days, and there to instruct and teach him or her. Jesus discipled those who followed him: he lived with them, traveled with them, worked and ministered with them, ate meals with them, and prayed with them. He was the Rabbi who said, "Follow me!" He not only taught his followers; he modeled for them the life of the kingdom and told them to do the same.

Our primary assignment of making disciples of all nations has two supporting tasks: baptizing and teaching. "Therefore go and make disciples of all nations, *baptizing* them in the name of the

Father and of the Son and of the Holy Spirit, and *teaching* them to obey everything I have commanded you" (Matt. 28:19–20). In this chapter I will discuss the first of these tasks, showing that the sense of baptism Jesus stressed can be captured by the phrase "living a life that baptizes."

We are to *demonstrate* the kingdom of God so that people can *see* it before we *teach* the kingdom for them to *hear* it. Jesus' baptism marked the beginning of his public ministry of daily sacrifice and ultimately his death on the cross. As believers, we are to follow him in this baptism.

The Nature of Baptism

Baptism has three major understandings, all true and valid. First, baptism is an ordinance of the church, initiation into the body of Christ. Second, baptism symbolizes the believer's identification with Jesus Christ. The act of going down into water and rising up again is visual identification with the death, burial, and resurrection of Christ. This is a significant *public renunciation* of one's past life and a *public confession* of one's new identity and life in Christ. In free societies baptism often has little cost, but in totalitarian societies it may be seen as rebellion against the social order, possibly bringing severe penalties, including death.

The third understanding of baptism is an extension of the first two; it is the idea of entering into an ongoing, vital, life-giving relationship with Christ and a kingdom-oriented community. This understanding emphasizes Christ's headship of the church, his body.[1] He fills it with his life; he is in a vital and organic union with it. We identify ourselves with him, and he identifies himself with us. Dr. William Hendriksen, professor of New Testament exegetical theology and author of several volumes in the New Testament Commentary series, writes: "'Being baptized into the name of,' therefore means 'being brought into vital relationship with' that One. . . . The one who submits to it [baptism] . . . is proclaiming that he has broken with the world and has been brought into union with the Triune God, to whom he intends to devote his life."[2]

The apostle Paul captures this as he writes to the church at Rome: "Or don't you know that all of us who were baptized into Christ Jesus were baptized into his death? We were therefore buried with him through baptism into death in order that, just as Christ was raised from the dead through the glory of the Father, we too may live a new life" (Rom. 6:3–4).[3]

Missions Pastor Robert Lynn, a fellow of the Wilberforce Forum, writes of the connection between baptism, the cross, Christ's mission, and ours: "[Christ's] baptism is the beginning of His ministry of giving Himself in suffering love for the sake of the world. . . . The cross is the meaning of His baptism. . . . [Our] journey begins with our own baptism. We have known water, and by that water we are incorporated into a people whose life together looks like Jesus' life, a life given away in suffering love for the sake of a world so desperately in need of healing and transformation."[4]

Baptism marks the beginning of a journey, a mission from another place—the kingdom of God—and for this world (to use N. T. Wright's phrasing, quoted earlier). The baptized person is committing to live in union with the triune God and in accordance with the laws and ordinances of his kingdom. We see this connection in John 15:5 where Jesus says, "I am the vine; you are the branches. If you remain in me and I in you, you will bear much fruit; apart from me you can do nothing." The first two meanings of baptize mark an event. This third concept is a process of believers abiding in Christ and is significant in the discussion of the Great Commission.

The word baptize in Greek is baptizō. Nicander of Colophon, a second-century BC Greek poet and physician, has given us a clear understanding of this word by way of a metaphor: making pickles.[5] Two steps are required to pickle a cucumber. First, the cucumber is dipped into boiling water. The Greek word for this action is baptō. But baptō doesn't turn the cucumber into a pickle; it simply prepares the cucumber for pickling. The second step is to immerse the cucumber into the pickling juice, typically vinegar and spices, and to leave it there. Over time, the juice permeates the cucumber and transforms it into a pickle. The Greek word for this process is *baptizō*. While *baptō* is a short-term process resulting in temporary change, *baptizō* is a long-term process resulting in permanent change.

When Jesus said, "baptize them," he used the word *baptizō*. Christians are to be the agents of transformation. Our vital relationship with Christ is the "solution" in which we are to baptize nations. Over time, this baptizing process will bring about permanent change.

Someone told me about a computer sales and service representative named Bob. One of his customer accounts was a company that made pickles. Whenever Bob visited the pickle factory, he was overwhelmed by the stench of the pickling solution. The smell permeated the walls, equipment, and furniture. Later, when Bob arrived at home, his wife would know immediately he had been at the pickle factory! Christians are to be the pickling solution: we are to live a life that baptizes.

Baptō is an event; *baptizō* is a comprehensive process. God wants to see nations transformed, changed from one thing into another. That happens when nations are overwhelmed and transformed by the nature and character of God.

The Significance of a Name

We are baptized in the *name* of the Father and of the Son and of the Holy Spirit. The name of God and the place where God dwells play a significant role in the transformation of nations. Israel was transformed from a slave nation to a free nation. Following the exodus from Egypt, the Hebrews were nomads, living in tents and wandering from one watering hole to the next. God journeyed with them and led them. To demonstrate his identification with his people, he gave them instructions for building a tabernacle: "Then have them make a sanctuary for me, and I will dwell among them" (Exod. 25:8).[6] The people had their tents, and God would have his tent, the tabernacle. God wanted to dwell in the midst of his people, not far away on a holy mountain in a distant country.

Later, the temple became the place where God's name resided. "He [David] is the one who will build a house for *my name*. And I will establish the throne of his kingdom forever" (2 Sam. 7:13). "My father David had it in his heart to build a temple for *the name of the LORD,* the God of Israel" (2 Chron. 6:7–9).[7] Perhaps you can relate to this personally. People know my house as "the Millers." It is not only where the Miller family lives; it is the place identified with our name.

Zechariah connects the place where God resides with God's nature. "This is what the LORD says: 'I will return to Zion and dwell in Jerusalem. Then Jerusalem will be called the City of Truth, and the mountain of the LORD Almighty will be called the Holy Mountain'" (Zech. 8:3 NIV 1984). The mountain is holy and the city is truth because holiness and truth are the nature of the God who resides there. God's nature is to be manifested by his people who live in the place of his name. "'These are the things you are to do: Speak the truth to each other, and render true and sound judgment in your courts; do not plot evil against your neighbor, and do not love to swear falsely. I hate all this,' declares the LORD" (8:16–17).

Because the character of the city reflects the truth and goodness of God, nations will be drawn to the city with God's name and to Israel's God. "And many peoples and powerful nations will come to Jerusalem to seek the LORD Almighty and to entreat him" (Zech. 8:22). Israel's obedience to God ultimately leads to transformation so powerful that nations are drawn to God as moths are drawn to the light. We see the same theme in Deuteronomy 4:5–8:

> See, I have taught you decrees and laws as the LORD my God commanded me, so that you may follow them in the land you are entering to take possession of it. Observe them carefully, for this will show your wisdom and understanding to the nations,

who will hear about all these decrees and say, "Surely this great nation is a wise and understanding people." What other nation is so great as to have their gods near them the way the LORD our God is near us whenever we pray to him? And what other nation is so great as to have such righteous decrees and laws as this body of laws I am setting before you today?

When the people of Israel enter the Promised Land, they are to remove the worship places of the pagan animists so that God's dwelling place might be built and his name inhabit the place.

> Destroy completely all the places on the high mountains and on the hills and under every spreading tree where the nations you are dispossessing worship their gods. Break down their altars, smash their sacred stones and burn their Asherah poles in the fire; cut down the idols of their gods and *wipe out their names from those places.* You must not worship the LORD your God in their way. But you are to seek the place the LORD your God will choose from among all your tribes *to put his Name there for his dwelling.* (Deut. 12:2–5)

God says in effect, "When you go into the land, destroy the pagan altars and get rid of the pagan gods' names. Establish my tabernacle, the place where I will dwell, the place where my name will reside."

Dr. Christopher Wright, a British author and Old Testament scholar, comments: "To remove the names of Canaan's gods was to remove their presence and their power. Just as the putting of Yahweh's name in a place was to fill it with his availability and his nearness."[8] Our culture often does not recognize the power of a name, but the influence of a name is profound.

The Old Testament gives an example of what Wright is saying. The name Baal, one of the pagan gods of the Moabite people, means "owner, master."[9] He was a ruthless god, and the Jews began worshiping this god when they moved into the land. What happened when they rejected the worship of the living God, Yahweh? Their language and culture changed. The name for husband changed among the Hebrew people from *ish*, "loving, self-sacrificing head," to *baal*, "owner, master."[10] Throughout the Old Testament the Jewish husband is called *baal* because his behavior toward his wife is a reflection of Baal's behavior toward those who worship him. During this period, the husband became the owner/master of his wife.[11]

A modern example is the powerful impact that the name *Allah* has on Muslims. For jihadists, killing and bombing—acts of jihad—are all done in the "name of Allah."

Names are powerful. The United States and Europe are seeing immense changes today. Why? Because God's name has been removed and pagan animistic and secular gods are being worshiped. Instead of the living God, nature and man have become the center of the universe.

The Trinitarian Name of God

A name, whether of a person or an object, can reveal something of the nature of the person or object. In some cultures parents do not name a child for several years, until they have a sense of the child's personality. Then they give the child a name that reflects his or her nature. When God told Adam to name the animals in Genesis 2, Adam most likely did not simply pull names out of the air. To name something, one has to observe the characteristics and uniqueness of the thing being named. Adam must have studied the animals to see what made each one unique and then given each a name that related to the creature's nature.

God has revealed his nature and character through hundreds of names in the Bible. He is called YHWH (Yahweh), the name that was not to be spoken, meaning "I Am"; *elohim*, the one supreme Deity; holy; the Rock; the Provider; the Almighty; the Redeemer; the Savior; the Prince of Peace; the Alpha and Omega; and the good Shepherd. We could go on and on and on. Each of God's names reflects something of his nature and character. But Jesus specifically instructs us to baptize the nations "into the name of the Father and the Son and the Holy Spirit" (Matt. 28:19).[12]

The persons of the Trinity have distinct roles in creation, salvation, and the kingdom. In creation, the Father is the creator;[13] the creation was by and for the Son;[14] and the Holy Spirit was brooding over creation.[15] In salvation, the Father authored, led, and directed the plan; the Son executed the plan through his life, death, and resurrection; and the Holy Spirit sealed the plan through regeneration and sanctification. It is *in* Christ and *through* the indwelling of the Holy Spirit that the kingdom community lives in relationship *with* the Father.[16]

It is in the comprehensive Trinitarian name that we are to be the baptizing agents, the transforming agents of our societies. God's Trinitarian nature—one God in three persons, unity and diversity—is reflected in creation, as we will explore in chapter 14. In baptizing nations, we must recognize and value this unity and diversity.

Furthermore, as we will discuss in chapters 15 through 17, God's Trinitarian nature is manifested in culture through truth, goodness, and beauty. Christians are to embody and create culture that reflects these elements of God's nature.

In this chapter we have seen how the church lives in vital relationship with Christ and thus enters into the life of the Trinity. Our task is to baptize the nations in God's name, overwhelming them with the nature and character of God. How this can be done is our next subject.

CHAPTER 13

Living the Word:
Love and Service

*Don't look for big things, just do small things with great love. . . . The
smaller the thing, the greater must be our love.*
—MOTHER TERESA

In the Old Testament God instructed his people to build a tabernacle so that he could dwell in their midst. This theme continues
in the New Testament. John 1:14 says, "And the Word became flesh,
and did *tabernacle* among us, and we beheld his glory, glory as of an
only begotten of a father, full of grace and truth" (YLT). The Greek
word for "tabernacled" is the same word that was used in the Greek
translation of the Old Testament. God came from heaven and
incarnated himself as the person of Jesus Christ because he wanted
to live among his people. It is through the indwelling Holy Spirit
that God tabernacles in believers today.

In the last chapter we began to examine the theme of baptizing
the nations in the name of the Father, Son, and Holy Spirit. Now we

will examine how this may be done through love and truth actively lived out.

The Word Becomes Flesh

In his profound book *The Rise of Christianity: How the Obscure, Marginal Jesus Movement Became the Dominant Religious Force in the Western World in a Few Centuries*, Rodney Stark seeks to understand how a relatively small number of Christians were able to overcome Rome. Stark describes how Rome considered cruelty a virtue and compassion a vice, evidenced by the blood sports of gladiators and throwing people to lions. In this culture of cruelty, the God of compassion raised up a generation of worshipers who, like him, lived compassionately. Stark describes the impact of this compassion: "Christianity brought a new conception of humanity to a world saturated with capricious cruelty and the vicarious love of death. . . . What Christianity gave to its converts was nothing less than their humanity."[1]

What was it that led to the rise of Christianity? Stark answers: "Central doctrines of Christianity prompted and sustained attractive, liberating, and effective social relations and organizations. . . . It was the way these doctrines *took on actual flesh,* the way they directed organizational action and individual behavior, that led to the rise of Christianity."[2] The early church responded to pagan Rome with a better theology, a theology they lived out. They understood that the Word had become flesh in Christ; now the Word was to become flesh in their lives.

The Great Commission can only be fulfilled as the Word becomes flesh in the life of the church. To say it differently, both individual Christians and the local community of believers are to live, by God's grace, an embodied life. We are to abide in God's Word, obey the Word, and love in deed and in truth.[3] We cannot disciple individuals or nations with lies. <u>Freedom comes from the truth, and truth comes from the Word of God.</u>[4] We must not only actively study the Bible to know the truth; we must also apply what we have learned. The Greek mind was interested in *knowing* the truth, but the Hebrew mind was concerned with *doing* the truth. Too many Christians are like the ancient Greeks. We listen to expository preaching; we attend Sunday school classes and Bible studies. We fill our minds with knowledge about the Bible, yet struggle to apply what we have learned.

Many people outside the church are not ready to listen to our message; they want to see the truth lived out. Too often Christians want to evangelize with words. This is fine for people who are ready to hear the truth, but it will have no effect on people who want to see the truth. Similarly, we are not merely to pray but to put feet to our prayers. We are to live out the Lord's Prayer: "Your kingdom come, your will be done, on earth as it is in heaven."[5]

The Greek language distinguishes between three primary words for love: *eros*, the intimacy of sexual love between a man and a woman; *phileō*, friendship or brotherly love; and *agapē*, the self-sacrificing love of God. Christians are called upon to love as God loves, with selflessness and self-sacrifice.[6] A classic children's folk song captures the essence of this love:

> Love, love, love, love,
> The Gospel in one word is love
> Love your neighbor as yourself
> For God is love

The Scriptures call us to love comprehensively. We are to love our family, our neighbors, our countrymen, and strangers.[7] And, yes, we are to love our enemies.[8]

American pastor John Piper calls for "persistent public love."[9] Love needs to be translated into action. Persistent public love drove William Wilberforce to fight to end the slave trade in the British Empire. Persistent public love led William Carey to fight to end widow burning in India. Persistent public love caused Martin Luther King Jr. to lead the civil rights movement in the United States.

Love Cells

The Starfish and the Spider by Ori Brafman and Rod A. Beckstrom relates an intriguing fact.[10] If you cut off the legs of the spider it will die, whereas if you cut off the legs of a starfish, the legs grow back. If you have a large enough piece of a leg, the leg will grow a whole new starfish. While the two animals have a similar profile viewed from above, they are structured very differently.

Brafman and Beckstrom tell the story of a group of Australians who were concerned about a starfish population destroying the Great Barrier Reef. The group tried to save the reef by cutting the starfish into pieces. A year later they were shocked to find three to four times the number of starfish as before. Instead of killing the starfish, they had multiplied them!

From this biological concept, the authors make a case for "leaderless organizations." A hierarchal organization with a top-down structure is a spider. If the legs are cut off, the organization dies. Starfish-like organizations, on the other hand, have DNA that permeates the group and allows it to replicate itself even if the legs are taken off. Brafman and Beckstrom suggest that al-Qaeda is a starfish, while the US Army is a spider. If everything else were equal, who would win? The starfish!

What about the church? I would suggest that the early church was a starfish, while today's church is more hierarchical, like a spider. What would happen if today's church became a starfish? The jihadists use the starfish model for terror cells. What would happen if the church spawned a starfish model of *love cells?* What if the DNA of Christ permeated the church in small cells that loved their enemies and nurtured kingdom values in their members?

Dutch theologian Hendrik Berkhof describes the potential impact of love cells: "It can happen that Christ's church, *by her preaching, her presence, and the patterns of life* obtaining within her fellowship, may represent such a mighty witness and so forcefully address the consciences of men far beyond her borders, that they generally orient themselves by this reality, tacitly accepting it as a landmark. . . . They do so because they know of no better guarantor of *a decent life, of mercy, freedom, justice, and humanity* than a certain general acknowledgement of the sovereignty of Christ."[11]

Cyprian (200–258), the bishop of Carthage, describes the nature and extent of the call to Christian love: "The people being assembled together, he first of all urges on them the benefits of mercy. . . . Then he proceeds to add that there is nothing remarkable in cherishing mercy on our own people with the due attentions of love, but that one might become perfect who should do something more than heathen men or publicans, one who, *overcoming evil with good,* and *practicing merciful kindness* like that of God, should *love his enemies* as well. . . . Thus the good was done to all men, not merely to the household of faith."[12]

Love cells are viral by nature. Jesus uses four analogies of the organic (non-programmatic) nature of such cells. Christians are to function as salt, light, yeast, and mustard seeds.[13] They are to take on a life of their own and have a positive impact in the community. One of my hero churches is the Watoto Church mentioned earlier. This cell-based church in Kampala, Uganda, is outwardly focused to meet needs in their community. The five hundred cells in the church were challenged to love someone dying of AIDS. Each cell cared for a person while he or she was dying and then supported the family after the family member's death. We are motivated to love in this way by Christ's example[14] and by God's command.[15]

Another hero church comes from the past. German Count Nikolaus Ludwig von Zinzendorf (1700–1760) became a social reformer and founded the Moravian church, making his estate at Herrnhut available to shelter the poor and homeless. The Moravians were known, among other things, for engaging in wholistic mission. They sent out businessmen to start businesses and plant churches. At a time when most churches deployed one member cross-culturally for every thousand at home, the Moravians deployed one for every sixty. The Moravian community also prayed twenty-four hours a day, seven days a week . . . for one hundred years![16]

The Moravian legacy includes the story of two young men

who wanted to minister to the two to three thousand black slaves on British plantations in the Caribbean. The slave owners forbade missionaries, so these young men sold themselves into slavery and with the proceeds bought one-way passage to the Caribbean. As the ship pulled away from the dock in Copenhagen, the two young men waved and shouted at their weeping friends and family on the pier, "May the Lamb that was slain receive the reward of his suffering!"

This is love in action! This is how the invisible kingdom of God becomes visible through our lives. If love cells engaged the two wars of our generation, what might be the result?

Responding to the War from the East

How can Christians respond to the war from the East? Government has the responsibility to defend its nation against terrorist enemies. But the church has a different responsibility: to love. Christ calls us to love even our enemies. The church responds to the violence of the sword with the vulnerability of the cross; to the culture of death with the culture of life; to hatred with love, injustice with justice, tyranny with freedom.

Andrew van der Bijl (b. 1928), known as Brother Andrew, smuggled Bibles into communist countries during the height of the Cold War. After the fall of communism, he turned his attention to the Middle East. "We cannot win the war on terror with guns and bombs," he says, "because everyone we kill is replaced by dozens more who seek revenge. . . . We believe that if millions of Christians would respond to Muslims with the love of Christ, that would do far more to remove the threat of terror than our military activities.[17] Brother Andrew challenges Christians to say, "'I Sincerely Love All Muslims (I.S.L.A.M.)' and to prove it by putting their arms around Muslims and say, 'God loves you; therefore I love you.'"[18]

Liberato (not his real name) is a pastor from the Philippines and part of the minority Christian community on an island with a Muslim majority. He told me how his church became a love cell.

Muslims wanted to overrun the central government and set up an Islamic state on the island. They sought to drive the Christians out by burning down their homes. (Imagine if someone in your community hated you enough to burn down your home, simply because you were a Christian.) The Philippine army arrived to crush the Muslim rebellion by blowing up the terrorists' homes. Liberato responded by saying, "We need to love our enemies. We need to demonstrate God's love." None of the other pastors in the community agreed, but Liberato organized his church to rebuild the terrorists' homes. Eventually other churches joined them. When I heard the story, they had rebuilt the homes of forty Muslim families. Not surprisingly, the attitude of the Muslim community toward Christians was changing dramatically.

I received a letter from a friend named Chris who works with the Disciple Nations Alliance affiliate in Africa. Chris had the privilege of speaking to pastors in Malakal, in what is now South Sudan, on the need for the church to minister to the needs of the larger community, including the Muslim minority. Chris describes a thrilling moment in the closing ceremony: "The highlight of the celebration was when a mosque preacher, an imam, who we did not know was a participant, walked forward and said, 'Having listened to the wholistic message of loving one's neighbor as oneself, including loving your enemies, and the rest of the transformational messages, I hereby openly declare my departure from the Islamic faith and identify myself with the family of Jesus Christ.'"

Abba Love, a large cell church in Jakarta, Indonesia, ministers to neighboring slums inhabited by Muslims. The church has started schools, soup kitchens, literacy programs, and skills training for unemployed Muslims. When a group of radicals came to burn down Abba Love's building, they were prevented by poor Muslims who streamed out of the community and surrounded the building, saying, "You are not going to touch this church. These people love us."

May these examples be multiplied a million times over everywhere a church touches a Muslim community. The war in the East will be won through the self-sacrificial love of the church, through the Word becoming flesh in God's people.

Responding to the War in the West

How does the Word become flesh in the midst of the war in the West? In her book *Eve's Revenge: Women and a Spirituality of the Body*, Lilian Calles Barger suggests: "We do this by living little acts of resistance—everyday acts done in our bodies. . . . Our protest must be based on faith that an invisible kingdom is being made visible in the bodies of the men and women who actively follow the crucified and resurrected one."[19] The church must not be a spectator of the decline of the West; it must proactively engage as the conscience of the nations, the inhibitor of that decline. The Reverend Martin Luther King Jr. used a powerful metaphor: "The church was not merely a *thermometer* that recorded the ideas and principles of popular opinion; it was a *thermostat* that transformed the mores of society."[20]

The church is to counter the modern and postmodern culture. It is to lead the resistance. God has hardwired human beings for freedom. At times, Christians must form the core of the resistance to political, social, and economic tyranny. Rick Pearcey, editor of *The Pearcey Report*, makes a clarion call to stand against tyranny and injustice:

> Human beings are creatures of resistance. There is a sense in which we are hardwired to rebel—not against good, but against evil. Not against life in community with our Creator and our neighbor, but against that which, if not resisted, alienates us from the good, the true and the beautiful—including freedom. So of course a creature destined for freedom is a creature of resistance against tyranny. And so the founders in the Declaration affirm the "right" and "duty" to "throw off" a government

that has as its "direct object . . . the establishment of an absolute Tyranny."

How can the New Resistance win the culture war? First, do not allow a demonizing name-calling to slow you down. Second, stand up, proudly, *as citizens* of resistance. And third, stand up, magnificently, *as human beings*—as creatures of resistance "blessed" that way by the Creator to say "no!" to tyranny and "yes!" to freedom.[21]

The points of resistance are grounded in the kingdom culture of truth, goodness, and beauty. First, we are to speak truth to power. This may be as simple as starting a blog or writing letters to the editor to challenge prevailing opinions. It may be homeschooling children or establishing charter schools that function from a biblical worldview and principles. Or it may be to serve on a school board or introduce a supplemental curriculum into a public school setting.[22] Second, we are to confront corruption, injustice, and evil with goodness, justice, and wholesomeness. The civil rights and pro-life movements are examples of this. We might choose to have a larger family (being fruitful and multiplying) in the face of the anti-family movement. Third, we are to habitually bring beauty into the "small places" of home, work, school, and recreation. We are to model excellent work in the marketplace.

In carrying out the Great Commission, we are to live the Word so that it becomes flesh to the world around us, fulfilling the first secondary task of baptizing nations. This brings us to the other secondary task: teaching the nations.

CHAPTER 14

Teaching the Nations: The Comprehensive Task

One desire has been the ruling passion of my life.... That is in spite of all worldly opposition, God's holy ordinances shall be established again in the home, in the school, and in the State for the good of the people: to chisel as it were into the conscience of the nation the ordinances of the Lord.

—ABRAHAM KUYPER

When I was a young man, my friend Bob and I arrived for an appointment and were kept waiting for half an hour. While I stared at the wall, Bob pulled a book out of his back pocket and read. For me the time was wasted. Bob spent the time learning.

God has created us to learn and grow in wisdom and knowledge. Education is the art of lifelong learning, not simply formal schooling. It begins before formal schooling and continues until the day we die. Francis Schaeffer used to say, "Don't let your children's schooling get in the way of their education."[1] We must distinguish between schooling and education.

Nations, like people, are to learn. In the twin secondary tasks of the Great Commission, Christ calls us first to *demonstrate* the truth (living a life that baptizes) and then to *teach* the truth (teaching that which transforms). Having looked at the first task, we now turn our attention to the second: "teaching them to obey everything I have commanded you" (Matt. 28:20). Instruction in truth is foundational to the primary task of discipleship.

This chapter aims to show how God's commands are beautifully simple and wonderfully profound. Through obedience to God's commands—in all their fullness—people and nations find freedom, life, and peace.

"Teaching Them to Obey Everything"

Let's examine this passage by looking at a number of key words. The first key word in the passage is *teaching*, which comes from a Greek word meaning "to hold discourse with others in order to instruct them, deliver didactic discourses."[2] The second key word is *obey*, which in Greek means "to attend to carefully, take care of, to guard."[3] The things that Christ has commanded are precious, to be guarded and taken care of.

Both "teaching" and "obey" are present tense (ongoing action, no end in sight) and active voice (the subject is actively involved). Disciples are to actively and continually engage in teaching the nations. Nations are to actively and continually obey all that Christ has commanded. Teaching and obeying are to continue "to the very end of the age" (Matt. 28:20), when Christ returns to bring his kingdom to fruition.[4]

What are the nations to obey? What is the "everything" Jesus has commanded us? The answer requires a firm grasp of two other key words, *everything* and *commanded*.

The word translated "everything" comes from the Greek word meaning "every, any, all, the whole."[5] Earlier we saw this word (or one of its forms) used seven times in Colossians 1:15–20 to reflect Christ's sovereignty over *all* things. In Matthew 28:18–20 the word is used three times: *all* authority has been given to Christ; *all* nations are to be discipled; and *everything* Christ commanded is to be taught and obeyed. The passage is comprehensive, speaking of all commands, not some; all nations, not a few; all authority, not partial or limited. We can connect this to the other Great Commission passages, which describe the three dimensions: to all the earth, to all creation, and to all nations.

The Greek word for "commanded" comes from *entellomai*, "to order, command to be done."[6] This word is derived from *telos*, "the end," that by which a thing is finished, the end to which all things relate, the aim, the purpose. We explored this word family in chapter 10, noting that history is moving toward the fulfillment of God's purposes. What is that purpose? Nothing less than "your kingdom come, your will be done, on earth as it is in heaven." *Telos* is the eschatological end to which all of history is moving, and *teleios* is the anthropological purpose for each human being.[7] How do individuals and nations move toward the fulfillment of their God-given purpose? By obedience, by keeping all that Christ has commanded—*entellomai*.

All authority in heaven and on earth has been given to Christ. He employs that authority by sending us to make disciples of all nations, teaching them to obey "everything I have commanded you," to extend his rule on earth. The kingdom of God (the reign of Christ) is the *framework* for our obedience; Christ's saving work on the cross (our salvation) is the *foundation* of our obedience; and nations keeping all that Christ commanded produces the *fulfillment* of obedience—"your kingdom come, your will be done, on earth as it is in heaven!"

When we examined the task of baptizing nations in the name of the Father, Son, and Holy Spirit, we noted that God wants his name over the nations. This reality will reach its consummation with the return of Christ, when "the LORD will be king over the whole earth.

On that day there will be one LORD, and his name the only name"
(Zech. 14:9). We are to give our lives for the achievement of this
vision: God's name and glory filling the earth.[8]

Acts 5 records that the civil authorities brought Peter and the
other apostles before the Sanhedrin, the religious authorities. The
apostles were living according to this compelling vision and thus
had violated local restrictions. The high priest told them, "We gave
you strict orders not to teach in this name. . . . Yet you have filled
Jerusalem with your teaching and are determined to make us guilty
of this man's blood" (Acts 5:28). God's people were *filling* the city
and the nation with his glory and knowledge, teaching them to
obey all that Jesus had commanded.

Paul says he proclaims the message about Jesus Christ "so that
all nations might believe and obey him" (Rom. 16:26 NIV1984).
Individuals and nations are not only to know all that Christ commanded; they are to do—to obey—all that he commanded. Nations
are to make the law of Christ the root of their national order. The
results of this obedience are freedom, justice, peace, and bounty.

Obedience and Self-Government

Let's look more closely at the relationship between obedience,
freedom, and authority. We usually think of obedience in external
terms: obedience is when people submit to government or laws;
disobedience is when people do what is right in their own eyes.[9]
Christ calls us to a different kind of obedience: to freely and internally govern ourselves according to all that he has commanded.

We gain the sense of this internal self-government from the
opening of Psalm 119. Here we see the wonder of God's laws and
the willing obedience of those who follow them.

Blessed are they whose ways are blameless,
    who walk according to the law of the LORD.
Blessed are those who keep his statutes

and seek him with all their heart—
They do no wrong
    but follow his ways.
You have laid down precepts
    that are to be fully obeyed.
Oh, that my ways were steadfast
    in obeying your decrees!
Then I would not be put to shame
    when I consider all your commands.
I will praise you with an upright heart
    as I learn your righteous laws.
I will obey your decrees;
    do not utterly forsake me.

God's people are to live as free women and men as they "follow his ways" and build God's order in their lives. My good friend Dr. Elizabeth Youmans, founder of Chrysalis International, states: "The Christian principle of self-government is God ruling internally from the heart of the believer. In order to have true liberty, man must willingly (voluntarily) be governed internally by the Spirit and Word of God rather than by external forces. Government is first internal (causative), then extends outwardly (effect)."[10]

Youmans says that instead of having a self-governing mindset, we often have a victim mindset. When something goes wrong in our life or nation, we find someone to blame. "It's the government's fault." "If only the president had done x, things would have been better." But to put the responsibility for our lives on someone else is to have a slave mentality. In Christian internal self-government, people and nations do not put the responsibility on others; they themselves are free and responsible.

Hugo Grotius (1583–1645), Dutch theologian, lawyer, and educator, describes how self-government is the foundation of all other governing structures, from the largest to the smallest: "He knows not how to rule a kingdom, that cannot manage a Province; nor can he wield a Province, that cannot order a City; nor he order a City, that knows not how to regulate a Village. Nor he a Village, that cannot guide a Family; nor can that man Govern well a Family that knows not how to Govern himself; nor can he Govern himself unless his Reason be Lord, Will and Appetite be vassals; nor can Reason rule unless herself be ruled by God, and (wholly) be obedient to Him."[11]

Two words describe internal self-government: *virtue* and *habitus*. Virtue is "moral goodness; the practice of moral duties and the abstaining from vice, or a conformity of life and conversation to the moral law. . . . The practice of moral duties from sincere love to God and his laws, is virtue."[12] Virtue is voluntary obedience to truth—the very principle of internal self-government.

In his book *The Death of Character*, James Davison Hunter describes habitus as "the continuity and stability of a culture . . . [that] organizes our actions and defines our way of being."[13] Worldview is to habitus as cult (worship) is to culture. Speaking metaphorically, habitus is "the air we breathe." The habits of our heart establish the internal frame of our lives. Do we function by faith or fear, thrift or waste, hard work or laziness? Are we compassionate or cruel, just or corrupt? Do we trust or distrust, create beauty or create vulgarity? These are our habitus. We are to store up God's laws within our hearts and let them establish the habits of our lives.[14]

Whole cultures and nations are framed by habitus. For instance, how different is a nation built on thrift from one built on consumption! The United States became an economic powerhouse because of the virtues of hard work and thrift. Today the vices of laziness and consumption are growing, and the United States is losing its economic dominance.

As we have seen elsewhere, God has a heart for nations. He wants nations to flourish. His mission is to transform slave nations into free nations, just as he transformed the Hebrew nation, a people with a slavery mentality, into a free and great people, a model for the nations of the world. This transformation occurs through obedience.

The City on a Hill

Jesus created a powerful image when he told his disciples: "You are the light of the world. A town built on a hill cannot be hidden. Neither do people light a lamp and put it under a bowl. Instead they put it on its stand, and it gives light to everyone in the house. In the same way, let your light shine before others, that they may see your good deeds and glorify your Father in heaven" (Matt. 5:14–16). Christ is the light of the world, and so are his followers! We are to shine like a city on a hill, a light to guide other nations. Paul continues this theme: "so that you may become blameless and pure, 'children of God without fault in a warped and crooked generation.' Then you will shine among them like stars in the sky" (Phil. 2:15).

The English Puritans came to America enlivened by a proleptic vision—to live in the reality of the future, today; to build a nation that would be a city on a hill, a nation that would in some small way manifest God's coming kingdom.

Shortly before landing in the New World in 1630, John Winthrop, the governor of Massachusetts Bay Colony, stood on the deck of the Puritan flagship *Arabella* and preached a sermon titled "A Modell of Christian Charity." He took the image directly from Christ's vision, telling the community they would be "a city upon a hill" that would be watched by the whole world: "For we must consider that we shall be as a city upon a hill. The eyes of all people are upon us. So that if we shall deal falsely with our God in this work we have undertaken . . . we shall be made a story and a by-word throughout the world. We shall open the mouths of enemies to speak evil of the ways of God. . . . We shall shame the faces of many of God's worthy servants, and cause their prayers to be turned into curses upon us till we be consumed out of the good land whither we are a-going."[15]

The Puritan vision was not personal and pietistic but communal and corporate. They desired to create a community of believers that would transform the world, not in a triumphal sense, but in obedience to Christ's commands. In faith they expected to form a nation that would, by God's grace, draw people to Christ and his kingdom. This vision of freedom, this humble attempt of a people to work toward the kingdom of God, was manifested in the building of a nation that has since drawn "huddled masses" from all over the world.

Has America achieved its vision perfectly? No! Have there been mistakes and sins? Yes! But the Puritans envisioned the kingdom of God coming to earth, and that vision has profoundly shaped the American experiment.

President-elect John Kennedy delivered a speech on January 9, 1961, to the General Court of the Commonwealth of Massachusetts in which he referred to John Winthrop's sermon: "Today the eyes of all people are truly upon us—our government, in every branch, at every level, national, state, and local, must be *a city upon a hill*—constructed and inhabited by men aware of their great trust and their great responsibilities."[16]

President Ronald Reagan used the phrase in his farewell speech to the nation on January 11, 1989:

> The past few days when I've been at that window upstairs, I've thought a bit of the "shining city upon a hill." The phrase comes from John Winthrop, who wrote it to describe the America he imagined. . . .
>
> I've spoken of the shining city all my political life, but I don't know if I ever quite communicated what I saw when I said it. But in my mind it was a tall proud city built on rocks stronger than oceans, wind-swept, God-blessed, and teeming with people of all kinds living in harmony and peace, a city with free ports that hummed with commerce and creativity, and if there had to be city walls, the walls had doors and the doors were open to anyone with the will and the heart to get here. That's how I saw it and see it still.[17]

Kennedy and Reagan were likely speaking more from historic memory than personal Puritan-like faith. But Christians today are to live with biblical conviction, actively seeking to be a city on a hill. The church has embraced a dualistic paradigm that separates work from worship and wealth from nation-building. We need to return to the richness of the biblical paradigm. We need to leave behind the anemic vision of simply "saving souls for heaven" and take up the Great Commission of discipling *all* nations, teaching them to obey *all* of God's commands.

How do we go about doing this immense task?

The Minimum and Maximum

We need to grasp Jesus' words "everything I have commanded" from two perspectives: their *irreducible minimum* and their *comprehensive maximum*.

When a Jewish lawyer asked Jesus to identify the greatest commandment, Jesus reduced God's law to two commands: "'Love the Lord your God with all your heart and with all your soul and with all your mind.' This is the first and greatest commandment. And the second is like it: 'Love your neighbor as yourself.' All the Law and the Prophets hang on these two commandments'" (Matt. 22:36–40).[18]

The apostle Paul reduces these two commands to one, the irreducible minimum: "The entire law is summed up in a single command: 'Love your neighbor as yourself'" (Gal. 5:14).[19] John explains how the two commands—love God and love your neighbor—can be simplified to the one: "Whoever claims to love God yet hates a brother or sister is a liar. For whoever does not love their brother and sister, whom they have seen, cannot love God, whom they have not seen. And he has given us this command: Anyone who loves God must also love their brother and sister" (1 John 4:20–21).

The irreducible minimum of all God's laws is to love your neighbor. On the simplest level, this is what all nations are to be taught. How different would the world be if individuals and nations obeyed this one simple command?

Christ speaks of the intricate nature of the law: "Truly I tell you, until heaven and earth disappear, not the smallest letter, not the least stroke of a pen, will by any means disappear from the Law until everything is accomplished" (Matt. 5:18). In saying this, Christ calls attention not only to the irreducible minimum but also to the comprehensive scope of God's laws. If "love your neighbor" is the irreducible minimum of "everything that I have commanded," what is the comprehensive maximum—the fullest, most profound expression?

The answer to this lies in recognizing that the entire universe was created and is governed by God. Every aspect of the universe and the world in which we live plays a part in the comprehensive maximum of "everything that I have commanded" because God spoke (commanded) the universe into existence. "By faith we understand that the universe was formed at God's command, so that what is seen was not made out of what was visible" (Heb. 11:3).

The nature of the universe revealed in the Bible shows us that nothing is outside of God's control or God's plan. First, the universe is *real*, not an illusion (Hinduism).[20] Second, the universe is *good*, not intrinsically broken and something from which to escape (Eastern religions) nor inherently evil (false Christian view).[21] Third, the universe is an *integrated whole*, a unity with diversity, with physical elements (stars, planets, molecules, atoms) and spiritual elements (angels, demons, human spirits) that are unique and that interact.[22] The universe is not ultimately spiritual (Eastern religions) nor only physical (materialism); nor is the spiritual realm "higher" than the natural realm (dualistic philosophy). Fourth, the universe is *rational* and *ordered*; it is not chaotic, controlled by capricious gods (Eastern and animistic faiths), nor empty of meaning (nihilism).[23] Fifth, the universe is *progressive* and purpose-filled, not circular (Eastern religions).[24]

The comprehensive maximum is reflected not only in the nature of the universe but also in God's governing of the universe, which he does in three ways: the laws of creation, his providence, and human wisdom and obedience.

First, God governs the universe through the *laws of creation*. Earlier, we saw that a name often reveals the nature of what is named. God's names include Truth,[25] Goodness,[26] and Beauty.[27] These names correspond to God's laws of creation. Truth is reflected in God's physical and metaphysical laws. Goodness (justice) is reflected in God's moral laws. Beauty is reflected in God's aesthetic laws. The laws of creation form the infrastructure upon which individual lives and nations are built. Physical laws govern the physical world, moral laws promote human development, and metaphysical and aesthetic laws help societies blossom.

Second, God governs the universe though his *providence*. The Bible reveals God as both transcendent and immanent. God's transcendence means that he existed before creation, is independent of creation, and stands outside creation. His immanence refers to his providential governance of creation: God is active in creation, working in space and time. This concept opposes animism, which affirms God's immanence but denies his transcendence. It opposes deism, which affirms his transcendence but denies his immanence. And it opposes secular humanism, which denies the existence of God altogether.

The laws of creation and God's providence come together this way: God works *providentially* to govern the universe *through* his laws. Deists acknowledge creation laws but deny God's engagement with creation. Atheists deny the Lawgiver, rationally severing him from the laws of creation. But the profound biblical revelation stands: God created the universe *and* he providentially sustains. Paul wrote, "For in him all things were created . . . and in him all things hold together" (Col. 1:16–17).

Third, *human wisdom and obedience* is a means for stewarding God's creation. It is imperative for human beings to discover and apply the ordinances of creation in personal and national life. Only through wisdom—living in the framework of God's creation—can people and societies become all that God intends. Moses highlights the inseparable link between human wisdom and God's laws: "I have taught you decrees and laws as the Lord my God commanded me. . . . Observe them carefully, for this will show your wisdom and understanding to the nations" (Deut. 4:5–6).

Moses also captures the comprehensive maximum of obeying all that Christ commanded: "For I command you today to love the LORD your God, to walk in obedience to him, and to keep his commands, decrees and laws; then you will live and increase. . . . I have set before you life and death, blessings and curses. Now choose life" (Deut. 30:16, 19). God's commands divide truth from falsehood, good from evil, beauty from ugliness. The person or nation who understands and applies them moves toward life. Those who don't, move toward death. To try to live outside the framework of God's universe is folly.

The Driving Vision

Christ's commands propel creation to its grand finale—the City of God, the New Jerusalem, God coming to dwell forever among men. This vision drove Abraham into the desert: "For he was looking forward to the city with foundations, whose architect and builder is God" (Heb. 11:10). Seeking, finding, and applying wisdom allows human beings to engage in this grand story. Through wisdom we can discover that order and glorify God by developing our lives (gifts and talents), communities, cultures, and nations within the framework of that order.

God's glory is the end and purpose of creation. God created the universe, sustains the universe, and calls people to engage in history and the consummation of all history. As we explore creation, we see more and more of God's glory. God has hidden himself all around us and is waiting for the wise person to seek and to find.[28] Wise people grow to understand the laws of creation (discovering God's thoughts after him) and to know the One who is wisdom so that their lives and governments will be rightly ordered.

Here's a slightly different perspective on this truth. When God made human beings, he made them in his image to rule creation as his vice-regents, to manage his household (*oikos*). As we saw in chapter 10, *oikonomia* can mean "household management," specifically the management, oversight, and administration of others' property. God's house (*oikos*) is to be stewarded by humans, built up (*oikodomeō*) to reach its God-given potential. Humans are to "administer the house" through "house laws," the laws God established to govern his creation from the beginning. These were laid down at creation and built into creation as a reflection of God's nature. These are the laws *through which* God governs the creation by means of his vice-regents.[29]

This is the meaning of Christ's words "*all* I have commanded." Just as loving one's neighbor is the irreducible minimum of God's commands, administering all the laws of creation is the comprehensive maximum of God's commands. God's commands belong to all people; they are not the exclusive right of Christians or Jews. Furthermore, these invisible laws are immutable. They cannot be broken. Like gravity, they "work"! When a person or nation lives by these laws, the result is more justice, wealth, health, and social peace.

We are to teach nations to obey everything that Christ has commanded. This is a simple as loving your neighbor as yourself. It is as profound as using our rational minds to discover and apply all the metaphysical, moral, and aesthetic laws of creation. In the following chapters, we will examine each of these laws, seeking to understand further how to make disciples of all nations.

CHAPTER 15

Truth:
The Metaphysical Order

*Faith and reason are like two wings on which the human spirit rises
to the contemplation of truth; and God has placed in the human
heart a desire to know the truth—in a word, to know himself—so
that, by knowing and loving God, men and women may also come
to the fullness of truth about themselves.*
—JOHN PAUL II

I had been a Christian for over ten years, was discipled by an evangelical student ministry, and had studied at an evangelical seminary before I realized that I had a born-again heart and an atheistic mind. I viewed repentance as an emotion: feeling sorry for sin. This conformed to a life driven by feelings and emotions. My mind needed to be born again.[1]

Then the moment came when a friend, Udo Middelmann, confronted me: "You know, Darrow, Christianity is true, even if you don't believe it!" After two sleepless nights I understood what Udo was saying. I had been taught that Christianity was true precisely *because* I believed it, but Christianity is true even if no one in the world believes. It is a description of reality. It is true because God exists. We know things because they are, and as Augustine said, "Things are because God knows them."[2]

I also came to realize I needed to repent as the Bible teaches repentance. The Greek word for "repent" means "to change one's mind."[3] To repent means to let God tell us what is real and true. It means to conform our thinking, values, and lifestyle to what is true, good, and beautiful. Like reason and faith, repentance is rooted in the mind.

As J. B. Phillips writes in his paraphrase of 1 John 2:4, "The man who claims to know God but does not obey his laws is not only a liar but lives in self-delusion." To know God is to obey his laws. If we say we know God but do not obey his laws, we are living in *a world of illusion,* our own make-believe world.

If we are to live in God's world rather than a world of illusion, we must repent. The American poet and physician William Carlos Williams, though not a Christian, caught the need for repentance: "Unless there is a new mind there cannot be a new line, the old will go on repeating itself with recurring deadliness."[4]

As we saw in the previous chapter, the irreducible minimum of all that Christ commanded is simply to love your neighbor as yourself; the comprehensive maximum of all that Christ commanded is to administer the laws of creation—the metaphysical, moral, and aesthetic laws. This requires great thinking.

The laws of creation relate to what I will call the "cultural trinity" and what the ancients called the three great transcendentals—truth, goodness, and beauty. Earlier I described these as the elements of kingdom culture; they capture the comprehensive maximum of teaching nations to obey all that Jesus commanded. Just as humans are hardwired for life, they also thirst for truth, goodness, and beauty. These are the ultimate human desires. Human sinfulness, however, has distorted what God has made; in the reality of our fallen world, sin produces deceit, evil, and hideousness. Our task in creating kingdom culture means combating lies with truth, evil with goodness, and the hideous with beauty.

In this chapter we will begin our discussion with truth, as it pertains to the metaphysical order. Metaphysics deals with first causes, fixed principles. As I have said, we are faced with a battle for the mind, a battle for ideas and ideals. Ideas have consequences! Truth leads to life, and lies lead to death. Truth, arrived at through both revelation (accepted in faith) and reason, is the basis of free societies.

The Biblical View of Mind

We live in an increasingly anti-intellectual society. A culture once concerned with truth is now interested only in pragmatics and emotions. We no longer ask, "Is it true?" but "Does it work?" or "Is it fun?" or "Does it feel good?" We are more concerned with subjective experience than with objective reality. Our minds have atrophied.

Our post-Christian world has artificially separated faith from reason and nature from grace. Atheistic science, with its assumption that there is no God and hence nothing other than physical matter, has no place for faith or grace (as we saw in chapters 4 and 6). Unfortunately, too many Christians also separate faith from reason and grace from nature. The result: an increasingly irrelevant church in the modern world.

The Bible makes no such separations. God gave us minds, and Jesus calls us to love God with all our minds.[5] Thus the human mind is of utmost importance to any exploration and comprehension of truth. Both reason and faith involve the mind, and both stand before the bar of God's self-revelation. To reason means to ask questions, to challenge oneself and others with the facts. Faith is conviction of the truth of something. Faith is not irrational or devoid of objectivity. Rather, faith is the conviction, based on evidence, of the truth of a thing or a claim.

The New Testament writers reflect the importance of this truth in the extraordinary number of words related to *reason, intellect,* and *mind.* There are forty different Greek terms used 1,500 times. For example: *ginōskō* (know, recognize, understand);[6] *gnōsis* (knowledge);[7] *epignōsis* (full knowledge, worldview, conscious awareness);[8] *gnōmē* (purpose, decision, judgment, advice);[9] *gnōrizō* (to make known);[10] *logikos* (reasonable, logical);[11] *dokeō* (to think);[12] *logos* (account, reason);[13] *nous* (mind or understanding);[14] and *phronimos* (wise person).[15]

Many Christians who quote Romans 12:1–3 probably do not realize that these three short verses use eight words related to the mind.

> Present your bodies a living and holy sacrifice, acceptable to God, which is your spiritual [*logikos*] service of worship.... Be transformed by the renewing of your mind [*nous*], so that you may prove [*dokimazō*: to test, examine] what the will of God is.... I say to everyone among you not to think more highly [*huperphroneō*] of himself than he ought to think [*phroneō*]; but to think [*phroneō*] so as to have sound judgment [*sōphroneō*], as God has allotted to each a measure of faith [*pistis*: conviction of the truth]. (NASB)

British-Canadian theologian and Bible expositor J. I. Packer challenges Christians to use their minds: "The Evangelical is *not afraid of facts* ... nor is he afraid of thinking, for he knows that *all truth is God's truth,* and right reason cannot endanger sound faith. ... When confronted by those who ... take exception to Christianity, he must ... *out-think them.*"[16]

One hundred years ago, J. Gresham Machen (1881–1937), American theologian and New Testament scholar, said something still highly appropriate for the church today: "It is a great mistake ... to suppose that we who are called 'conservatives' hold desperately to certain beliefs merely because they are old, and are opposed to the discovery of new facts. On the contrary ... *we welcome new discoveries with all our hearts. . . .* We are seeking . . . to arouse youth from its present uncritical repetition . . . into some genuine examination of the basis of life; and we believe that *Christianity flourishes not in the darkness, but in the light.*"[17]

Christians are to love God with all their minds, to function within the framework of reason and revelation. There is no contradiction between science and faith, reason and revelation. As we explore with a Bible in one hand and a microscope in the other, we discover the order God has built into the universe. When the apostle Paul writes of "taking every thought captive to Christ," he does not mean, as many Christians suggest, only spiritual or religious thought. He means *every* thought, whether of history, science, the arts, agriculture, health care, education, family, engineering, business, communication, ethics, or beauty. All of it is our concern.

Revelation and Reason

God has revealed himself to human beings in two primary ways. The first way, *general revelation,* occurs in two ways—one interior and one exterior. The apostle Paul writes: "because what may be known of God is *manifest in them,* for God has *shown it to them.* For since the creation of the world His invisible attributes are clearly seen, being understood by the things that are made, even His eternal power and Godhead, so that they are without excuse" (Rom. 1:19–20 NKJV).

First, knowledge of God is *manifest in them.* Human beings are made in the image of God; thus, as a person reflects on her own existence, she can see in her intellect, emotions, and will the echoes of God's intellect, emotions, and will. In addition, God's moral laws are written in human hearts: "Indeed, when Gentiles, who do not have the law, do by nature things required by the law, they are a law for themselves, even though they do not have the law. They show that the requirements of the law are written on their hearts, their consciences also bearing witness, and their thoughts sometimes

accusing them and at other times even defending them" (Rom.
2:14–15). Many have called this "natural law."[18]

Second, knowledge of God exists because he has *shown it to
them*. God has revealed himself through the things he has made.
The psalmist describes this beautifully:

> The heavens declare the glory of God;
>   the skies proclaim the work of his hands.
> Day after day they pour forth speech;
>   night after night they display knowledge.
> They have no speech, they use no words;
>   no sound is heard from them.
> Yet their voice goes out into all the earth,
>   their words to the ends of the world.
> (Ps. 19:1–4)

God designed creation for a purpose, building laws, structure,
and function into the universe to fulfill its design. Human beings can
observe the design of a created object and learn not only about the
object, but also about its maker. Human reason can discover truths
made self-evident by God. Self-evident truth is clear enough that
the common person can see, understand, and be "without excuse."

The other primary way in which God makes himself known is
through the *special revelation* of his Word—both the living Word
(Christ) and the written Word (the Bible). The living Word, the
Son of God who became incarnate as Jesus Christ, reveals God.[19]
While creation and conscience attest to God's existence and reveal
some of God's characteristics, the Son of God reveals God fully.[20]

We encounter the living Word through the written Word (the
Bible) and the Holy Spirit's internal witness. The Bible is the record
of God's acts throughout human history, including the climac-
tic event of the incarnation of the Word, and reveals more about
God's nature and characteristics than creation alone does.[21] As the
inspired Word of God, the Bible contains all the information necessary for our salvation from sin and death and our growth in God.[22]

General revelation—knowing God through the facts of creation and human reason—*supplements* but does not *supplant* special revelation. On the other hand, at times faith transcends the rational, but it is never inconsistent with reason.

While reason and revelation are available to all human beings, not everyone employs both. Blaise Pascal (1623–62), the French mathematician, scientist, and philosopher, operated from both reason and faith. He writes in *Pensées*, "Faith certainly tells us what the senses do not, but not the contrary of what they see. It is above them, not against them."[23]

We can distinguish four contemporary views of revelation and reason and the way in which truth is discovered.

1. Biblically faithful Christians and Jews, as well as moderate and reformed Muslims, hold that truth is found through both reason and revelation.
2. Atheists and secularists of the post-Christian West deny God and thus deny revelation, seeking truth from reason alone. Many liberal Christians also deny revelation.
3. Postmodernists, animists, and New Agers deny revelation and abandon reason. In their search for truth, they conclude there are no reasonable and rational answers: all is mystery! From such a beginning what other conclusion could they reach?
4. Jihadists, many fundamentalist Muslims, some traditional religions, and many Christians embrace revelation but deny any place for reason in the search for truth. They tend toward an anti-intellectual mindset of "Don't ask questions, only believe." Faith, to them, is a subjective experience with no objective reality.

Human beings were made to think, to reason, to reason with God.[24] We have minds, yet our intellect is limited. Because we are made in the image of God, we can ask questions our finite minds cannot answer. So it is with every inquisitive child: Why does the sun come up over there? How far away is the moon? Why do I bleed? Even when his parents cannot answer, he keeps inquiring. He does not conclude that no answers exist. When we can articulate a question for which we can't find answers, we must simply recognize our limitations rather than assume there are no answers. We continue to inquire and pursue truth.

Principles of Free Societies

We have seen that God has a big agenda throughout history. His intention is to see people in personal relationship with him through the salvation secured by the death and resurrection of Jesus Christ. He has also called the saved to be transforming agents in society. God's revelation, together with human reason, enables us to discern truth and apply it to the ordering of free and just societies.

Jesus made the connection between truth and freedom: "To the Jews who had believed him, Jesus said, 'If you hold to my teaching, you are really my disciples. Then you will know the truth, and the truth will set you free.'"[25] Note the distinction between believers and disciples. Many had believed, but few were disciples. A disciple holds to Jesus' teaching. When we continue in the word of Christ, we know the truth and the truth sets us free.[26]

The Bible does not promote any one system of governance. However, it does highlight social, economic, and political principles that, when applied, create more health, justice, and economic bounty for a nation. Ideas have consequences! As we have said, spiritual realities impact the social, political, and economic institutions of a society through culture. Nations that adopt biblical principles will flourish; those that build on counterfeit principles will languish. A classic example of such failure is communism, built on an atheistic closed system. Communism has collapsed because its metaphysical infrastructure did not comport with reality.

We will now examine some key principles of free societies, with reference to the United States as one imperfect example of applying biblical truth in establishing a nation. The American model is far from flawless. Its founders were imperfect in their understanding and application of the principles they built on. Many who affirmed that "all men are created equal" owned slaves. Yet flawed people creating an imperfect experiment set a new standard for freedom and civil governance.

Following are some of the key principles articulated by the founders of the American experiment of liberty and some reflections on how they apply to our study of the war from the East and the culture wars in the West.

Individuality

Every human being is made in God's image, endowed with dignity and honor, equal before God and equal before the law.[27] Professor of American history K. Alan Snyder says, "The Biblical concept of individuality can be stated succinctly: *God has created all things distinct and unique and for a specific purpose.* He has given an identity to all parts of His creation, whether material objects, animals, or of human beings."[28] God has given each individual a unique combination of skills and abilities to advance his kingdom.[29] Each individual has a distinctive and equally important contribution to God's purpose.

While the United States has not modeled these principles perfectly, it has set a new standard. Its concept of individuality opposes the uniformity of countries like Japan, communist China, and Islamic nations. It also contrasts with societies that ground an individual's value in caste, wealth, gender, or race. Tragically, postmodern, politically correct America is abandoning this principle and instead adopting the egalitarian view that everyone is the same and people are interchangeable.

Inalienable Rights

To be made in the image of God is to receive inalienable rights. As the Declaration of Independence states: "We hold these truths to be self-evident, that all men are created equal, that they are endowed by their Creator with certain unalienable rights." This decree—described as "one of the best-known sentences in the English language"[30] and "the most potent and consequential words in American history"[31]—set the moral vision for a new nation and defined a "gold standard" for other nations.

Rights endowed by God are inalienable; they "may not be transferred."[32] They were written into the universe at creation. They are granted by God—not, as statists would argue, by government.[33] Imbued in the human frame, they cannot be confiscated by government.

The Declaration of Independence identifies three inalienable rights: life, liberty, and the pursuit of happiness (which we discussed in chapter 5). The pursuit of happiness is not hedonistic license. Happiness is another word for *blessed*, as indicated in Young's Literal Translation of the Beatitudes (Matt. 5:3–7): "Happy the poor in spirit—because theirs is the reign of the heavens. Happy the mourning—because they shall be comforted. Happy the meek— because they shall inherit the land. Happy those hungering and thirsting for righteousness—because they shall be filled. Happy the kind—because they shall find kindness." Happiness is not license; rather, it is the product of discipline.

Rights demand responsibility. Every freedom has its corresponding responsibility; freedom without moral responsibility leads to license. Without responsibility, society deteriorates into anarchy leading to tyranny.

Human rights stand in contrast to the slavery of ancient societies (Egyptian, Greek, Roman, Mayan, Incan) as well as ancient and modern examples of tribalism, caste, race, and misogyny. The concept of human rights was born from the Bible, not from Greece or Rome, not from Mao, Hitler, or Stalin. Secularism produces euthanasia, embryonic stem-cell research, abortion on demand, and cloning—all of which deny basic human rights.

Family

The family, the first institution established by God, is the building block of nations. Marriage is a sacred institution based on a lifetime covenant relationship between a man, a woman, and God. The strength of the family determines the strength of the nation: free societies require virtuous citizens, and the first lessons of virtue and citizenship are taught and modeled in the home.

Early Americans saw love more as a frame of mind to nurture than an emotion to fall in and out of. Family worship was critical for spiritual and moral formation. The father led worship: singing hymns, praying, and reading the Scriptures. The virtuous woman of Proverbs 31 was emulated. Women were strong in character and convictions and managed their households as co-equals with their husbands. Education happened primarily in the home, where future citizens learned self-governance for a free society. Parents also helped their children discover their vocations. Every child had a part in advancing the kingdom. When they discovered that call, children were blessed to pursue it.

What a contrast to the modern redefinition of marriage and the family! In some countries the state has even usurped parents' responsibilities for educating and rearing their children.

Education

Free nations require virtuous and wise citizens who can carry out self-governance. Such citizens are the product of religious education, which provides moral vision, metaphysical capital (the infrastructure of the mind), and virtue.

In his farewell address, President George Washington established the connection between religion and national morality and warned against merely secular education: "And let us with caution indulge the supposition, that morality can be maintained without religion. Whatever may be conceded to the influence of refined education on minds of peculiar structure, *reason and experience both forbid us to expect, that national morality can prevail in exclusion of religious principle.*"[34] Similarly, Dr. Benjamin Rush (1746–1813), an educator, physician, and one of the founding fathers, writes, "The only Foundation for a useful education in a republic is to be laid in religion. Without it there can be no virtue, and without virtue there can be no liberty."[35]

Moral and religious education based on God's revelation builds intelligent, virtuous citizens capable of governing themselves, their families, and their nation. Citizens who learn morals and ethics are able to *master themselves* and acquire knowledge and skills to *master the world*; they can confront individual and institutional sinfulness, thus establishing free societies.

Contrast today's Western education system, based on atheistic premises, which prepares people for work and consumption. We are a consumer-based society. The educational system exists to prepare people to produce and spend. For this end, knowledge and technical skill take precedence over understanding and wisdom. Schools are platforms for social engineering and training people for passive acceptance of cultural relativism, political correctness, and tolerance. The modern intellect gives little thought to wisdom or virtue. Indeed, the measure of a person is experience, and ignorance is often seen as a virtue.

Contrast also the education that many fundamentalist Muslims receive in the madrassas. In these Islamic schools, Muslim students pursue religious studies primarily through reading, reciting, and memorizing the Qur'an. Math and science and what the West calls the humanities, subjects that open students to a wider world, are not part of the madrassas' education.

Community

Human beings, made in the image of the triune God who eternally exists in community, are to be in relationship in families and communities. God made each person unique for a special purpose, which is fulfilled in union with the body. An individual cannot thrive apart from community, yet the community does not supplant the individual. The person finds fulfillment, and the community is blessed.

Community implies unity of diversity, where people freely work together for the benefit of all. Several years ago a tornado ripped through Amish country in the Midwest. Within a year the Amish had worked together to rebuild their homes and barns, but their non-Amish neighbors were still waiting for government assistance. Many people in today's modern world have lost their sense of unity, replacing it with an individualistic entitlement mentality.

French historian, political thinker, and cultural observer Alexis de Tocqueville recorded his observation of early American unity: "Americans of all ages, all conditions . . . constantly form associations. They have not only commercial and manufacturing associations . . . but associations of a thousand other kinds—religions, moral. . . . Wherever, at the head of some new undertaking, you see the government of France, or a man of rank in England, in the United States you will be sure to find an association."[36]

These voluntary associations (sometimes called mediating institutions) form a core of relationships neither governmental nor personal. America's great variety of voluntary associations involves religion (churches and synagogues); service (Lions Club, Rotary Club); youth (Boy Scouts, Girl Scouts, 4H); and work (labor unions, professional associations). Historically, these associations cultivated virtue and morals. Functioning organically, they provided voluntary solutions to community problems without state intervention, which is so often more bureaucratic, more expensive, and less effective.

Community stands in contrast to the individualism of modern Western society and also to the conformity of many traditional societies that disregard the uniqueness of the individual.

Separation of Church and State
The concept of separation of church (i.e., organized religion) and state is derived from the Bible. When the Pharisees question Jesus about paying taxes, he responds, "Give back to Caesar what is Caesar's, and to God what is God's" (Matt. 22:21).

Martin Luther developed the connection between Scripture and human governance by distinguishing God as Creator from God as Redeemer. God as Creator provides the *laws of nature* that govern creation, including human beings and society. God as Redeemer provides what some call *divine law* for the rescue of humans from the effects of sin and rebellion, including brokenness in all relationships. Luther's Creator/Redeemer distinction led to the "two kingdoms" concept, church and state as separate and essential entities. Each derives its authority from God with equal but distinct functions. The state wields the sword to protect her citizens and provide for peace and tranquillity. The church wields the Word of God to shape godly citizens who govern themselves and their nation. In this view, both church and state are to function from biblical principles. Neither is to dominate the other.

Following Scripture and principles of the Reformation, America's founders resisted those who wanted the state to dominate the church or the church to dominate the state. The First Amendment reads in part, "Congress shall make no law respecting an establishment of religion, or prohibiting the free exercise thereof." Government is forbidden to interfere with the free exercise of religion or to impose a national religion (including secular humanism).

Separation of church and state leads to freedom of religion. Atheism leads to a political philosophy and a policy of freedom *from* religion, completely removing religious belief from the public square and the marketplace. Freedom *of* religion (ironically derived from the nonpluralistic foundation of Judeo-Christian theism) means freedom to be a Jew, Muslim, Buddhist, Christian, Hindu, or atheist.

Separation of church and state stands in stark contrast to tyranny, both religious tyranny (religious authority controlling the state, as in Iran under the ayatollahs or in Afghanistan under the Taliban) and secular tyranny (the state controlling religion, as in communist countries and, increasingly, in democracies). This principle also counters Christians who privatize their faith and leave God out of the marketplace of ideas.

Human Sinfulness

Though at first this may seem like a strange principle, the recognition of human depravity is necessary for free societies.[37] This principle contrasts with the humanist concept of the perfectibility of human nature, which underlies socialism and communism.[38] Government structures and laws must reckon with the reality of sin rather than embrace the false notion of human perfectibility, for "power tends to corrupt and absolute power corrupts absolutely."[39]

Recognizing that the tyranny of a majority is little better than the tyranny of one, the American founders designed a constitutional republic, ensuring the protection of the rights of the minority. American citizens elect representatives to speak for them in the various government bodies. These representatives are held accountable by frequent elections that terminate or reinstate their authority. The founders also created checks and balances to diffuse power: a legislative branch writes laws, an executive branch administers laws, and a judicial branch interprets laws. A free press was empowered to expose corruption, injustice, and lawbreaking.

When a nation has no such safeguards in place, those in power—corruptible human beings—often become tyrants, hoarding power and resources and taking away the rights of the citizens.

The Rule of Law

Because all people are sinners, a healthy society requires the rule of law. The Bible reveals a just God who built the universe on laws and who shows no partiality.[40] To prosper, societies must be built on the rule of law. The founding fathers understood this. President John Adams stated, "The very definition of a republic is 'an empire of laws and not of men.'"[41]

Samuel Rutherford's groundbreaking work *Lex Rex (The Law and the Prince)*, published in 1644, states that the law should be higher than anyone, including monarchs. From medieval times, nations practiced the "divine right of kings": since God had granted governing power to the king, the king was above the law, subject only to God. He could establish any law, and everyone except him was responsible to obey it. One can only imagine the resulting injustices and corruption.[42] Rutherford's *Lex Rex* reversed the "divine right" concept.

The founding fathers of the United States implemented the rule of law. Presidents and legislatures must obey any law they make. Citizens are to abide by the civil law,[43] but God's universal moral law (exhibited in the Ten Commandments) is higher. If the state calls us to violate God's law, resistance (civil disobedience) is not only allowed but required.[44] The United States was born out of civil disobedience.

New England pastor Jonathan Mayhew, a graduate of Harvard, preached a sermon in 1750 that would influence the thinking of the American founders: "No civil rulers are to be obeyed when they enjoin things that are inconsistent with the commands of God: All such disobedience is lawful and glorious.... All commands running counter to the declared will of the supreme legislator of heaven and earth, are null and void: And therefore disobedience to them is a duty, not a crime."[45]

The laws of nature and of nature's God justified the ultimate civil disobedience: the declaration of the independence of the United States. The Declaration of Independence begins: "When in the Course of human events, it becomes necessary for one people to dissolve the political bands which have connected them with another, and to assume among the powers of the earth, the separate and equal station to which *the Laws of Nature and of Nature's God* entitle them, a decent respect to the opinions of mankind requires that they should declare the causes which impel them to the separation" (emphasis added).

Benjamin Franklin proposed emblazoning the seal of the new country with the words "Rebellion to tyrants is obedience to God."[46]

The Declaration of Independence continues: "Whenever any Form of Government becomes destructive of these ends, it is the Right of the People to alter or to abolish it, and to institute new Government, laying its foundation on such principles and organizing its powers in such form, as to them shall seem most likely to effect their Safety and Happiness."

From a Birmingham jail, Baptist pastor and civil rights leader Dr. Martin Luther King Jr. (1929–68) wrote one of the clearest rationales for civil disobedience: "One may well ask: 'How can you advocate breaking some laws and obeying others?' The answer lies in the fact that there are two types of laws: just and unjust. . . . One has not only a legal but a moral responsibility to obey just laws. Conversely, one has a moral responsibility to *disobey* unjust laws."[47]

In the twenty-first century, the foundations of law and liberty have been undermined. Harvard University professor of law Harold Berman (1918–2007) describes what the future holds when the foundations are destroyed:

> The law is becoming more fragmented, more subjective, geared more to expediency and less to morality, concerned more with immediate consequences and less with consistency or continuity. Thus the historical soil of the Western legal tradition is being washed away in the twentieth century, and the tradition itself is threatened with collapse. . . . This did not occur at once, since the predominant system of beliefs throughout the West remained Christian. It is only in the twentieth century that the Christian foundations for Western law have been almost totally rejected. . . . Thus not only legal thought but also the very structure of Western legal institutions have been removed from their spiritual foundations.[48]

The rule of law contradicts the arbitrary absolutes of modern political correctness. The rule of law challenges the naked appeals to power made by the French Revolution, the bloody Bolshevik revolution, the fascists in Italy, and national socialists in Germany. Are we willing to obey just laws and disobey unjust ones?

Covenant

God has ordained three institutions that are founded on the concept of covenant: family, church, and civil government. The word *covenant* appears thirty-three times in the New Testament and over four hundred times in the Old.[49] A covenant, established between parties before God, binds the relationship and functions with the force of law. Each party agrees to certain actions. The covenant is so forceful that parties who verbally agree and shake hands are bound for life.

This covenant concept was applied to American government through something called "the consent of the governed." The Declaration of Independence asserts "that to secure these rights [to life, liberty, and the pursuit of happiness], Governments are instituted among Men, *deriving their just powers from the consent of the governed*" (emphasis added).

People voluntarily submit to covenants they have established. The first American covenant was the Mayflower Compact of November 1620, which founded Plymouth Colony. The signers pledged to "solemnly and mutually in the presence of God and one of another, Covenant and Combine ourselves together into a Civil Body Politic."[50]

Puritan Thomas Hooker (1586–1647), founder of the Colony of Connecticut, explained the consent of the governed: "there must of necessity be mutuall ingagement [*sic*], each of the other, by their free consent."[51]

The founders of the United States used covenantal relationships to establish their state and federal charters.

Joseph G. Lehman, president of the Mackinac Center for Public Policy, summarizes the distinction between governments of coercion and those of freedom: "Governments near the compulsion pole require expansive governments powerful enough to force people to do what they might otherwise not do. Societies near the voluntary pole have more limited governments. Put another way, in some societies the government constrains its people. In others, the people constrain their government."[52]

The Declaration of Independence and the Constitution are not secular documents derived from an atheistic enlightenment, but compacts patterned on biblical covenants between God and his people. A covenantal relationship of consent among the governed stands in contrast to the state or the church as sovereign over the affairs of men and also to the anarchy of each man doing what is right in his own eyes. The concept of covenant relationships is one of the significant distinguishing factors between the United States and many nations.

Work Ethic

Before the Protestant Reformation, all the world's nations were poor.[53] A small ruling class was wealthy; all others were indentured servants and slaves. Work was seen as a curse. The Reformation changed all that. German sociologist and political economic philosopher Max Weber (1864–1920), exploring why some nations were rich and others poor, concluded that the Protestant work ethic—work as man's dignity—made the difference. Weber recognized poverty's root in the absence of moral vision. A work ethic proclaimed from Reformation pulpits sparked the economic revolution that lifted nations from poverty.

Business and financial professionals Kenneth and William Hopper have extended Weber's thesis to a study of the organizational and management practices of the Puritans that led to generations of bountiful economic activity in the United States. Four characteristics of the Puritans shaped this culture: "a conviction that the purpose of life . . . was to establish the Kingdom of Heaven on Earth; an aptitude for the exercise of mechanical skills; a moral outlook that subordinated the interests of the individual to the group; and an ability to assemble, galvanize and marshal financial, material and human resources to a single purpose."[54]

Farmers, shopkeepers, and tinkerers founded the United States. Their lives and policies repudiated the two-tiered, aristocracy/ peasant society of Europe. Their ideal was a nation of social equals. "A willingness to get their hands dirty distinguished managers from their European equivalents; this distinction reflected the relative lack of social stratification in the New World, the men at the top and bottom being considered to be made from the same common clay."[55]

America's founders understood that all labor, not just ecclesiastical work, is sacred. Not only religious leaders but every human being has a vocational calling. This counters the dominant belief of the pre-Reformation world and many nations today that work is a blight, that people who work with their hands are cursed. It also contradicts the idea held by many Christians today that "spiritual" work is higher than "secular" work.[56] Every follower of Christ is called to "full-time" Christian work because all work is sacred.

Property Rights

The concept of property rights is conveyed in the Bible. As discussed in chapter 10 on the Cultural Commission, God delegated to women and men the stewardship of his house and blessed (called and equipped) them to fulfill that responsibility. Two clauses in the Ten Commandments relate to private ownership of property: "You shall not steal" and "You shall not covet."[57] Christ told two parables to show the importance of wise management of property.[58]

Too often in the modern materialistic paradigm, property is reduced to material things, but the biblical concept of property is much more comprehensive and dynamic.[59] Property is both internal and external to human beings. Internal property is that with which a person is born, or that bestowed at the new birth: a mind to reason, a spirit to savor, freedom of conscience, moral responsibility, imagination to create, natural talents and interests. Internal property also includes accumulated capital: knowledge; skills; enculturation; the virtues of hard work, thrift, and charity; character; and a family name. In addition, we have our bodies and five senses and the ability to work and to procreate.

We have external property in creation (natural resources), in our homes (material assets), and in communities (libraries and museums, tools and equipment, and social capital). In addition to the assets in space, we also have the underrecognized and underutilized asset of time. Each of us is given the days of our lives with which to create history and wealth.

It is the wise administration of our internal property that develops the requisite skills to manage our external property.

This stewardship is to be based on the biblical principle of *oiko-nomia*, management of a household so as to increase its value to all of its members over the long run. The wealth generated through moral stewardship is to benefit the entire community. We have a moral responsibility to feed the hungry, clothe the naked, welcome the stranger, give cold water to the thirsty, and care for the widow and the orphan.[60] This stands in stark contrast to modern hedonism that is characterized by *chrematistics*, the manipulation of property and wealth so as to maximize short-term exchange values and focus on personal consumption.[61]

The American founders instituted the principle of property rights into the governing policies of the new nation. John Adams writes that "the moment the idea is admitted into society that property is not as sacred as the Laws of God, and that there is not a force of law and public justice to protect it, anarchy and tyranny commence. Property must be sacred or liberty cannot exist."[62]

The founders promoted the principle of private ownership of property. Personal wealth is to be freely and generously given.[63] Wealth generated by individuals does not belong to the government, and it is not to be coercively taken to be "redistributed." Today's atheistic West, with its closed system of limited resources, demands "equality" for each individual as a starting point, thus justifying government confiscation of private property to redistribute wealth. This was not the founders' view of economic justice; they worked from an open system in which wealth is created by free and morally responsible people. Economic justice assures that people are *equal before the law*. The fruits of their labor and creativity are their property to use as they see fit. All people are equal in their value and equal before the law, but all people are not the same. They are not identical in their skills, abilities, intellectual capacity, wealth, race, gender, background, desires, initiative, and so on.

This concept of justice comes first from our equality in the eyes of God and the inalienable rights thereby granted to all people. Second, it comes from the rule of law, the equality before the law that protects the weakest, most vulnerable, and disadvantaged in birth and allows them to reach their full potential. The role of a free and just government is to guarantee equal rights for all, not to provide equal things for all.

A precursor of Jefferson's Bill of Rights, the Virginia Declaration of Rights, written by George Mason, states that "all men are by nature equally free and independent, and have certain inherent rights ... namely, the enjoyment of life and liberty, *with the means of acquiring and possessing property,* and pursuing and obtaining happiness and safety."[64]

Private property and equality before the law allow the poorest to labor, be creative, and generate wealth to lift themselves out of poverty. Property rights include the freedoms to choose one's work, to establish binding contracts, and to receive the rewards of one's work without confiscation of wages from unjust employers or taxation by tyrannical governments.

The conscious founding of the United States as a nation built on biblical principles has created, though imperfectly, a light to the world. In a tragedy of epic proportions, Americans are abandoning the faith of their ancestors for a nation ruled by people and not by laws. The consequences will be increased poverty, social unrest, and tyranny.

In teaching the nations "all that Christ has commanded," we must not only bring truth; we must also bring goodness. From the metaphysical order, we now turn to the moral order.

CHAPTER 16

Goodness: The Moral Order

*The Ten Commandments . . . are not a set of harsh prohibitions
imposed by an arbitrary tribal deity. Instead, they are liberating
rules that enable a people to diminish the tyranny of sin; that teach
a people how to live with one another and in relation with God,
how to restrain violence and fraud, how to know justice and to raise
themselves above the level of predatory animals.*
—RUSSELL KIRK

The Ten Commandments are a gift from the Jews to the world.
They provide a moral framework for governing our lives and
a foundation for building just societies. By these commands God
intended to transform a slave society, bound by Egyptian tyranny,
into a free, model nation for the world.

The laws were inscribed on two stone tablets. The first tablet
deals with piety, our responsibilities toward God; the second with
morality, our duties toward our fellow human beings. The first
instructs us to love God; the second commands us to love our
neighbor. As we saw in the "irreducible minimum," Jesus reduced
the Ten Commandments to two: love God and love your neighbor.

Before etching the commandments into stone, God wrote them on the human heart.[1] The Ten Commandments, or the Decalogue, are the negative form of the positive statement already written on the conscience. Human beings, however, refuse to heed God's law of love, so a sterner statement is required. Hence, the moral law becomes a framework for the lives of individuals and of nations.

What is Christ's relationship to the Law? First, he came to fulfill the law, not destroy it.[2] Second, he expected his followers to go beyond the standard of the scribes and Pharisees.[3] Jesus set a higher benchmark—heart obedience rather than legalistic obedience—in several areas, including murder, adultery, divorce, oaths, retribution, and love of enemies.[4]

There is a direct correlation between the moral righteousness of individuals and the well-being of society.

As we have said elsewhere, discipleship is an inside-out process, beginning in the individual, moving to the family, the vocational sectors or other *ethnē*, and then to the larger society. Virtue in society is a product of virtue in the souls of its citizens. Said differently, development of citizens' morality precedes national development.

Michael Metzger, president and senior fellow of the Clapham Institute, writes on the loss of moral virtue not only in the West but also in the Western church: "From antiquity until the close of the Middle Ages, knowledge required *fact, myth,* and *truth* coiled together. Real knowledge begins with *facts,* or *experiences,* as the Latin 'fact' means 'something happened.' Knowledge requires the whole body, not just the brain. *Myth* is *imagination,* the songs and stories shaping how individuals *imagine* their experiences. *Truth* is *reason,* rational capacities making sense of our imagination."

The early European understanding was changed at the time of the Enlightenment, when man became the center of the universe. Metzger continues: "The deepest knowledge became cerebral, not necessarily *doing* anything. As a result, individuals and institutions could claim to know all sorts of things without getting their hands dirty. The tightly wound coil of knowledge—fact, myth, and truth—was unraveling."

This has a resulting impact on the modern church in the West: "The modern church can claim to 'know God' without experiencing or obeying him. Modern believers can claim to be 'servants of Christ' by simply studying 'servanthood' rather than serving others."[5]

Moral development precedes social, economic, and political development. The more internal self-governance people practice (based on God's laws), the freer, more prosperous, and more just their society will be. Conversely, the less people restrict their appetites, the more laws, courts, and jails will be required to maintain order.

As we have seen earlier, God has called us to pursue virtue and to flee vice. The fact that these two words have been almost totally erased from Western life and culture is a testimony to the grip that amoral atheistic culture has on our nations. An example of how different the West is today from as little as two hundred years ago is found in the character of George Washington. The man who became the first president of the United States believed that moral character was so important that as a young teenager he studied the subject and compiled, for popular consumption, a book of virtues titled *Rules of Civility*. Washington was so impressed with a set of guidelines originating in a French Jesuit community from the 1500s that he both collected and commented on them. Many are not only still pertinent, but their broad application would help transform any society today:

- Sleep not when others speak, sit not when others stand, speak not when you should hold your peace, walk not when others stop.
- Show not yourself glad at the misfortune of another though he were your enemy.
- When you see a crime punished, you may be inwardly pleased; but always show pity to the suffering offender.
- It is good manners to prefer them to whom we speak before ourselves.

- Strive not with your superiors in argument, but always submit your judgment to others with modesty.
- Undertake not to teach your equal in the art himself professes; it flavors of arrogancy.
- Wherein you reprove another be unblameable yourself; for example is more prevalent than precepts.
- Use no reproachful language against any one, neither curse nor revile.
- In your apparel be modest and endeavor to accommodate nature.
- When another person is speaking, be attentive yourself and disturb not the audience if any hesitate in his words help him not nor prompt him without desired, interrupt him not, nor answer him till his speech be ended.
- Undertake not what you cannot perform but be careful to keep your promise.[6]

Virtue is found in the moral habits of the individual and the "moral ecology" of a nation. When the majority of a nation's people pursue virtue, the nation grows in social, political, and economic health. When the people follow their base instincts, the nation suffers. The Western world is focused on natural ecology and the survival of the planet. She would do well to consider the moral ecology so fundamental to the survival of a nation.

Life or Death

God has built a real, objective universe based on physical, metaphysical, moral, and aesthetic laws. Observing these laws leads to life; ignoring them leads to death. God longs for people to choose life. It is worth listening to the words of Moses:

Now what I am commanding you today is not too difficult for you or beyond your reach. . . . No, the word is very near you; it is in your mouth and in your heart so you may obey it.

See, I set before you today *life and prosperity, death and destruction.* For I command you today to love the LORD your God, to walk in obedience to him, and to keep his commands, decrees and laws; then you will live and increase, and the LORD your God will bless you in the land you are entering to possess.

But if your heart turns away and you are not obedient, and if you are drawn away to bow down to other gods and worship them, I declare to you this day that you will certainly be destroyed. You will not live long in the land you are crossing the Jordan to enter and possess.

This day I call the heavens and the earth as witnesses against you that I have set before you *life and death,* blessings and curses. Now *choose life,* so that you and your children may live and that you may love the LORD your God, listen to his voice, and hold fast to him. For *the LORD is your life.* (Deut. 30:11, 14–20)

When I was a younger Christian reading passages like this, I envisioned God zapping disobedient people with thunderbolts or blessing them if they obeyed. Such a picture misses the point. The universe has a natural cause-and-effect relationship. Based on the moral laws God built into creation, some actions lead to prosperity and blessings and others to destruction and curses.

Pastor and revivalist Charles Finney (1792–1875) says that moral law is fundamental for establishing civil law in a nation: "It follows that no government is lawful or innocent that does not recognize the moral law as the only universal law, and God as the Supreme Lawgiver and Judge, to whom nations in their national capacity, as well as individuals, are amenable. The moral law of God is the only law of individuals and of nations, and nothing can be rightful government but such as is established and administered with a view to its support."[7]

This leads to the question of why some historically non-Judeo-Christian nations—such as Japan and Singapore—have prospered. The answer to this is that moral principles and laws do not "belong" to Christians and Jews. They are transcendent laws that belong to all humankind. When people or nations employ these laws, whether they are believers or not, they will reap positive consequences.[8] Yet Jews and Christians, God's covenant people, have a fundamental understanding because they have received God's revelation in creation and in his Word.

Goodness

Atheists have rejected the Judeo-Christian faith, as we have said elsewhere, for moral reasons. They want license to live for themselves, engage in sex without limit, and rid their consciences of life in a moral universe. But as the character Mitya Karamazov so prophetically perceives in Dostoyevsky's novel *The Brothers Karamazov*, if God does not exist, everything is permitted.[9] Without God, without a moral universe, human behavior has no limits on murder, sexual slavery, or pedophilia.

In chapter 6 we quoted President Teddy Roosevelt, who said, "There is only one morality. All else is immorality. There is only true Christian ethics over against which stands the whole of paganism."[10] This one morality is derived from the nature of God. God is *good*. "Teach them to obey all that I have commanded" includes teaching the moral vision to *be good* (Christian internal self-government) and to *do good* toward others and toward creation. We can contrast this one morality with the reigning immorality in the West today.

The riots in London and other English cities in the summer of 2011 were a testament to the narcissistic climate of self-absorption, instant gratification, and lawlessness found in many Western cities. Such vices have largely displaced commonly held virtues of the past: family and community, thrift and saving, and respect for the law.

The US National Drug Intelligence Center reported that in 2008, 14.2 percent of individuals twelve years of age and older had used illicit drugs during the past year. Marijuana led the list, used by 25.8 million people twelve years of age and older. Recreational use of prescription drugs ranked second, at 15.2 million. Some 5.3

million individuals used cocaine, 850,000 used methamphetamine, and 453,000 used heroin.[11] The financial cost of drug abuse in the United States is 215 billion dollars;[12] few have counted the cost in terms of lost health, early death, broken families, and the emotional and economic impact on the larger community. In addition, consider the cost in human life from the drug wars in Mexico: 28,000 people from 2006 to 2010.[13] The fact is, we do not have a drug problem; we have a moral problem that manifests itself in this kind of destruction.

In a country that was founded on the sacredness of life, we are confronted with trends that may only be called diabolical. At the beginning of life, social Darwinism demands the death of the weakest, the unborn baby. The fact that nearly half of pregnancies in America are "unintended" reflects a casual view of sex. Instead of the beauty of sexual intimacy within marriage, sex at the beginning of the twenty-first century has been reduced to recreation and entertainment. That about four in ten of these "accidental" conceptions are terminated by abortion indicates profound disrespect for the most vulnerable among us. Nearly one in four babies conceived in America are deliberately terminated. Between 1973 and 2008 nearly 50 million legal abortions were performed in the United States.[14] Horribly, in 2011 the Guttmacher Institute reported that 37 percent of women obtaining abortions identify as Protestant and 28 percent as Catholic—a total of 65 percent, or two out of three women, identifying as Christian.[15] Another indication of the appalling impact of social Darwinism on the church is seen in a 1996 study, which found that "one in five women having abortions [in the United States] are born-again or Evangelical Christians."[16]

At the other end of life, social Darwinism calls societies to destroy those who are weak, sick, or no longer productive. States and physicians are beginning to "experiment" with euthanasia and physician-assisted suicide. In the 1990s Dr. Jack Kevorkian assisted over forty people in committing suicide in Michigan. His first public assisted suicide was in 1990. Later he crossed the narrow threshold of assisting suicide to actually murdering a patient. Thankfully, the state of Michigan found him guilty of second degree murder and sent him to prison. The movement that Kevorkian publicized has led to the legalization of physician-assisted suicide in Oregon, Washington, and Montana. A nation that no longer sees life as sacred has justified murder at both ends of life.

Another decline in virtue is seen in our treatment of the earth. We have been placed on the planet to be stewards of the land, to conserve and prosper it. Too often Americans have raped the land by clear-cutting forests and polluting lakes, rivers, and the air with industrial waste. In the name of efficiency, we have reduced animals to machines of production rather than creatures made by God. We have viewed farming as an industrial rather than a family enterprise. Rather than leaving the land in better condition for the next generation, we often leave it poorer. The lifestyles of many in the West reflect conspicuous consumption and a "throwaway" culture, which lead to the wasting of water, energy, land, and other precious, God-given resources. The narcissism that produced riots in England has also led to the destruction of creation.

What does goodness look like for us today as we engage the war from the East and the war in the West? Each of the preceding examples of immorality reveals opportunities to spread and embody goodness in our societies. Christians are to stand for freedom, order, and justice; for communities and families; and for the sanctity of human life from beginning to end. We are to create peace, health, and prosperity and to care for God's creation and every individual.

Having examined the first two components of the cultural trinity—truth and goodness—we now turn to the final element, beauty.

CHAPTER 17

Beauty: The Aesthetic Order

The aesthetic dimension of reality is the vessel within which the
infinitely free, invisible God graciously becomes visible.
—JOHN R. SACHS

In the beginning God created the heavens and the earth" (Gen.
1:1). The Bible's very first words disclose what the storyline will
be about: creativity, art, and beauty. The early chapters of Genesis
begin the revelation that God existed before the universe and created all things out of nothing—the invisible making the visible—
bringing form to the formless and light to the darkness.[1] God's
creation is beautiful because it reflects his nature: it is permeated
with light, structure, order, harmony, and goodness. God is the First
Artist, the author of all things beautiful.

The most beautiful thing you have ever seen is beautiful because
it reflects God. The most hideous thing you have ever seen is hideous because it distorts God's nature. Part of our task in the Great
Commission, connected to the Cultural Commission, is to create
beauty.

The Nature of Beauty

God's beauty is marked by his light, glory, splendor, and radiance. He shines greater than the greatest splendor in his creation. The splendor we see in the night sky, in the Grand Canyon, or in a mother caring for her child is only a small reflection of the divine, just as the moon is a pale reflection of the sun.

God is light![2] There is no darkness in him; in fact, darkness flees the light. *Illumination* existed before the sun and moon and will exist when there is no more sun and moon.[3] Why? Because God is glorious! His light so shines that there is no need for another source of light. God's glory is brightness and splendor,[4] and infinite perfection.[5] Jesus is also light,[6] the brightness of the father's glory.[7]

Zion, the City of God (the place of his name) is "perfect in beauty."[8] We are called to worship the Lord in the "splendor of his holiness."[9] When we look at God, we see his beauty and glory.[10]

Cynthia Pearl Maus (1880–1970) was an author and editor who inspired many. Much of her writing focuses on beauty and the arts. She describes the nature of beauty this way:

> We are so accustomed to thinking of beauty as merely decorative and ornamental that we forget that beauty is a moral necessity. God wrought beauty in the structure of the universe. Beauty is the high form of righteousness. Beauty and truth are not separated in God's world, and they are not to be in human thought. . . . God, who gave as much care to paint a lily as to forming the eternal hills, joined truth and beauty in holy union; and what God has joined together man ought not attempt to put asunder, because beauty has a moral value for truth.[11]

Beauty is a moral necessity, fused with goodness and truth. On the other hand, the hideous is not simply ugly; it is fused with evil and lies.

Beauty brings hope into places of poverty and life to places of hideousness. Congregationalist pastor W. M. O'Hanlon, writing about the immense poverty and degradation in the nineteenth-century slums of Belfast, profoundly said, "Beauty is God's Messenger."[12] Beauty brings light into dark places and hope to the hopeless. Dr. Larry Ward, founder of Food for the Hungry International, was fond of saying that he wanted FHI to be the relief organization that planted flower seeds in refugee camps.

God's Art

The Bible describes how the First Artist communicates through his artistry.

> Lift your eyes and look to the heavens:
>> Who created all these?
> He who brings out the starry host one by one,
>> and calls them each by name.
> Because of his great power and mighty strength,
>> not one of them is missing.
> (Isa. 40:26)

> The heavens declare the glory of God;
>> the skies proclaim the work of his hands.
> Day after day they pour forth speech;
>> night after night they reveal knowledge.
> (Ps. 19:1–2)

> But the basic reality of God is plain enough. Open your eyes and there it is! By taking a long and thoughtful look at what God has created, people have always been able to see what their eyes as such can't see: eternal power, for instance, and the mystery of his divine being. So nobody has a good excuse. (Rom. 1:19–20, *The Message*)

God's art (creation) reveals his existence and the elements of his transcendent nature. It reveals the design, structure, and purpose of humankind and the wonder and nature of creation.

Many years ago I was standing in our yard in Denver, Colorado, with a good friend, Darrell Phippen. It was spring and the snow cover was slowly receding. Bulbs were beginning to flower in red, yellow, and white. As we admired their beauty, Darrell, an engineer, said in wonder: "Look at this! Look at the colors coming out of the brown soil! How did God do this? How could a brown bulb growing in brown soil produce such beautiful colors?"

The Scripture begins and ends with beauty. It begins in a garden and ends in a garden-city.[13] It begins with the wedding of the first couple, Adam and Eve, and ends with the royal wedding of the last couple, Christ and his bride, the church. With the ingathering of the nations (see the next chapter), the glory of each nation is given to Christ and his bride on their wedding day. The unique splendor of each nation is a gift to Christ.

Only a humble heart can fully recognize and appreciate beauty. Pride rebels against the created order, substituting evil for good, the hideous for beauty. To recognize beauty "demands the humility to sit at the foot of a dandelion"[14] or, I might add, before the face of God.

Franciscan theologian Saint Bonaventure captured so poetically the power of God's self-revelation in creation:

> Whoever, therefore, is not enlightened by such splendor of created things is blind; whoever is not awakened by such outcries is deaf, whoever does not praise God because of all these effects is dumb; whoever does not discover the First Principle from such clear signs is a fool. Therefore, open your eyes, alert the ears of your spirit, open your lips and apply your heart so that in all creatures you may see, hear, praise, love and worship, glorify and honor your God, lest the whole world rise against you.[15]

Human Art

Human beings were given the task of creating godly culture. They were equipped with hands to cultivate the *soil* and with minds and hearts to cultivate the *soul*.[16] People can use their senses and creativity to compose a song no one has ever heard, write a poem no one has ever read, paint a picture no one has ever seen, choreograph a dance no one has ever danced, or create a play no one has ever performed.

The fundamental question is: Will these works of art reflect beauty or the hideous? Will they breathe life or bring death? In making life-affirming art, the artist—*the secondary creator*—reveals the *Primary Creator*. The artist's secondary world reflects the wonder and reality of the primary world.

Many Roman Catholic writers have given us profound insights into the nature of beauty and art. Biographer Thomas of Celano wrote of Saint Francis: "In every work of the artist he praised the Artist; whatever he found in the things made he referred to the Maker. He rejoiced in all the works of the hands of the Lord and saw behind things pleasant to behold their life-giving reason and cause."[17]

J. R. R. Tolkien (1892–1973), author of *The Hobbit* and The Lord of the Rings trilogy, reflected on the relationship between the primary creation and the artist's secondary creation. Tolkien says we were made to live in the framework of Creation's Order.

> Probably every writer making a secondary world, a fantasy, every sub-creator, wishes in some measure to be a real maker, or hopes that he is drawing on reality: hopes that the peculiar quality of this secondary world (if not all the details) are derived from Reality, or are flowing into it. If he indeed achieves a quality that can fairly be described by the dictionary definition: "inner consistency of reality," it is difficult to conceive how this can be, if the work does not in some way partake of reality.[18]

Art begins with what God has provided, with the principles of aesthetics and the resources found "in the garden." All that the secondary artist creates is a new expression of the timeless and transcendent. C. S. Lewis (1898–1963), Christian apologist, medievalist, author, and academic, describes the work of the artist: "An author should never conceive of himself as bringing into existence beauty or wisdom which did not exist before, but simply and solely as *trying to embody in terms of his own art some reflection of that eternal Beauty and Wisdom.*"[19]

Working within the circle of reality and beauty, the secondary artist is to pursue excellence in his artistic discipline. Biblical scholar, commentator, and author, Frank E. Gaebelein (1899–1983) explains why the artist should seek excellence: "It is because of who and what God is, it is because of the beauty and truth manifest in his Son, it is because of the perfection of his redeeming work, that evangelicals can never be content with the mediocre in aesthetics. Here, as in all else, the call is to the unremitting pursuit of excellence to the glory of the God of all truth."[20]

Life or Death

An artist's expression is a reflection of her worship. Art will contribute either to a toxic culture or a healthy one; it will promote life or death. When laws of creation are honored and biblical principles applied, the artist's expression will glorify God and contribute to the building of a godly nation.

Dr. Elizabeth Youmans writes of the influence of the Bible on art: "In nations where the Bible has highly influenced language, law, and culture, the fine arts reflect beauty, truth, and moral goodness. When the Bible has not been an influence or has been removed as the seedbed of language and culture, the fine arts reflect the corruption and debasement of beauty, truth, and moral goodness."[21]

As truth stands opposed to lies, and good to evil, so does beauty to the hideous. Just as there is an *objective* truth and goodness, so there is a tangible standard of beauty. Relativists claim that "beauty is in the eye of the beholder." But absolute beauty has an objective standard: the glory and splendor of God. True beauty is permeated with truth and goodness just as God is beautiful, true, and good.

In their creativity, people contribute to culture that either edifies or tears down. They create culture that either nurtures the human spirit and refines nations, or poisons the soul and pollutes society. Father Thomas Dubay writes about the power of music to influence us: "In touching the inner core of our beings beautiful music ennobles and uplifts. It possesses a persuasive power towards the good, while coarse and barbaric music cheapens, degrades, and promotes evil."[22]

On the scale with the hideous and beauty on opposite ends, each person may evaluate where they are in terms of their cultural contribution. They may also ask, "Am I moving toward beauty and life or toward the hideous and death?" A life-enhancing culture begins with worship of the Creator, finds its basis in reality, imparts joy and hope, transforms, and leads people into edifying life. On the other hand, death-producing culture begins with worship of man or nature or the demonic, finds its basis in illusion, leads to hopelessness and despair, deforms, and draws people into evil and harm.

The Aesthetic Order: Elements of Beauty

As we have mentioned, good art reveals the nature of the Creator and the Primary Creation. Cynthia Pearl Maus says, "The principle of fine arts is the embodiment of the universal and eternal to render visible that which is Divine."[23]

The apostle Paul provides what John Erickson, creator of the children's book series Hank the Cowdog, describes as the "Great Commission" to the artist: "Finally, brothers, whatever is true, whatever is noble, whatever is right, whatever is pure, whatever is lovely, whatever is admirable—if anything is excellent or praiseworthy—think about such things."[24] These are the marks of art that edifies.

At least four critical ingredients characterize good art: artistry, content, order, and technique.

Artistry is the ability to stir the soul. Erickson writes, "Young writers should be speaking out against stories that are formless, chaotic, selfish, and disgusting. Their mission should be to do what artists deserving of the title have always done: bring light into the world, find order in chaos, and provide nourishment, hope, and meaning to people who need it."[25]

The *content* of the artist's expression reveals reality and the glory of God. Joy is found when a creation reveals something of God's glory. God's artistry reveals his glory. It is found when *reality* is discovered in the midst of artistic expression. In his treatise on fantasy, Tolkien writes: "The peculiar quality of the 'joy' in successful Fantasy can thus be explained as a sudden glimpse of the underlying reality or truth. It is not only a 'consolation' for the sorrow of this world, but a satisfaction, and an answer to that question, 'Is it true?' The answer to this question that I gave at first was (quite rightly): 'If you have built your little world well, yes: it is true in that world.' That is enough for the artist (or the artist part of the artist)."[26]

The *order* of the artistic expression moves toward coherence and harmony. Physicist Paul Davies describes the relationship between beauty and order: "Time and again, the artistic taste has proved a fruitful guiding principle and led directly to new discoveries, even when it at first sight appears to contradict the observational facts. . . . Central to the physicist's notion of beauty are harmony, simplicity, and symmetry."[27]

Similarly, Sir Archibald Russell (1904–95), British aerospace engineer, writes that things are beautiful as they comport with the laws of nature: "When one designs an airplane, he must stay as close as possible to the laws of nature. . . . It so happens that our ideas of beauty are those of nature. Every shape and curve of the Concorde [the world's first supersonic passenger jet] is arranged so it will conform with the natural flow as conditioned by the laws of nature."[28]

The *technique* of the artist is to reveal excellence. Not only the art's content but also its excellencies bring joy to the observer because they point to the glory of the First Artist. Dubay describes the radiance of perfection in a piece of art: "Michelangelo's Pieta is light in stone. Its radiance not only delights the observer but also simultaneously shouts that it came about not by a chance erosion caused by unknowing elements of water and wind. Its form, integrity, proportion, and radiance declare both its message and the design of the master who produced it."[29]

Individuals and nations can live in a more beautiful world. They can produce more beauty and less vulgarity, more wholesomeness and less decadence, more splendor and less dreariness, more anticipation and less tediousness, and more harmony and less dissonance.

With her late husband Francis, Edith Schaeffer founded L'Abri Fellowship. One of the hallmarks of L'Abri was the beauty brought into everyday life. The Schaeffers understood that God is beautiful and his nature should be reflected in one's home. Examples abounded at L'Abri. Meals were beautifully prepared and served. Fresh-cut flowers adorned the table. The soft glow of candlelight set the ambience for quiet, stimulating conversation in the evening. The garden produced fresh fruit, vegetables, and flowers. Classical music hung in the air of the chalet homes. Such beauty costs little money but requires intentionality. In *Hidden Art,* Edith describes this common expression of beauty.[30]

From L'Abri, I visited a mission base in Austria that smuggled Bibles behind the Iron Curtain. The disparity was striking. Neither L'Abri nor this base had much money, but in contrast to the simple beauty at L'Abri, the base meals were like army rations. The food was served in cooking pots placed unceremoniously on the table and eaten from plastic plates. The dining room was dark and drab. What made the difference in these two expressions? This mission base was functioning from a stark war mentality. To be sure, we are in a conflict, as we have seen. But beauty can be brought even to the battle.

Muslim fundamentalists oppose the immorality, vulgarity, and crudeness spread by so much of the West's artistic expression. One can think of this in fashion (e.g., the *Sports Illustrated Swimsuit Issue* and Victoria's Secret, which exalt immodesty and objectify women; and Gothic fashion, which is characterized by darkness, morbidity, and eroticism); in music (e.g., gangster rap, which promotes male chauvinism, sexual immorality, drugs, and violence); and in theater (e.g., *The Vagina Monologues*, which promotes promiscuity, lust, and homosexuality). These expressions of art are steeped in lies and darkness rather than truth and light. They lead to bondage and death rather than freedom and life. We should oppose such false forms of beauty in our society.

We must recognize that we are all culture makers, given the task of creating beauty marked by goodness and truth. We are artists in our homes as we prepare and present meals, decorate, and choose the fabrics, flowers, and pieces of art we display. In the office we can transcend mere functionality to create an aesthetically pleasing workplace with quiet music, artwork, and plants. The factory can be a clean, healthy environment for workers with splashes of beauty.

Let us be creators of beauty. Let us "teach them to obey all I have commanded." Let us live out the aesthetic order, together with the moral and metaphysical orders, as we anticipate the fulfillment of God's kingdom, to which we now turn.

CHAPTER 18

The Consummation
of the Kingdom

*The treasure that men find laid up in heaven turns out to be the
treasures and wealth of the nations, the best they have known and
loved on earth redeemed of all imperfections and transfigured by the
radiance of God.*

—G. B. CAIRD

Jesus Christ has made no mystery about what he wants for his
creation: the Great Commission is his big agenda for the world.
By embracing that agenda—by binding themselves to the framework of God's created order—nations can flourish.

God's agenda is *simple,* but its implementation is not *easy.* We
are called to a war, a cosmic battle. A battle of worldviews. A battle
for the hearts and minds of people. A battle for the very souls of
nations. We who follow Jesus Christ are the vanguard. We must
think and *act.* We must engage the battle for the souls of nations and
the future of the world.

Some parties are using bullets and bombs, but such will not win this war. This war will be won by lives invested well and sacrificed for others. It will be won by truth over falsehood, justice over corruption, freedom over tyranny, liberty over license, love over hate, and beauty over vileness. It will be won by those who proclaim by their words and lives the truth, goodness, and beauty of the coming kingdom in the midst of our poor and broken world.

As we have mentioned elsewhere in this book, Christians are to live with the end of history in mind. We are to live "proleptic lives" in anticipation of the reality of the end of the age. Our lives *now* are to reveal the *not yet* of the final completion of the kingdom of God.

"And Behold, I Am with You Always"

At the end of our study of the Great Commission, we now consider Jesus' parting words: "Behold, I am with you always, to the end of the age" (Matt. 28:20 ESV). Some versions translate "behold" as "surely," stripping the original of its force. The Greek word is in the imperative mood,[1] with all the power of "Go and make disciples." Christ is saying, "Hey, pay attention! Look!"

Are we so preoccupied with our own lives and circumstances that we fail to focus on Christ and his coming kingdom? Do we fail to recognize Christ's presence and purpose in our lives because our thoughts are elsewhere?

Look! Jesus is with us always . . . to the very end of the age. His power, authority, love, and grace abound. Behold! He is king of heaven and earth and of *time*.

How does Jesus characterize his commitment to be with us? Always, daily—literally "all the days"! Think of traditional wedding vows: "I take you to be my wife/husband, to have and to hold *from this day forward*, for better or for worse, for richer, for poorer, in sickness and in health, to love and to cherish; *from this day forward* until death do us part." The promise is for the good days and the bad days—for all the days. Jesus will be with us all the days.

We began our study by examining Jesus' *great claim:* all authority in heaven and on earth has been given to him. He is king of
all.[2] Christ is king of heaven and earth today. He has already won
the battle! In his victory we have certain hope. From his example
we take courage. Our task—discipling nations—is done by living
lives that baptize and by teaching that which transforms (i.e., God's
truth). We are to go forth under Christ's banner to settle the final
skirmishes, to prepare for the glorious appearing of our great God
and Savior, Jesus Christ.

The extraordinary ending of the Great Commission brings us
full circle in our study. Matthew begins his gospel by announcing
that Christ is Immanuel, *God with us.*[3] He concludes with Jesus'
pronouncement that *he is with us* until the end of the age. What is
the very end of the age? Toward what is all history moving?

The Consummate Vision

From the beginning of Scripture to its end we see God's love for the
nations. God raised up Abraham and his descendants *to be a blessing to all nations.*[4] Centuries later, the apostle Paul remarkably connects the gospel to the blessing of nations: "Scripture foresaw that
God would justify the Gentiles by faith, and announced the gospel
in advance to Abraham: 'All nations will be blessed through you'"
(Gal. 3:8). Now, in these last days, God has raised up the church to
disciple the nations.

A number of passages picture the glory of Christ's return and
the consummation of his kingdom. The curtain is pulled back and
we glimpse the glorious vision. Psalm 47 captures one of the most
inspiring visions of the end of time.

> Clap your hands, all you nations;
> shout to God with cries of joy.
> For the LORD Most High is awesome,
> the great King over all the earth!

He subdued nations under us,
　　peoples under our feet. . . .
For God is the King of all the earth;
　　sing to him a psalm of praise.
God reigns over the nations;
　　God is seated on his holy throne.
The nobles of the nations assemble
　　as the people of the God of Abraham,
for the kings of the earth belong to God;
　　he is greatly exalted.
(vv. 1–3, 7–9)

The consummation of history and culture is further revealed in the parallel visions of Isaiah 60 and Revelation 21. These visions merit further examination.

The Gates Are Never Shut

Both prophecies tell us that the gates of the City of God never need to be shut.

Your gates will always stand open,
　　they will never be shut, day or night.
(Isa. 60:11)

On no day will its gates ever be shut, for there will be no night there. (Rev. 21:25)

Gates are closed at night to keep enemies out. But there will be no enemies and no night! So the gates will no longer need to be shut against attack.[5] Swords will be turned into plowshares, and shalom will abound.[6]

God Is the Light of the City

The sun and moon won't be needed in the new heaven and earth.

The sun will no more be your light by day,
    nor will the brightness of the moon shine on you,
for the LORD will be your everlasting light,
    and your God will be your glory.
Your sun will never set again,
    and your moon will wane no more;
the LORD will be your everlasting light,
    and your days of sorrow will end.
(Isa. 60:19–20)

The city does not need the sun or the moon to shine on it, for the glory of God gives it light, and the Lamb is its lamp. (Rev. 21:23)

God's glory provided light[7] before he created the sun and the moon.[8] At the end of time, we will have no need of sun or moon; the glory of God will be the source of light.

At the end of history, the whole earth will be filled with his glory.[9] The nations will be filled with knowledge of the Lord "as the waters cover the sea" (Isa. 11:9; Hab. 2:14), an image of baptism. The transformation, or baptism (recall the pickling metaphor in chapter 12), of the nations will be complete. The glory of God will be the light of the City.[10]

Nations will be drawn by the light of God's glory.[11] The prophet Isaiah beautifully writes:

The LORD rises upon you
    and his glory appears over you.
Nations will come to your light,
    and kings to the brightness of your dawn.
(Isa. 60:2–3)

Light attracts. A moth in the darkness is drawn to the light, a lost person to the proverbial light at the end of the tunnel. The light of God's glory will draw the nations and kings of the earth to the City of God.

No More Suffering and Pain

The end of history means no more tears, death, hunger, or suffering.

> I will make peace your governor
>   and well-being your ruler.
> No longer will violence be heard in your land,
>   nor ruin or destruction within your borders,
> but you will call your walls Salvation
>   and your gates Praise.
> (Isa. 60:17–18)

And I heard a loud voice from the throne saying, "Look! God's dwelling place is now among the people, and he will dwell with them. They will be his people, and God himself will be with them and be their God. He will wipe every tear from their eyes. There will be no more death or mourning or crying or pain, for the old order of things has passed away." (Rev. 21:3–4)

This is the picture of the new heaven and the new earth, the fulfillment of shalom. Old things will pass away and all things become new.[12] Mel Gibson powerfully captures this truth in *The Passion of the Christ*. Jesus, beaten raw by the Roman guards, stumbles toward Golgotha carrying his cross. As he falls under the weight, his eyes meet his mother's and he utters, "Behold, Mother, I make all things new." Gibson's artistic license of putting Revelation 21:5 into Jesus' mouth at Calvary conveys a powerful truth: the cross of Christ reversed the consequences of the fall and made all things new.

The Ingathering of the Nations for Worship

At the *teleios*—the consummation of history—the nations will gather to worship Christ:

Arise, shine, for your light has come,
　　and the glory of the LORD rises upon you.
See, darkness covers the earth
　　and thick darkness is over the peoples,
but the LORD rises upon you
　　and his glory appears over you.
Nations will come to your light,
　　and kings to the brightness of your dawn.
(Isa. 60:1–3)

Psalm 86:9 and other passages capture the sense of rapturous worship: "All the nations you have made will come and worship before you, Lord; they will bring glory to your name."

The Scriptures speak of the *registry of nations* (or peoples). One of the clearest references is Psalm 87:3–7:

Glorious things are said of you,
　　city of God:
"I will record Rahab and Babylon
　　among those who acknowledge [or know] me—
Philistia too, and Tyre, along with Cush—
　　and will say, 'This one was born in Zion.'"
Indeed, of Zion it will be said,
　　"This one and that one were born in her,
　　and the Most High himself will establish her."
The LORD will write in the register of the peoples:
　　"This one was born in Zion."
As they make music they will sing,
　　"All my fountains are in you."

This passage includes several noteworthy elements about this registry or enrollment of the people. First, note that God is the great Census Taker. Second, the criterion for inclusion is the acknowledgment, or possession of intimate knowledge, of God.[13] Qualifying nations include some Gentile people and peoples: Rahab,

Babylon, Philistia, Tyre, and Cush. Gentile nations are usually seen as enemies of God, but these will come to the Lord en masse at the end of time.[14] God covenants with Abraham to bless "all nations." He covenants not with the Jews for the Jews but with the Jews for the nations. He intends to make one people out of many.[15]

Third, those in the registry are acknowledged three times to have been "born in Zion." This is remarkable: Gentiles are registered as born in the City of God! The Hebrew word translated "born" means "to bring forth, to be a descendant, to tell of ancestry."[16] A modern equivalent might be a hospital registry that records the names of all those born in the entire city or state. This heavenly roster credits Gentiles as having been born (metaphorically) in Zion, the City of God. The righteous individuals in the nations, whose names are in the registry of nations, will enter the City of God.[17]

Finally, the nations will joyously gather for celebration.[18] They will sing of the fountain of their joy flowing from God and his throne.[19] This is pictured most beautifully in the last chapter of the Bible, another full-circle text. Genesis 2 spoke of the tree of life in the garden. In Revelation we see the tree growing beside the river of life in the New Jerusalem for the healing of nations:

> Then the angel showed me the river of the water of life, as clear as crystal, flowing from the throne of God and of the Lamb down the middle of the great street of the city. On each side of the river stood the tree of life, bearing twelve crops of fruit, yielding its fruit every month. And the leaves of the tree are for the healing of the nations. (Rev. 22:1–2)

The Gifts of the Nations

At the great ingathering of the nations to worship Christ and celebrate his magnificent nuptial,[20] the kings of the earth will present him with the glory of their nations as wedding gifts.

> Then you will look and be radiant, your heart will throb and swell with joy; the wealth on the seas will be brought to you,

to you the riches of the nations will come. Herds of camels will cover your land, young camels of Midian and Ephah. And all from Sheba will come, bearing gold and incense and proclaiming the praise of the LORD. All Kedar's flocks will be gathered to you, the rams of Nebaioth will serve you; they will be accepted as offerings on my altar, and I will adorn my glorious temple. (Isa. 60:5–7)

The nations will walk by its light, and the kings of the earth will bring their splendor into it. . . . The glory and honor of the nations will be brought into it. (Rev. 21:24, 26)

Cultures throughout history have celebrated and presented gifts. Early in the biblical narrative we witness the giving of gifts from one tribal leader to another.[21] When God calls the Hebrew people to build him a tabernacle, the people bring gifts for its construction and furnishing.[22]

Two other notable illustrations are the gifts of the Queen of Sheba to Solomon and the gift of the Magi to the child Jesus. The book of 1 Kings records the great Queen of Sheba (from present-day Yemen) recognizing in Solomon a king above all human kings.[23] She arrived in Jerusalem with a large caravan of camels carrying spices, large quantities of gold, and precious stones. She brought gifts representing the glory of her nation.

Similarly, the Magi came from the East to pay homage to the royal sovereign, the baby Jesus. Matthew records the coming of these Gentile ambassadors to the King of the Jews.[24] The gospel, announced beforehand to Abraham, was good news not merely to the Jews but to all the nations of the earth. The Magi brought the best their nations had to offer as gifts of tribute to King David's heir: gold, incense, and myrrh.[25] These ambassadors, presenting gifts to Christ at his nativity, prefigure the kings of the earth who will bring the glory of their nations to the King of kings at his wedding.

David wrote of the glory of the ingathering of the nations to pay tribute to God:

Because of your temple at Jerusalem
    kings will bring you gifts. . . .
Envoys will come from Egypt;
    Cush will submit herself to God.
Sing to God, you kingdoms of the earth,
    sing praise to the Lord.
(Ps. 68:29, 31–32)

The book of Revelation foresees kings bringing their splendor, the glory and honor of their nations, into the City of God. The Greek word for "splendor" (Rev. 21:24) and "glory" (21:26) is *doxa*. Often used of God's splendor, the word reflects a person's godly character and reputation. The Greek word for "honor," *timē*, means preciousness, value, the worth of something, the price paid. Here it specifically means "the festive honour to be possessed by nations, and brought into the Holy City, the Heavenly Jerusalem."[26]

The gifts are given to honor the king. Even conquered kings will bring gifts and will bend the knee before the sovereign King of kings, Jesus Christ. Righteous gifts will come even from the unrighteous: "When you ascended on high, you took many captives; you received gifts from people, even from the *rebellious*—that you, LORD God, might dwell there" (Ps. 68:18).[27] "Rebellious" in Hebrew means stubborn, defiant, obstinate, that is, in open defiance to authority.[28] Even the defiant will bow and give their best to pay tribute to Christ.

The Glory of the Nations

He who is Lord of all declares, "I am coming soon. I am the Alpha and the Omega, the First and the Last, the Beginning and the End" (Rev. 22:13). What was begun at creation is now finished at the end of time. We have come full circle. With the last marriage, the marriage of the Lamb,[29] we are reminded of the first marriage of Adam and Eve in the garden. We are reminded by the New Jerusalem, the heavenly city,[30] that the new creation replaces the original. The Cultural Commission to develop the earth in Genesis is consummated with the City of God and the ingathering of the nations. The first vice-regents (Adam and Eve) and their descendants were tasked with creating artifacts to be brought by the last vice-regents to adorn the New Jerusalem.

What "artifacts" will Adam and Eve's progeny bring? The fruits of their cultural creativity, the wealth of their nations![31] God did not intend people and nations to be poor. He established a set of creation laws. When wise people discover his laws and obey them, wealth grows, wealth of individuals and of nations. The unique glory of each nation is established.

Professor of Christian philosophy and president of Fuller Theological Seminary, Dr. Richard J. Mouw, writes: "Jesus died to save sinners—but he is also the Lamb who serves as the lamp in the transformed City. As the Lamb of God he will draw all of the goods, artifacts, and instruments of culture to himself."[32] The unique wealth of each nation is brought to adorn the City of God. Not only will we see people from every tribe and nation, but the glorious gifts of each nation.

Dr. Anthony Hoekema (1913–88), the Dutch-born professor of systematic theology, captures the essence of the adornment of the City of God with the godly elements of cultural creativity:

> One could say that according to these words, the inhabitants of the earth will include people who attained great prominence and exercised great power on the present earth—the kings, leaders and the like. One could also say that whatever people have done on earth which glorified God will be remembered in the life to come (see Revelation 14:13). But more must be said. Is it too much to say that, according to these verses, the unique contribution of each nation to the life of the present earth will enrich the life of the new earth? Shall we then perhaps inherit the best products of culture and art this earth has produced?[33]

C. S. Lewis has captured this sense of awe and wonder in his children's book *The Last Battle*. Peter, Edmund, and Lucy are taken into Aslan's Country (heaven). (Susan does not join them, because she ceases to believe in Narnia.) As Aslan—the figure of Christ— calls them to "come further up and further in," they sense that they "have been there before." Continuing their journey, they find they are in England in all her glory. All the dross has been burned off; only the unique beauty of England is left. With this image Lewis captures how the goodness of each culture will be redeemed and purified in the light of the glory of God.

What might these gifts of the nations be? Here are some possibilities:

- *Natural resources* (animals, plants, minerals) that people have developed and stewarded.[34] Perhaps we will relish coffee from Ethiopia, Kenya, Yemen, or Colombia. Maybe we will enjoy tulips from Holland and roses from Texas. The finest wines from France, South Africa, Chile, or California may be among the gifts.

- *Cultural artifacts* (products made from natural resources) such as art, music, poetry, dance, and cuisine. Perhaps the richly colored and patterned fabrics from the indigenous peoples of Guatemala and Ghana, the rich music of African harmonies, or the symphonies of J. S. Bach will be among the gifts.

- The application of *biblical ideals* such as freedom, peacemaking, justice, and beauty. Perhaps New Zealand and Denmark will carry the flag of justice, Norway the flag of peacemaking, the United States the flag of freedom, and Japan the flag of beauty.

- *Discoveries in science and technology* such as the herbal and medicinal cures that have contributed to the healing of nations. Perhaps the wonder of human flight will be presented to the King.

Note the symbiotic relationship. The glory of each nation, shining in the light of the glory of God, is reflected glory, as the moon mirrors the sun's glory. Paul writes, "And we, who with unveiled faces all *reflect the Lord's glory,* are being transformed into his likeness with *ever-increasing glory,* which comes from the Lord, who is the Spirit" (2 Cor. 3:18 NIV 1984). It is the glory of the nations that brings glory to God.

A good friend of mine, Dr. Gila Garaway, is a Messianic Jew whose home overlooks beautiful Lake Tiberias (the Sea of Galilee). She told me of the privilege she had of introducing her beloved Israel to a group of Burundian pastors. One day they were outside the city of Bethlehem overlooking a forest that had been planted by the Jews in the rocky hillside. The pastors marveled at what they saw. They told Gila that in Burundi the forest grew in dark rich soil. They had never seen a forest growing in a desert before. They asked Gila to explain this phenomenon. She told them that God had given each people in the world a land. To the Jews he had given a desert. When he returns at the end of time, she said, he will ask each nation, "What have you done with the land I have given you?"

G. B. Caird (1917–84), professor of exegesis at Oxford University, reminds us: "Nothing from the old order which has value in the sight of God is disbarred from entry into the new. John's heaven is no world-denying Nirvana, into which men may escape from the incurable ills of sublunary existence, but the seal of affirmation on the goodness of God's creation."[35]

God has placed human beings in this world as his vice-regents and co-creators. In the Cultural Commission he equipped us with all we need to develop the earth's abundant potential. In the Great Commission he called and empowered his followers to bring good news—through words and actions—to a broken and fractured world. Since the creation, he has been watching to see what his creatures bearing his image will do with these assets. Today he watches still.[36]

At the end of the age, when the glory and honor of the nations are presented to Christ and his bride, the Holy City,[37] what part will you play in that cosmic celebration? What is the wealth of your nation? Is your nation prepared for the glorious return of the King?

"A Garment of Praise instead of a Spirit of Despair"

Our journey began with the troubled context of our world. The defining movements of the opening of the twenty-first century are the war from the East, jihad, and the war in the West, the culture wars. These wars are related through the moral and spiritual unraveling of the West and the core visions of three vastly different narratives: radical Islam, secular fundamentalism, and Judeo-Christian theism. Only one of these visions produces freedom; the other two result in anarchy and tyranny. Only one of these visions will survive this conflict.

The journey through the modern context of our mission could lead any sane person to despair.[38] But we have hope! Our hope is found in *Christus Victor*. He has conquered both the fear of death and death itself to "free those who all their lives were held in slavery by their fear of death" (Heb. 2:15). We have been set free, not *from* suffering, but *for* suffering.[39] We have been redeemed, not for a life of ease, but for a life of rebellion against the status quo.

Enough of a passive life, waiting for the return of Christ! Enough of seeking personal peace and affluence! Enough of an anemic gospel that may bring hope for eternity but brings no hope in time, leaving human lives, communities, and nations trapped in ignorance, poverty, injustice, and despair!

No! The kingdom is on the offensive. Christ is King of heaven *and earth*. He has unfurled the banner of the kingdom of God, the flag of freedom. And he cries out, "Follow me." He is leading us. The place that he is taking those who would follow is toward the compelling vision of the coming of the kingdom of God. He is calling us, commanding us, to follow him into the midst of the battle, into the hard and dark places. In those spaces we are to live lives that baptize and teach that which transforms. Our lives, in some small way, are to captivate the imagination of people trapped in hopelessness and emancipate people in the prison of despair. And he promises us that he will be with us always and that even *the gates of hell will not prevail against us.*[40]

The prophet Isaiah writes of the compelling vision at the consummation of all history:

> The Spirit of the Sovereign LORD is on me,
>   because the LORD has anointed me
>   to proclaim good news to the poor.
> He has sent me to bind up the brokenhearted,
>   to proclaim freedom for the captives
>   and release from darkness for the prisoners,
> to proclaim the year of the LORD's favor
>   and the day of vengeance of our God,
> to comfort all who mourn,
>   and provide for those who grieve in Zion—
> to bestow on them a crown of beauty
>   instead of ashes,
> the oil of joy
>   instead of mourning,
> and a garment of praise
>   instead of a spirit of despair.
> They will be called oaks of righteousness,
>   a planting of the LORD
>   for the display of his splendor.
> They will rebuild the ancient ruins
>   and restore the places long devastated;
> they will renew the ruined cities
>   that have been devastated for generations. . . .
> For as the soil makes the sprout come up
>   and a garden causes seeds to grow,

so the Sovereign LORD will make righteousness
    and praise spring up before all nations.
(Isa. 61:1–4, 11)

These words were lived by Christ and are to be lived by those who profess his name. Do you see the unfurled banner of freedom? Your King is calling: "Follow me!"

APPENDIX: STARTING LOVE CELLS

In chapter 13 we discussed the power of self-sacrificial love in the battle against tyranny. The church, I suggested there, should start "love cells." Similar to the idea of terrorist cells—but opposite in intention—love cells are small groups that love their enemies and nurture kingdom values in their members.

Here are some guidelines for Christians who want to form love cells:

- Start small (remember the mustard seed)
- Be organic (starfish, not spiders)
- Be viral (brushfires, not campfires)
- Pray, seeking to understand where God is already working and join him there
- Work quietly, seeking no power or glory
- Lead with demonstration rather than proclamation
- Work collaboratively with other believers and churches
- Be innovative and creative, thinking outside the box
- Give away things and self (time, energy, reputation)
- Be neighborly (love and serve)

In creating an offensive of kingdom culture, remember that baptizing nations means overwhelming them with truth, goodness, and beauty.

- Challenge lies and illusions with truth telling
- Defy the hideous and mundane with the creation of beauty
- Confront corruption, injustice, and evil with goodness, justice, and wholesomeness

One place to start is to build an outward focus into your existing small group, Bible study, or church committee.

Some excellent resources for beginning love cells can be found in the Materials section of the Harvest Foundation website (http://harvestfoundation.org/593954.ihtml). Look at the "Discipline of Love" and "Seed Projects" materials. Also, be encouraged by what others are doing by looking at the stories in the Stories section of both The Harvest Foundation (http://harvestfoundation.org/619156.ihtml) and the Disciple Nations Alliance (http://www.disciplenations.org/stories) websites.

NOTES

Introduction: A Clash of Civilizations

1. Samuel P. Huntington, *The Clash of Civilizations and the Remaking of World Order* (New York: Simon and Schuster, 1996).

2. We must distinguish between *moral anarchy* as the absence of moral restrictions and *political anarchy* as the absence of government. Most Western secularists are moral anarchists but not political anarchists.

3. As we will see later, moral anarchy ultimately leads to tyranny: when all values are relative and there is no objective truth, those in power will impose their values on others. Communism and fascism were both atheistic ideologies that led to tyranny.

4. Luke 4:18–19.

5. Readers more interested in the timelessness of the Great Commission and less concerned about the contemporary context may want to begin with Part 2.

6. Russell Kirk, *The American Cause* (Wilmington, Del.: Intercollegiate Studies Institute, 2002), x.

7. Ronald Reagan, "Inaugural Address, January 5, 1967," *Text of Speeches and Statements by Ronald Reagan, 33rd Governor of California*, Ronald Reagan Presidential Library, http://www.reagan.utexas.edu/archives/speeches/govspeech/01051967a.htm.

8. Kirk, *The American Cause*, 4; emphasis added.

9. Paul Berman, "The Philosopher of Islamic Terror," *New York Times Magazine*, March 23, 2003.

10. See my book *LifeWork: A Biblical Theology for What You Do Every Day* (Seattle: YWAM Publishing, 2009).

11. Matt. 28:18–20; Mark 16:15; Acts 1:8.

12. See chapter 10.

13. Col. 2:15.
14. I prefer the word *wholistic* to the more common spelling *holistic*, which has taken on the New Age connotation of unity without diversity. *Wholism* conveys the idea of the whole of God's Word to the whole person in the whole world.
15. Psalm 119:68 says, "You [LORD] are good, and do good; Teach me Your statutes" (NKJV).

1. The War from the East: Is This War?

Epigraph: Akbar S. Ahmed, *Islam Today: A Short Introduction to the Muslim World* (New York: I.B. Tauris, 1999), 1.

1. "Bin Laden's Fatwa," PBS NewsHour, August 1996, http://www.pbs.org/newshour/terrorism/international/fatwa_1996.html.
2. Dr. Matthew Robinson, "9/11: Threats about Airplanes as Weapons Prior to 9/11," Justice Blind?, http://www.justiceblind.com/airplanes.html.
3. World Islamic Front, "Jihad against Jews and Crusaders," Federation of American Scientists, February 23, 1998, http://www.fas.org/irp/world/para/docs/980223-fatwa.htm.
4. Bernard Lewis, "Europe and Islam," Irving Kristol Lecture, March 7, 2007, 1.
5. Thomas Friedman, *Longitudes and Attitudes: The World in the Age of Terrorism* (New York: Anchor Books, 2002), 323.
6. Newt Gingrich, "A Third World War," *Human Events*, July 17, 2006, http://www.humanevents.com/article.php?id=16065.
7. Rom. 11:17; Eph. 2:11–13.
8. It is worth noting that God saw Hagar in her distress. In Genesis 16:8 he calls her by name. What kind of God is this? The infinite creator God recognizes a female, a servant? He talks with her, calls her by name? This was unheard of at the time. Even today in many parts of the world, women and servants are considered second-class citizens. However, the living God addressed by name a person whom the world would not acknowledge. Hagar recognized what had just happened when she cried out, "You are the God who sees me" (Gen. 16:13). This beautiful story establishes the dignity of women, including the Arab daughters of Hagar and all Muslim women.
9. E. A. Hammel, "Kinship-based Politics and the Optimal Size of Kin Groups," PNAS, June 30, 2005, http://www.pnas.org/content/102/33/11951.full. Historian Mary Habeck relates how Muslims believe that "God ordained a law of enmity between human beings at the beginning of time so that 'it is in the nature of the unbeliever to hate Islam and Muslims'" (Mary Habeck, *Knowing the Enemy: Jihadist Ideology and the War on Terror* [New Haven: Yale University Press, 2006], 84). Similarly, the late Harvard University political science professor Samuel Huntington describes the reality of the

"wild donkey" today: "Wherever one looks along the perimeter of Islam, Muslims have problems living peaceably with their neighbors. . . . Muslims make up about one-fifth of the world's population but in the 1990s they have been far more involved in intergroup violence than the people of any other civilization. The evidence is overwhelming" (Samuel Huntington, *The Clash of Civilizations and the Remaking of World Order* [New York: Simon & Schuster, 1996], 256).

10. "Translation of the Inscriptions at the Dome of the Rock (Jerusalem)," Columbia University, http://www.learn.columbia.edu/courses/islamic/pdf/Inscrip_Dome.pdf.

11. The Battle of Vienna took place over two days, ending on September 12, 1683.

12. Hasan al-Banna, quoted in R. Scott Appleby, "History in the Fundamentalist Imagination," in Joanne Meyerowitz, ed., *History and September 11th: Critical Perspectives on the Past* (Philadelphia: Temple University Press, 2003), 166.

13. Hashemi Rafsanjani, quoted in Mike Scruggs, "Deep Roots of Crisis in the Middle East," *The Tribune Papers*, http://www.ashevilletribune.com/asheville/terrorism/Middle%20East%20Crisis%201%20RTF.htm.

14. Robert Fulford, "A War between Civilizations," *The National Post*, October 9, 2001, http://www.robertfulford.com/Civilizations.html.

15. Habeck, *Knowing the Enemy*, 7.

16. "Napolitano Warns against Anti-Muslim Backlash," *Fox News*, November 8, 2009, http://www.foxnews.com/politics/2009/11/08/napolitano-warns-anti-muslim-backlash/.

17. Kim R. Holmes, "Who Links Terrorism to Islam? Not America," *The Washington Times*, February 19, 2010, http://www.washingtontimes.com/news/2010/feb/19/who-links-terrorism-to-islam-not-america/.

18. Robert Spencer, "Does America Have a 'Muslim Problem'?" *FrontPageMagazine.com*, September 9, 2005, http://archive.frontpagemag.com/readArticle.aspx?ARTID=7325.

19. George Santayana, *The Life of Reason*, vol. 1, 1905.

20. Daniel Boorstin, "Losing Our Sense of History," *Newsweek*, July 6, 1970, quoted in Doug's Blog, http://www.visionforum.com/news/blogs/doug/2009/03/4967/.

2. The Fight for the Soul of Islam

Epigraph: M. Zuhdi Jasser, *The Third Jihad*, directed by Wayne Kopping and Erik Werth (Public Scope Films, 2008), DVD.

1. "Major Religions of the World Ranked by Number of Adherents," Adherents.com, August 9, 2007, http://www.adherents.com/Religions_By_Adherents.html.

2. Pew Forum on Religion and Public Life, *Mapping the Global Muslim Popula-tion: A Report on the Size and Distribution of the World's Muslim Population,* October 2009, 4, http://www.pewforum.org/newassets/images/reports/ Muslimpopulation/Muslimpopulation.pdf.

3. Ibid., 5.

4. Ibid., 6.

5. Christopher M. Blanchard, *Islam: Sunnis and Shiites,* Congressional Research Service, January 28, 2009, 4, http://fas.org/irp/crs/RS21745.pdf.

6. Shiites recognized the Ayatollah Ruhollah Khomeini as the first legitimate religious authority since the disappearance of the twelfth imam. Since Kho-meini's death in 1989, Seyed Ali Hoseyni Khāmene'i has been recognized as his successor. While the Shiites believe that *divine* intervention will begin the conflict that triggers the return of the Mahdi, their theology allows the possibility of *human* action launching that conflict. Such action might be a nuclear attack by Iran against the state of Israel. This explains the flammable rhetoric of Iranian president Mahmoud Ahmadinejad.

7. M. Zuhdi Jasser, "It's Time to Root Out Political Islam," *The Arizona Repub-lic,* January 9, 2010, www.azcentral.com/arizonarepublic/opinions/articles /2010/01/08/20100108jasser09.html.

8. Scott Helfstein et al., "Deadly Vanguards: A Study of al-Qai'da's Vio-lence Against Muslims," Combating Terrorism Center at West Point, December 2009, 2, http://www.ctc.usma.edu/posts/deadly-vanguards-a -study-of-al-qaidas-violence-against-muslims.

9. Ayaan Hirsi Ali, *Infidel* (New York: Free Press, 2007).

10. It is a minority of Muslims who are radicalized. Estimates range from a low of 1 percent and a high of 10 percent. That means between 1.3 million and 13 million Muslims are Islamists.

11. Joel C. Rosenberg, *Inside the Revolution: How the Followers of Jihad, Jefferson & Jesus Are Battling to Dominate the Middle East and Transform the World* (Carol Stream, Ill: Tyndale, 2009), 36.

12. Mary Habeck's chapter "From Mecca to Medina" in her book *Knowing the Enemy: Jihadist Ideology and the War on Terror* helped me understand the his-torical root of the differences between reform-minded and jihadist Muslims.

13. M. A. Muqtedar Khan, "Two Theories of Jihad," Ijtihad, www.ijtihad.org/ ijtihad.htm.

14. Ibid.

15. Brigitte Gabriel, *Because They Hate: A Survivor of Islamic Terror Warns Amer-ica* (New York: St. Martin's Press, 2006), 152, citing Ibn Warraq, *What the Koran Really Says.*

16. Will Durant, *The Age of Faith,* The Story of Civilization, vol. 4 (New York: Simon and Schuster, 1950), 341.

17. Dean Derhak, "Muslim Spain and European Culture," www.load-islam

.com/artical_det.php?artical_id=492&section=indepth&subsection=Isla mic%20history.

18. Kenneth Latourette, *A History of Christianity, Volume I: Beginnings to 1500* (New York: Harper, 1953), 497.

19. JB, e-mail message to author, June 22, 2010.

20. *Arab Human Development Report 2002* (New York: United Nations Development Programme, 2002), 8, http://hdr.undp.org/en/reports/ regionalreports/arabstates/RBAS_ahdr2002_EN.pdf.

21. It should be noted that this evaluation of the poverty of the Muslim world is one made by Western standards; jihadists would never agree with such an assessment.

22. Fouad Ajami, *The Foreigner's Gift: The Americans, the Arabs and the Iraqis in Iraq* (New York: Free Press, 2006), 60–61.

23. *Arab Human Development Report 2002*, 5.

24. *The Report in Numbers: Selected Data from the Arab Human Development Report 2009* (New York: United Nations Development Programme, 2009), 10, http://www.arab-hdr.org/publications/contents/2009/ahdrnumbers -e.pdf.

25. Ibid., 12.

26. Freedom House, *Freedom in the World 2012,* http://www.freedomhouse .org/report/freedom-world/freedom-world-2012.

27. *Arab Human Development Report 2002*, 2; emphasis added.

28. *The Report in Numbers*, 24.

29. Ibid.

30. Ibid., 25.

31. Ajami, *The Foreigner's Gift*, 61.

32. *Arab Human Development Report 2002*, 3.

33. Daniel del Catillo, "The Arab World's Scientific Desert," *The Chronicle of Higher Education*, March 5, 2004, quoted in Richard Rupp, "Higher Education in the Middle East: Opportunities and Challenges for U.S. Universities and Middle East Partners," *Global Media Journal* 8, no. 14 (Spring 2009), http://lass.calumet.purdue.edu/cca/gmj/sp09/gmj-sp09-rupp.htm.

34. *Arab Human Development Report 2003* (New York: United Nations Development Programme, 2003), http://www.arab-hdr.org/publications/other/ ahdr/ahdr2003e.pdf.

35. Personal electronic correspondence, June 22, 2010.

36. Citizens Against Sharia, *Sharia Utopia Is a Myth Part 1: Muslim Countries Among Most Corrupt*, http://citizensagainstsharia.wordpress.com/2008/ 03/14/sharia-utopia-is-a-myth-part-1-muslim-countries-among-most -corrupt/.

37. Athar Osama, "Muslim Science Must Join the 21st Century," SciDev.net, November 3, 2006, http://www.scidev.net/en/opinions/muslim-science -must-join-the-21st-century.html.

3. The Tyranny of Jihad

Epigraph: Syrian Defense Minister Hafez al-Assad, 1966, quoted in Daniel Pipes, *Syria Beyond the Peace Process,* Policy Paper Number 40 (Washington, DC: The Washington Institute for Near East Policy, 1996), 89.

1. Mary Habeck, *Knowing the Enemy: Jihadist Ideology and the War on Terror* (New Haven: Yale University Press, 2006), 65.

2. Ibid., 153.

3. Ibid., 125.

4. Stuart Robinson, *Mosques and Miracles: Revealing Islam and God's Grace* (Upper Mount Gravatt, Aus.: City Harvest Publications, 2004), 310; emphasis added.

5. The British novelist Salman Rushdie was declared apostate after he published his fourth novel *The Satanic Verses* in 1988.

6. Anwar Sadat, the third president of Egypt, signed a peace treaty with Israel, was then declared apostate, and was assassinated.

7. Lawrence Wright, *The Looming Tower: Al-Qaeda and the Road to 9/11* (New York: Knopf, 2006), 142.

8. Imam Khomeini, *Excerpts from Speeches and Messages of Imam Khomeini on the Unity of Moslems* (Tehran: Ministry of Islamic Guidance, 1979), 2, 4, quoted in George Grant, *The Blood of the Moon: The Roots of the Middle East Crisis* (Brentwood, Tenn.: Wolgemuth & Hyatt, 1991), 72.

9. Osama bin Laden, "Declaration of War against the Americans Occupying the Land of the Two Holy Places," August 1996, http://www.pbs.org/ newshour/terrorism/international/fatwa_1996.html.

10. "Golda Meir on Peace," Jewish Virtual Library, http://www.jewishvirtual library.org/jsource/Quote/MeironPeace.html.

11. Ibid.

12. "Controversial Imams," *Telegraph,* July 20, 2005, http://www.telegraph .co.uk/news/1400034/Controversial-imams.html.

13. Walid Phares, *The War of Ideas: Jihad against Democracy* (New York: Palgrave Macmillan, 2007), 40.

14. *Obsession: Radical Islam's War against the West,* directed by Wayne Kopping, 2006, www.obsessionthemovie.com.

15. Robinson, *Mosques and Miracles,* 212.

16. Friedman, *Longitudes and Attitudes,* 342–43.

17. Alex Alexiev, *Wahhabism: State-Sponsored Extremism Worldwide,* US Senate Subcommittee on Terrorism, Technology and Homeland Security, Thursday, June 26, 2003, http://kyl.senate.gov/legis_center/subdocs/ sc062603_alexiev.pdf.

18. Oren Dorell, "'Honor Killings' in USA Raise Concerns," *USA Today,* November 30, 2009, http://www.usatoday.com/news/nation/2009-11-29 -honor-killings-in-the US_N.htm.

19. David Bukay, "Defensive or Offensive *Jihad*: Classical Islamic Exegetes vs. the New Islamists' Propaganda," 4, http://www.acpr.org.il/ENGLISH -NATIV/11-issue/bukay-11.doc.

20. Kirk Semple, "Iraq Bombers Blow Up 2 Children Used as Decoys," *The New York Times*, March 21, 2007, http://www.nytimes.com/2007/03/21/ world/middleeast/21iraq.html.

21. Walid Phares, "The Caliph-Strophic Debate," *History News Network*, October 22, 2006, http://hnn.us/articles/31036.html.

22. Ibid.

23. President George W. Bush, address, Islamic Center of Washington, DC, September 17, 2001, http://www.americanrhetoric.com/speeches/gwbush 911islamispeace.htm.

24. *Dictionary of Biblical Languages with Semantic Domains: Hebrew.* s.v. "shalom."

25. *Dictionary of Biblical Languages with Semantic Domains: Greek,* s.v. "eirēnē."

26. *American Dictionary of the English Language,* s.v. "peace."

27. Syed Kamran Mirza, *An Exegesis of Islamic Peace,* http://www.faithfreedom .org/Articles/SKM/islamic_peace.htm.

28. Abidullah Ghazi and Tasneema K. Ghazi, *Teachings of Our Prophet: A Selection of Ahadith for Children* (Skokie, Ill: IQRA International Education), 3.

29. Uwe Siemon-Netto, "Scholar Warns West of Muslim Goals," *United Press International,* June 18, 2002, http://www.hvk.org/articles/0602/180.html.

30. Ibid.

31. Tahera Rahman, "Boom in UK Converts to Islam," *Al Jazeera,* January 5, 2011, http://www.aljazeera.com/news/europe/2011/01/201115141940 879721.html. The report, entitled "A Minority within a Minority: A Report on Converts to Islam in the United Kingdom," was written by Kevin Brice of Swansea University in Wales.

32. "NBC News: 20,000 Americans Convert to Islam Each Year," http://www .youtube.com/watch?v=Rfx4glTU5JQ.

33. Amil Imani, "Islam-Bashers Repent," *American Thinker,* November 19, 2009, http://www.americanthinker.com/2009/11/islam_bashers_repent.html.

34. *The Third Jihad,* directed by Wayne Kopping (Public Scope Films: 2008), DVD, http://www.thethirdjihad.com/about.html.

35. Nissan Ratzlav-Katz, "American Jihadist Cell Planned Attacks in Israel, Jordan, Kosovo," *Israel National News,* July 28, 2009, http://www.israelnational news.com/News/News.aspx/132611#.TpTCeHH1uHl.

36. "Rehabbing the D.C. Snipers," *Investors Business Daily,* October 17, 2007, available at http://sweetness-light.com/archive/ibd-cnn-drops-jihad-from -dc-sniper-story.

37. Adam Liptak, "Virginia Justices Set Death Sentence in Washington Sniper Case," *The New York Times,* April 23, 2005, http://www.nytimes .com/2005/04/23/national/23sniper.html?_r=1.

38. Al-Awlaki was later forced to flee to Yemen where, until his death in September 2011, he continued to recruit and train al-Qaeda operatives, including Nigerian Umar Farouk Abdulmutallab, who attempted to bomb Northwest Airlines Flight 253 over Detroit, Michigan, on Christmas Day 2009.

39. The slide presentation can be found at http://www.washingtonpost.com/wp-dyn/content/gallery/2009/11/10/GA2009111000920.html.

40. Gary Bauer, "Waiting for the American Jihad," *Human Events*, March 13, 2009, http://www.humanevents.com/article.php?id=31057.

41. "Prison Radicalization: Are Terrorist Cells Forming in U.S. Cell Blocks?" Committee on Homeland Security and Governmental Affairs (September 19, 2006), 18.

42. Frank Cilluffo et al., "Out of the Shadows: Getting Ahead of Prisoner Radicalization," Critical Incident Analysis Group and Homeland Security Policy Institute, 2006, i.

4. The War in the West: The Culture Wars

Epigraph: Janeane Garofalo, quoted in Marcus Rubyman, "Janeane Garofalo: Flag-Burning Chokes Me with Pride!" Hollywood Investigator, July 30, 2002, http://www.hollywoodinvestigator.com/2002/garofalo.htm.

1. Of course, the United States is not the only nation with Judeo-Christian values and contributions in the world, but because I necessarily write from an American perspective, much of the following material directly refers to the history and culture of the United States.

2. "John Adams: The Foundation of Government," *Encyclopædia Britannica*, http://www.britannica.com/presidents/article-9116853.

3. Aleksandr Solzhenitsyn, "Our Own Democracy," *National Review*, September 23, 1991, 44.

4. Bruce Frohnen, "T. S. Eliot on the Necessity of Christian Culture," Family Research Council Witherspoon Lectures, January 5, 2001, http://www.freerepublic.com/focus/fr/548010/posts.

5. Russell Kirk, "Civilization without Religion?" The Heritage Foundation, August 21, 1992, http://www.heritage.org/research/lecture/civilization-without-religion.

6. Patrick J. Buchanan, "The Aggressors in the Culture Wars," The American Cause, March 8, 2004, http://www.theamericancause.org/patculturewars.htm.

7. Daniel Lapin, *America's Real War* (New York: Multnomah Books, 1999), 45.

8. François Heisbourg, quoted by E. J. Dionne Jr., "God and Foreign Policy: The Religious Divide between the U.S. and Europe," event transcript, July 10, 2003, http://pewforum.org/Politics-and-Elections/God-and-Foreign-Policy-The-Religious-Divide-Between-the-US-and-Europe.aspx.

9. "Lincoln's 'House Divided' Speech," PBS Online, http://www.pbs.org/wgbh/aia/part4/4h2934t.html.

10. Francis A. Schaeffer, *A Christian Manifesto* (Wheaton, Ill: Crossway Books, 1981), 18.

11. For more on this shift, see my book *Discipling Nations: The Power of Truth to Transform Culture*, 2nd ed. (Seattle: YWAM Publishing, 2001).

12. Milan Kundera, *The Book of Laughter and Forgetting*, trans. Aaron Asher (New York: Perennial Classics, 1999), 159.

13. James Kurth, "The American Way of Victory," *National Interest*, Summer 2000, 5, quoted in Pat Buchanan, *The Death of the West: How Dying Populations and Immigrant Invasions Imperil Our Country and Civilization* (New York: Thomas Dunne Books, 2002), 243.

14. William Lind, "Turn Off, Tune Out, Drop Out: A Cultural Conservative's Strategy for the 21st Century," *Against the Grain*, Free Congress Foundation, Washington, DC, 1998, quoted in Buchanan *The Death of the West*, 84.

15. Jim Nelson Black, *When Nations Die* (Wheaton, Ill.: Tyndale House, 1994), xix, quoted in Buchanan, *The Death of the West*, 187.

5. The Freedom of Biblical Theism

Epigraph: Will Durant, quoted in "Teachers: The Essence of the Centuries," *Time*, August 13, 1965.

1. David Aikman, *Jesus in Beijing: How Christianity Is Transforming China and Changing the Global Balance of Power* (Washington, DC: Regnery, 2006), 5; emphasis added.

2. The full text of the Declaration of Independence is available at http://www.archives.gov/exhibits/charters/declaration_transcript.html.

3. Francis Schaeffer, *How Should We Then Live?* (Old Tappan, N.J.: F. H. Revell, 1976), chapter 11, "Our Society."

4. We will see in later chapters that God built his universe around laws—physical, moral, aesthetic, and metaphysical. We reach our God-given potential—we are happiest—when we choose to live within the framework of God's laws. We are most miserable when we violate creation's ordinances. Thus the "pursuit of happiness" must be defined within the context of the founders' biblical understanding and not the modern secular amoral mindset. For more on this see my three sabbatical reflections on the pursuit of happiness on the Darrow Miller and Friends Blog, http://disciplenations.wordpress.com/2009/06/12/sabbatical-reflections-3a-the-pursuit-of-happiness/.

5. William Blackstone, *Blackstone's Commentaries with Note of Reference to The Constitution and Laws of the Federal Government of the United States and of the Commonwealth of Virginia*, http://www.constitution.org/tb/tb-1102.htm.

6. A. James Reichley, *Religion in American Public Life* (Washington, DC: Brookings Institution, 1985), 348.

7. Ps. 19:1–4; 111:2; Prov. 25:2; Rom. 1:20.

8. Thomas Jefferson, Query XVIII of his notes on the State of Virginia, quoted in William Federer, *America's God and Country* (St. Louis: Amerisearch, 2000), 323. In 1802 Jefferson assured his friends at the Danbury Baptist Association that America would not establish religion as had the British (the monarch of the Church of England was head of both church and state). In his letter he referred to a "wall of separation" between church and state: no state church is to dominate, but all citizens have freedom of conscience to practice any or no religion (Thomas Jefferson, "Letter to the Danbury Baptist Association, 1802," http://oll.libertyfund.org/index.php?Itemid= 264&id=1067&option=com_content&task=view).

    Modern secularists have twisted Jefferson's meaning to forbid faith in public life. Jefferson, as we have seen, recognized that Christian principles establish freedom of conscience and religion. Secular humanists deconstruct Jefferson and American history to purge biblical principles from the public square and fill that square with atheistic ideas. They oppose freedom *of* religion and promote freedom *from* religion.

9. Noah Webster, *History of the United States, to which Is Prefixed a Brief Historical Account of Our [English] Ancestors* (New Haven: Durrie & Peck, 1832), 310.

10. Jürgen Habermas, *Time of Transitions* (Malden, Mass.: Polity Press, 2006), 150–51; emphasis added.

11. Kenneth Woodward and David Gates, "How the Bible Made America," *Newsweek*, December 27, 1982, 44.

12. Donald Lutz, quoted in D. James Kennedy, "Hardly a 'Godless Constitution,'" *The Christian Index*, 2005, http://www.christianindex.org/1470.article.

13. *The Impact of Christianity*, Faith Facts, http://www.faithfacts.org/christ -and-the-culture/the-impact-of-christianity#government.

14. D. James Kennedy and Jerry Newcombe, *What If Jesus Had Never Been Born?* (Nashville: Thomas Nelson, 1994), 70.

15. Loraine Boettner, "Calvinism in America," *Studies in Reformed Theology* 8, no. 16, http://www.reformed-theology.org/html/issue06/calvin.htm.

16. George Bancroft, "A Word on Calvin the Reformer," in *Literary and Historical Miscellanies* (New York: Harper and Brothers, 1855), 406.

17. Noah Webster, *History of the United States* (New Haven: Durrie & Peck, 1832), 339.

18. John Adams, *The Works of John Adams, Second President of the United States*, vol. 2 (Boston: Little, Brown, and Company, 1865), 6–7.

19. "The Faith and Wisdom of George Washington," The George Washington Society and Foundation, http://www.georgewashingtonsociety.org/ Mission.html.

20. Robert Winthrop, *On Religious Support to the State*, speech to the Annual

Meeting of the Massachusetts Bible Society, Boston, Mass., May 28, 1849, http://www.fortifyingthefamily.com/religion_state.html.

21. *The American Heritage Dictionary of the English Language*, 4th ed., s.v. "pluralism."

22. Ibid.

23. D. James Kennedy, "The New Tolerance," *The Christian Post*, May 17, 2007, http://www.christianpost.com/news/the-new-tolerance-27459/.

24. Richard Dawkins, *The Selfish Gene*, 30th anniversary ed. (New York: Oxford University Press, 2006), 2.

25. Judg. 21:25.

26. Allegra Stratton, "David Cameron on Riots: Broken Society Is Top of My Political Agenda," *The Guardian*, August 15, 2011, http://www.guardian .co.uk/uk/2011/aug/15/david-cameron-riots-broken-society.

27. Francis Schaeffer, *How Should We Then Live?* (Old Tappan, N.J.: F. H. Revell, 1976), chapter 11, "Our Society."

28. A. James Reichley, *Religion in American Public Life* (Washington, DC: Brookings Institution Press, 1985), 347.

29. Freedom House, *Freedom in the World 2012*, http://www.freedomhouse .org/report/freedom-world/freedom-world-2012.

6. The Tyranny of Fundamentalist Atheism

Epigraph: Fyodor Dostoevsky, *The Brothers Karamazov*, trans. Constance Garnett (Ware, UK: Wordsworth, 2007), 72.

1. Umberto Eco, *Foucault's Pendulum*, trans. William Weaver (San Diego: Harcourt, 1989), 604.

2. Raymond Bragg, "Humanist Manifesto I," American Humanist Association, http://www.americanhumanist.org/Who_We_Are/About_Humanism/ Humanist_Manifesto_I.

3. Ibid.

4. Paul Kurtz and Edwin H. Wilson, "Humanist Manifesto II," *The Humanist*, September/October 1973, http://www.secularhumanism.org/index.php ?section=fi&page=kurtzmanifesto_28_6.

5. Daniel O. Conkle, "Secular Fundamentalism, Religious Fundamentalism, and the Search for Truth in Contemporary America" in *Law and Religion: A Critical Anthology*, ed. Stephen M. Feldman (New York: New York University Press, 2000), 330.

6. Richard S. Lindzen, "There Is No 'Consensus' on Global Warming," *Wall Street Journal*, June 26, 2006, http://online.wsj.com/article/SB115 127582141890238.html.

7. John J. Dunphy, "A Religion for a New Age," *The Humanist* 43, no. 1 (January–February 1983), 26.

8. Gary Wolf, "The Church of the Non-Believers," *Wired* 14, no. 11 (November 2006), 2, http://www.wired.com/wired/archive/14.11/atheism.html?pg=2&topic=atheism&topic_set=.

9. Donald Kagan, "Nihilism rejects any objective basis for society and its morality, the very concept of objectivity, even the possibility of communication itself," *Academic Questions* 8, no. 2 (Spring 1995), 56, quoted in Brannon Howse, *One Nation under Man: The Worldview War between Christians and the Secular Left* (Nashville: B&H Publishing Group, 2005), 22.

10. Professor of modern European history Richard Weikart connects Darwinism and Nazi Germany: "Among German historians, there's really not much debate about whether or not Hitler was a social Darwinist. He clearly was drawing on Darwinian ideas. It drove pretty much everything that he did. It was not just a peripheral part of his ideology. . . . [Hitler drew] on what many other scholars, biologists, and geneticists in Germany were . . . teaching" (Alexander J. Sheffrin, "'Expelled' Correct on Darwin, Hitler Link, Says Christian Group," *The Christian Post*, May 1, 2008, http://www.christianpost.com/article/20080501/-expelled-correct-on-darwin-hitler-link-says-christian-group/).

11. Taketoshi Nojiri, "Values as a Precondition of Democracy," *Democracy: Some Acute Questions*, 92, quoted in Michael Novak, *The Universal Hunger for Liberty: Why the Clash of Civilizations Is Not Inevitable* (Cambridge, Mass.: Basic Books, 2006), 164.

12. Alan Keyes, speech, Republican presidential candidates dinner, New Hampshire, February 19, 1995, Center for Reformed Theology and Apologetics, http://www.reformed.org/social/index.html?mainframe=http://www.reformed.org/social/keyes_on_abortion.html.

13. David Johnson, *Theodore Roosevelt: American Monarch* (Philadelphia: American History Source, 1981), 91.

14. Aldous Huxley, *Ends and Means: An Enquiry into the Nature of Ideals and into the Methods Employed for Their Realization* (London: Chatto & Windus, 1941), 272, 275.

15. David Kupelian, *The Marketing of Evil: How Radicals, Elitists, and Pseudo-Experts Sell Us Corruption Disguised as Freedom* (Washington, DC: WND Books, 2005).

16. Laura Schlessinger, "As Predicted, Bestiality Goes Mainstream," *Jewish World Review*, March 24, 2000, http://www.jewishworldreview.com/dr/laura032400.asp.

17. Such people are described in Rev. 6:16: "They called to the mountains and the rocks, 'Fall on us and hide us from the face of him who sits on the throne and from the wrath of the Lamb!'"

18. Edward Gibbon, *The Decline and Fall of the Roman Empire* (1788; repr. New York: Quill Pen Classics, 2008).

19. Jack L. Arnold, "Church History: The Fall of Rome, Early Church History, part 16," *Third Millennium Ministries Magazine Online* 1, no. 30 (September 20, 1999), http://reformedperspectives.org/newfiles/jac_arnold/CH.Arnold.CH.16.html.

20. Malcolm Muggeridge, "The Great Liberal Death Wish," *Imprimis* 8, no. 5 (May 1979), http://www.orthodoxytoday.org/articles/MuggeridgeLiberal.php.

21. Ibid.

22. Neal Postman, *Amusing Ourselves to Death: Public Discourse in the Age of Show Business* (New York: Penguin Books, 1986), 155–56.

7. The Connection between the Twin Wars

Epigraph: Will Durant, *Caesar and Christ*, vol. 3, *The Story of Civilization* (New York: Simon & Schuster, 1944), 665.

1. David Levinsky, "Practice for Worst-Case Scenario—Hostage-Crisis Drill Plays Out in Burlington Township," *Burlington County Times*, March 23, 2007, 1B.

2. See, for example, Bernd Debusmann, "Islam, Terror and Political Correctness," *Reuters*, February 19, 2010, http://blogs.reuters.com/great-debate/2010/02/19/islam-terror-and-political-correctness/.

3. Ayaan Hirsi Ali, *Infidel* (New York: Free Press, 2007), 257.

4. Robert B. Reich, "The Last Word: Bush's God," *The American Prospect*, June 17, 2004; emphasis added.

5. The signs point to misguided multiculturalism. Maybe we are also witnessing the influence of the abortion industry: the significance of a murder depends on the identity of the victim. Some murder victims don't matter. Note the racism implicit in those who profess tolerance.

6. Dr. Rowan Williams, interview, "Sharia Law in UK Is 'Unavoidable,'" *BBC News*, February 7, 2008, http://news.bbc.co.uk/2/hi/uk_news/7232661.stm.

7. Mathias Döpfner, "Europa—dein Name ist Feigheit," *Die Welt*, November 20, 2004. English translation from Snopes.com, updated July 29, 2006, http://www.snopes.com/politics/soapbox/dapfner.asp.

8. Mark Steyn, *America Alone: The End of the World as We Know It* (Washington, DC: Regnery, 2006), 56.

9. Given the replacement birth rate (2.33), even in the heartland, most families are not taking seriously the biblical charge to "be fruitful and multiply."

10. Malcolm Muggeridge, quoted in Ray Stedman, "Are These the Last Days," Ray Stedman Ministries, http://www.raystedman.org/thematic-studies/prophecy/are-these-the-last-days; emphasis added.

11. Margaret Wente, "A Wanderer from Islam with a Message for the West," *The*

Globe and Mail, June 8, 2010, text available at http://wwsg.com/a-wanderer
-from-islam-with-a-message-for-the-west.

12. Paul Berman, *Terror and Liberalism* (New York: W. W. Norton, 2003), 143.

13. Walid Phares, *The War of Ideas: Jihadism against Democracy* (New York: Palgrave Macmillan, 2007), 3.

14. Steyn, *America Alone,* 158.

15. Bernard Lewis, *The Crisis of Islam: Holy War and Unholy Terror* (New York:
Modern Library, 2003), 81.

16. Samuel Huntington, *The Clash of Civilizations and the Remaking of World
Order* (New York: Simon and Schuster, 1996), 213; emphasis added.

17. These words capture a profound irony. They come from one of the most
malevolent men in history, yet they remind me of the words that the apostle
Paul wrote in Romans 1:18–32. Paul describes what happens to a people's
behavior when they cease to worship the living God. The sum of it is captured in Romans 1:32: "And it's not as if they don't know better. They know
perfectly well they're spitting in God's face. And they don't care—worse,
they hand out prizes to those who do the worst things best!" (*The Message*).

18. Osama bin Laden, "Letter to the American People," Guardian.co.uk,
November 24, 2002, http://www.guardian.co.uk/world/2002/nov/24/
theobserver; emphasis added.

19. Matt C. Abbott, "The Pro-pedophilia Conference," Renew America, August
17, 2011, http://www.renewamerica.com/columns/abbott/110817.

20. Fifty-seven percent of pastors say that addiction to pornography is the most
sexually damaging issue to their congregation ("Statistics on Pornography,
Sexual Addiction and Online Perpetrators," Safe Families, http://www
.safefamilies.org/sfStats.php). Forty-four percent of young evangelicals support same-sex marriage (Bruce Nolan, "Gay Marriage Divides Evangelicals
along Generational Gap," *Huffington Post,* September 7, 2011, http://www
.huffingtonpost.com/2011/09/07/gay-marriage-evangelicals_n_952888
.html).

21. John F. Burns, "Bin Laden Stirs Struggle on Meaning of Jihad," *The New
York Times,* January 27, 2002, http://www.nytimes.com/2002/01/27/
international/asia/27JIHA.html?scp=8&sq=john%20burns%20january
%202002&st=cse.

8. Captivating Culture

Epigraph: John Paul II, *Address of His Holiness John Paul II to the Plenary
Assembly of the Pontifical Council for Culture,* March 18, 1994, http://www
.vatican.va/holy_father/john_paul_ii/speeches/1994/march/documents
/hf_jp-ii_spe_18031994_address-to-pc-culture_en.html.

1. James Davison Hunter, *Culture Wars: The Struggle to Define America* (New
York: Basic Books, 1991).

2. *Enhanced Strong's Lexicon,* s.v. "ochurōma."
3. *Strong's Exhaustive Concordance of the Bible,* electronic ed. (Ontario: Woodside Bible Fellowship), s.v. "logismos."
4. *Enhanced Strong's Lexicon,* s.v. "aichmalōtizō."
5. *American Dictionary of the English Language,* s.v. "captivate."
6. Sheikh Ahmad al Qataani, live interview on Al-Jazeera, December 2001, quoted in Salem Voice, "Millions of Muslims Converting to Christianity," *Islam Watch,* January 5, 2007, http://www.islam-watch.org/LeavingIslam/Muslims2Christianity.htm. The interview can be viewed at http://www.youtube.com/watch?v=pnAfsjZZ0c8.
7. Joel Rosenberg writes, "After criss-crossing the Islamic world over the last several years and interviewing more than 150 pastors and ministry leaders operating deep inside the most difficult countries for *Inside The Revolution,* I can report that in Iran, more than 1 million Shia Muslims have turned to Christ since 1979. In Pakistan, there are now more than 2.5 million followers of Jesus Christ. In Sudan, there are now more than 5 million followers of Christ. Not every country has seen millions leave Islam to become adherents of the New Testament teachings of Jesus. In Syria, there are between 4,000 and 5,000 believers, but this is up from almost none in 1967. In Saudi Arabia, there are about 100,000 followers of Jesus now, up from almost none in 1967. But overall, the trend has been dramatic and largely unreported" ("More Ex-Muslims Will Celebrate Easter This Year Than Any Other Time in History," *Joel C. Rosenberg's Blog,* April 10, 2009, http://flashtrafficblog.wordpress.com/2009/04/10/more-ex-muslims-will-celebrate-easter-this-year-than-any-other-time-in-history/). The website "Ex-Muslims" lists various sites referencing how Muslims are leaving Islam, http://www.formermuslims.com/forum/viewtopic.php?t=2133.
8. Matt. 26:47–56; Luke 22:41–53.
9. Lawrence E. Harrison, *The Central Liberal Truth: How Politics Can Change a Culture and Save It from Itself* (New York: Oxford University Press, 2006), 9.
10. Indian philosopher Vishal Mangalwadi asks, "Must the sun set on the West?" in a lecture series by that name. See his website: www.revelationmovement.com.

9. Christ and the Kingdom

Epigraph: Dallas Willard, *The Divine Conspiracy: Rediscovering Our Hidden Life in God* (New York: HarperCollins, 1998), 305.
1. *The Lord of the Rings: The Two Towers,* directed by Peter Jackson (Burbank, Calif.: New Line Cinema, 2002), DVD.
2. Reformed Episcopal Church, "A Pastoral Letter on Mission," http://rechurch.org/recus/ID84eb63aced10d3/?MIval=/recweb/articles.html&display=missions.

3. Matt. 28:16.

4. That is not to say that Jesus was afraid to die but that his victory over death included victory over the fear of death. He successfully faced down and overcame that fear as he overcame every temptation.

5. John Stott suggests that the cup Jesus dreaded "symbolized . . . the spiritual agony of bearing the sins of the world—in other words, of enduring the divine judgment that those sins deserved" (John Stott, *The Cross of Christ* [Downers Grove, Ill.: InterVarsity Press, 2006], 78).

6. Matt. 26:36–46.

7. Matt. 12:22–29.

8. Matt. 28:5–6.

9. Acts 2:24.

10. Col. 1:20.

11. Heb. 2:14–15.

12. Keith Green, "The Victor," *No Compromise*, Sparrow Records, 1978. To see a video of this powerful song, go to www.youtube.com/watch?v=Wil0PBylyW0.

13. G. K. Chesterton, quoted in John Warwick Montgomery, "The Un-Apologist," *Christian History* 21, no. 3, 39.

14. Isa. 9:7; Luke 1:32-33; Matt. 13:31–33.

15. Rev. 20:10.

16. Matt. 16:18.

17. N. T. Wright, interview by Tim Stafford, "Mere Mission," *Christianity Today*, January 5, 2007, http://www.christianitytoday.com/ct/2007/january/22.38.html?start=4; emphasis added.

18. Rom. 1:22–23.

19. Gen. 1:26–27; Gen. 12:2–3; Matt. 28:18–20; Col. 1:20.

20. Rev. 5:9–10.

21. Phil. 2:9–11.

22. All rulers create laws in order to rule. Jesus is the king and wants nations to be discipled by teaching them to obey all he has commanded. There is order in the kingdom of God, but we live in a fallen world where there is *dis*order because all people do not obey God's order. When people disobey God's order, disorder in life and nations is the result. This is corrected by a restoration of the Creator's order in our nations.

23. As told by Pastor Curi to Mandie Miller in Puerto Rico, September 15, 2008.

24. For more on this, see Vision Conference Notebook Materials: *The ABC's of Culture: The Web of Lies*, http://www.disciplenations.org/vc/host-tools.

25. Matt. 24:6–8; Rev. 6:1–8.

26. Mal. 3:2–4; 1 Cor. 3:12–13.

27. Dan. 7:14–27; Heb. 12:26–29.

28. St. Augustine, quoted in Charles Colson and Ellen Vaughn, *Being the Body* (Nashville: W Publishing Group, 2003), 3.

29. Dan. 2:35, 44–45; 7:27.
30. Isa. 9:6–7; Matt. 16:18; 28:20b; 1 Cor. 15:25–27; Rev. 11:15.
31. Matt. 13:31–33.
32. Isa. 25:8; 1 Cor. 7:31.

10. Reawakening the Cultural Commission

Epigraph: Herman Bavinck, *Our Reasonable Faith,* quoted in David Bruce Hegeman, *Plowing in Hope: Towards a Biblical Theology of Culture,* 2nd ed. (Moscow, Ida.: Canon Press, 2007), 31.

1. A more detailed discussion of the material in this section can be found in chapter 7, "The Essential Metanarrative," and part 3, "The Cultural Mandate," in my book *LifeWork: A Biblical Theology for What You Do Every Day* (Seattle: YWAM Publishing, 2009).
2. Gen. 1:4, 10, 12, 18, 21, 25.
3. Gen. 1:7, 9, 11, 15, 24, 30.
4. Gen. 1:31.
5. *Oikonomia* occurs nine times in the New Testament, including in the parable of the dishonest manager in Luke 16 and in four of Paul's letters. Note especially Paul's use in Ephesians 1:10 where he speaks of "an administration [*oikonomia*] suitable to the fullness of the times" (NASB), that is, the summing up of all things in Christ, things in the heavens and things on the earth. Similar uses occur in Ephesians 3:9, Colossians 1:25, and 1 Timothy 1:4.
6. Note the unique manner of man's creation. The text departs from the usual "let there be" and God says, "Let us make man." Robert L. Reymond writes that this language suggests "almost a pause in the divine activity for the purpose of solemn divine counsel" (Robert L. Reymond, *A New Systematic Theology of the Christian Faith,* 2nd ed. [Nashville: Thomas Nelson, 1998], 416).
7. Gen. 6:5–6; Rom. 3:23.
8. Gen. 3:16–18; Rom. 8:19–22.
9. Ezek. 22:29; Mic. 2:2.
10. Heb. 11:8–10, 13–16.
11. I have deliberately chosen the word *consummation* over the phrase *the return of Christ.* Too often when we think of the return of Christ, we think that things will get worse and worse and when they get bad enough, Christ will come back. This incorrect picture, in my view, leaves the church in a defeatist and defensive posture and disengaged from the task that Christ has given her. God is at work in history. Christ is king of heaven and earth now. When he returns at the end of history, all that he has been working toward will be consummated.

12. Col. 1:20; Rom. 8:18–23.

13. *Enhanced Strong's Lexicon*, s.v. "telos."

14. (1) Gen. 12:3–4; (2) Hab. 2:14; (3) Rev. 19:6–9; Eph. 5:22–33; (4) Rev. 21:1–4; (5) Isa. 60:1–3; Rev. 21:21–26; (6) Rev. 21:4.

15. *Vine's Expository Dictionary of New Testament Words*, s.v. "sunteleia." *Vine's* goes on to say, "The word does not denote a termination, but the heading up of events to the appointed climax."

16. Matt. 5:48; James 1:2–5; Rom. 8:28–30; Col. 1:28.

17. 1 Chron. 16:24–28; Ps. 67:1–4; 99:1–4; Isa. 60:1–3; Rev. 15:3–4; 21:24.

18. We could also call this the *ecological* commission.

19. Rom. 8:19–22.

20. Much of what follows was taken from Scott Allen's November 2, 2009, post on the DNA team blog, *The Cultural Mandate and The Great Commission*, http://disciplenations.wordpress.com/2009/11/02/the-cultural-mandate -and-the-great-commission/.

21. Christian Smith, *American Evangelicalism: Embattled and Thriving* (Chicago: University of Chicago Press, 1998), 198.

11. The Primary Task: Making Disciples of All Nations

Epigraph: Dietrich Bonhoeffer, *Prisoner for God: Letters and Papers from Prison*, ed. Eberhard Bethge, trans. Reginald H. Fuller (London: SCM, 1967), 211.

1. Abraham Kuyper, *Abraham Kuyper: A Centennial Reader*, ed. James D. Bratt (Grand Rapids: Eerdmans, 1998), 488.

2. John 1:1, 4–9, 14.

3. William Temple, quoted by Philip Yancey, "Denominational Diagnostics: What I Look for to Find a Healthy Church," *Christianity Today*, November 11, 2008, http://www.christianitytoday.com/ct/2008/november/27.119 .html?start=2.

4. Gary Skinner, quoted in "Model Church Profile: Watoto Church, Kampala, Uganda," Disciple Nations Alliance, http://www.disciplenations.org/ dna-news/stay-connect-with-the-dna/model-church-profile-watoto -church-kampala-uganda.

5. Acts 16:31.

6. *Dictionary of Biblical Languages with Semantic Domains: Greek (New Testament)*, s.v. "ethnos."

7. *Collins English Dictionary*, s.v. "ethos." The English word comes from the Greek word with the same spelling and meaning.

8. Matthew Henry, *Matthew Henry's Commentary on the Whole Bible: Complete and Unabridged in One Volume* (Peabody: Hendrickson, 1991), Matt. 28:16.

9. Matt. 5:15.
10. *Enhanced Strong's Lexicon*, s.v. "poreuomai."

12. Baptizing the Nations: Union and Transformation

Epigraph: Christopher Wright, *Deuteronomy,* New International Biblical Commentary (Peabody, Mass.: Hendrickson, 1996), 160.

1. John 15:1–8; 17:20-26; Eph. 1:22–23; 2:20-22; 4:15–16; 5:30; Col. 1:18; 2:19.
2. William Hendriksen, *The Gospel of Matthew,* The New Testament Commentary (Grand Rapids: Baker Books, 1979), 1000–1001.
3. Millard J. Erickson writes, "There is a strong connection between baptism and our being united with Christ in his death and resurrection. Paul emphasizes this point in Romans 6:1–11. The use of the aorist tense suggests that at some specific moment the believer actually becomes linked to Christ's death and resurrection" (*Christian Theology,* 2nd ed. [Grand Rapids: Baker Books, 2007], 1109–10).
4. Robert Lynn, "We Have Known Water: A Missional Reflection on Baptism," BreakPoint, January 19, 2007, http://www.breakpoint.org/component/content/article/104-worldview-church/944-we-have-known-water.
5. James Montgomery Boice, *Bible Study Magazine* (May 1989), quoted at Bible Study Tools, http://www.biblestudytools.com/lexicons/greek/kjv/baptizo.html.
6. Of course, God was speaking figuratively. As Stephen (among others) would later testify, "The Most High does not dwell in houses made by human hands" (Acts 7:48).
7. The place of the name marks the setting of God's presence: 1 Kings 8:43; 2 Chron. 6:33; 20:9; Dan. 9:18; Jer. 7:10, 11, 14, 30; 25:29; 32:34; 34:15.
8. Christopher Wright, *Deuteronomy,* New International Biblical Commentary (Peabody, Mass.: Hendrickson, 2006), 159.
9. *Strong's Enhanced Lexicon,* s.v. "Baal."
10. We see God's intention restored in Hosea 2:16–17.
11. For more on this see Darrow L. Miller, *Nurturing the Nations: Reclaiming the Dignity of Women in Building Healthy Cultures* (Colorado Springs: Paternoster, 2007), chapter 13.
12. Note that the verse does not say the *names* but rather the *name* of the Father, the Son, and the Holy Spirit, reflecting God's oneness.
13. Gen. 1:1; Ps. 33:6, 9; Mal. 2:10; 1 Cor. 8:6; Heb. 11:3.
14. John 1:3; Col. 1:16.
15. Gen. 1:2.
16. John 3:16; 1 Cor. 15:3–4; Eph. 1:13; 1 Pet. 3:18.

13. Living the Word: Love and Service

Epigraph: Mother Teresa, *Mother Teresa: Come Be My Light: The Private Writings of the "Saint of Calcutta,"* ed. Brian Kolodiejchuk (New York: Doubleday, 2007), 34.

1. Rodney Stark, *The Rise of Christianity: How the Obscure, Marginal Jesus Movement Became the Dominant Religious Force in the Western World in a Few Centuries* (New York: HarperCollins, 1996), 214–15.

2. Ibid., 211; emphasis added.

3. John 8:31–32; James 1:22–25; 1 John 3:17–18.

4. John 8:32; 17:17; 2 Tim. 2:15.

5. Matt. 6:10.

6. Phil. 2:1–8.

7. *Family:* Eph. 5:25; Titus 2:4; Col. 3:21; Luke 11:11–12. *Neighbors:* Matt. 19:19; Luke 10:29; Rom. 13:9; Gal. 5:13; James 2:8. *Countrymen:* Exod. 32:31–32; Rom. 9:2–3; 10:1. *Strangers:* Lev. 19:34; Deut.10:19; Heb. 13:2.

8. Exod. 23:4–5; Matt. 5:44; Luke 6:27; Rom. 12:14, 20; 1 Pet. 3:9.

9. John Piper, "The Spring of Persistent Public Love," sermon, January 14, 2007, http://www.desiringgod.org/resource-library/sermons/the-spring-of-persistent-public-love.

10. Ori Brafman and Rod A. Beckstrom, *The Starfish and the Spider: The Unstoppable Power of Leaderless Organizations* (New York: Penguin, 2006).

11. Hendrik Berkhof, *Christ and the Powers,* trans. John H. Yoder (Scottdale, Pa.: Herald Press, 1977), 58; emphasis added.

12. Cyprian, quoted in Stark, *The Rise of Christianity,* 87; emphasis added.

13. Matt. 5:13; 5:14–16; 13:33; 13:31–32.

14. John 13:1, 14–15, 34; 15:12; Eph. 5:2.

15. John 13:34–35; 14:15, 21–24; 15:9, 10–12; 1 John 3:23; 4:21.

16. Leslie K. Tarr, "A Prayer Meeting That Lasted 100 Years," *Christian History* no. 1, January 1, 1982.

17. Priya Abraham, "The Good Jihad," *World,* December 8, 2007, http://www.worldmag.com/articles/13572.

18. Stuart Robinson, *Mosques and Miracles: Revealing Islam and God's Grace* (Upper Mount Gravatt, Qld., Aus.: City Harvest, 2004), 298.

19. Lilian Calles Barger, *Eve's Revenge: Women and a Spirituality of the Body* (Grand Rapids: Brazos, 2003), 186.

20. Martin Luther King Jr., "Letter from Birmingham Jail," April 1963, http://www.stanford.edu/group/King/frequentdocs/birmingham.pdf.

21. J. Richard Pearcey, "How the New Resistance Can Win the Culture War," The Pearcey Report, March 26, 2010, http://www.pearceyreport.com/archives/2010/02/how_the_new_res_1.php.

22. Dr. Elizabeth Youman's AMO curriculum is designed "specifically to

cultivate a biblical, Christian mindset, Christian imagination and creativity, and Christian conscience and character," http://www.amoprogram.com/en/school.

14. Teaching the Nations: The Comprehensive Task

Epigraph: Abraham Kuyper, *Lectures on Calvinism* (1931; repr., Grand Rapids: Eerdmans, 2000), iii.

1. Dr. Schaeffer said this in my hearing in the late 1960s when my wife and I studied and worked at L'Abri Fellowship in Switzerland.
2. *Enhanced Strong's Lexicon,* s.v. "didaskō."
3. Ibid., s.v. "tēreō."
4. When Christ returns, what Satan is building will be utterly destroyed, while what God is building—his kingdom—will be consummated and will reach its fulfillment. All that God is doing in history will be completed. The church must stop her disengagement, her passive *waiting* for Christ to return, and follow him into battle. Christians have been called by Christ to engage in the Great Commission—to "come, follow me"!
5. Ibid., s.v. "pas."
6. *Strong's Enhanced Lexicon,* s.v. "entellomai."
7. Ibid., s.v. "teleios."
8. Ps. 72:19; Isa. 6:3; Isa. 11:9; Hab. 2:14.
9. Judg. 17:6.
10. Elizabeth L. Youmans, "The Christian Principle of Self Government," *AMO®️ Apprenticeship Manual* (Orlando: Chrysalis International, 2010), 127.
11. R. J. Slater, *Teaching and Learning America's Christian History* (San Francisco: Foundation for American Christian Education, 1960), 199, in Youmans, *The Christian Principle of Self Government,* 1.
12. *American Dictionary of the English Language,* s.v. "virtue."
13. James Davison Hunter, *The Death of Character: Moral Education in an Age Without Good or Evil* (New York: Basic Books, 2000), 222.
14. Deut. 6:6–9; Prov. 2:1; 3:1; 4:20–22; 6:21; 7:1–2.
15. John Winthrop, "A Modell of Christian Charity," 1630, Collections of the Massachusetts Historical Society (Boston, 1838), 3rd Series, 7:31–48, http://history.hanover.edu/texts/winthmod.html. I have updated the spelling in this quotation so that it is more readable.
16. John F. Kennedy, "City upon A Hill," speech, State House of Boston, January 9, 1961, http://www.kennedytour.com/city-on-a-hill.html.
17. Ronald Reagan, "Farewell Address to the Nation," speech, Oval Office, Washington, DC, January 11, 1989, http://www.reagan2020.us/speeches/farewell.asp.
18. See also Mark 12:28–31; Luke 10:26–28. "The Law and the Prophets" is

shorthand for the entire Old Testament, including the Books of Moses (the Torah, or Pentateuch), the Prophets, and the Writings.

19. Other passages that mark the irreducible minimum of one law are Matt. 7:12; Rom. 13:8–10; James 2:8.

20. Gen. 1; John 1:1–3.

21. Gen. 1:4, 10, 12, 18, 21, 25, 31. Too many Christians derive the view of the universe as evil by skipping over the first two chapters of Genesis and going immediately to chapter 3.

22. Gen. 1–2; Ps. 8.

23. Ps. 33:10–11; Isa. 46:10–11.

24. Job 19:25–27; Ps. 102:18–19; Dan. 2:45; Matt. 16:27–28.

25. Num. 23:19; Ps. 119:160; Isa. 65:16; John 14:6.

26. Deut. 32:4; Ps. 25:8; 92:15; 119:68; Isa. 5:16.

27. Ps. 27:4; 29:2; 48:1–2; 50:2; 145:5.

28. "It is the glory of God to conceal a matter; to search out a matter is the glory of kings" (Prov. 25:2).

29. To affirm that God actively governs creation through his laws is to refute deism. Deists acknowledge these natural laws but argue that God created the universe and then stepped back, allowing it to run on its own by the laws built into the system. The deist's God is Creator but not sovereign Lord. God as revealed in Scripture made creation laws, and he rules creation through these laws. If God were to withdraw his hand, these laws could not sustain the universe.

15. Truth: The Metaphysical Order

Epigraph: John Paul II, *Fides et Ratio,* Encyclical Letter, September 14, 1998, http://www.vatican.va/holy_father/john_paul_ii/encyclicals/documents/hf_jp-ii_enc_15101998_fides-et-ratio_en.html.

1. Rom. 8:5–6; 12:1–2; Eph. 4:22–24; Col. 3:10.

2. *Conf.* VII.4; XIII.38; *De Civ Dei* XI.10, quoted in Vivian Boland, *Ideas in God According to Saint Thomas Aquinas: Sources and Synthesis* (Leiden, The Netherlands: E. J. Brill, 1996), 78.

3. *Enhanced Strong's Lexicon,* s.v. "metanoeō."

4. William Carlos Williams, *Paterson,* rev. ed. (New York: New Directions Books, 1995), 50.

5. Matt. 22:37.

6. *Enhanced Strong's Lexicon,* s.v. "ginōskō."

7. Ibid., "gnōsis."

8. Ibid., "epignōsis."

9. Ibid., "gnōmē."

10. Ibid., "gnōrizō."

11. Ibid., "logikos."
12. Ibid., "dokeō."
13. Ibid., "logos."
14. Ibid., "nous."
15. Ibid., "phronimos."
16. J. I. Packer, *Fundamentalism and the Word of God* (Grand Rapids: Wm. B. Eerdmans, 1958), 34; emphasis added.
17. J. Gresham Machen, quoted in ibid., 27; emphasis added.
18. C. S. Lewis unpacks this concept in the appendix of *The Abolition of Man* and in the first chapter of *Mere Christianity*.
19. John 1:1–18.
20. Col. 1:15,19.
21. Col. 1:25–26.
22. Deut. 32:46–47; John 6:68; 2 Tim. 3:16–17.
23. Blaise Pascal, *Pensées,* trans. A. J. Krailsheimer (New York: Penguin Books, 1996), 56.
24. Gen. 2:19–20; Isa. 1:18 (NIV1984); Acts 17:2; 18:4.
25. John 8:31–32.
26. See also Ps. 119:43–48; Isa. 61:1; John 17:17; Acts 17:11; James 1:25.
27. As we shall see, this is different from everyone having equal conditions and equal material outcomes.
28. K. Alan Snyder, *If the Foundations Are Destroyed: Biblical Principals and Civil Government* (Longwood, Fla.: Xulon, 2010), 32; emphasis added.
29. Ps. 139:13–16; Matt. 25:14–15; Luke 19:12–13; Rom. 12:6–8.
30. Stephen Lucas, "Justifying America: The Declaration of Independence as a Rhetorical Document" in Thomas W. Benson, ed., *American Rhetoric: Context and Criticism* (Carbondale, Ill.: Southern Illinois University Press, 1989), 85.
31. Joseph J. Ellis, *American Creation: Triumphs and Tragedies in the Founding of the Republic* (New York: Vintage Books, 2008), 56.
32. *American Dictionary of the English Language,* s.v. "unalienable."
33. A statist believes the central control of the social, economic, and political life of a nation belongs to the government.
34. George Washington, "George Washington's Farewell Address to the People of the United States," http://www.earlyamerica.com/earlyamerica/milestones/farewell/text.html; emphasis added.
35. Benjamin Rush, 1798, quoted in Michael Novak, *On Two Wings: Humble Faith and Common Sense at the American Founding* (San Francisco: Encounter Books, 2003), 34.
36. Alexis de Tocqueville, *Democracy in America,* vol. 2, trans. Henry Reeve (Cambridge, Mass.: Sever and Francis, 1864), 129–30.
37. Gen. 3:1–7; 6:5–6; Isa. 6:1–5; Rom. 1:28–32; 3:23.

38. Michael Novak explains in *The Spirit of Democratic Capitalism*: "Whereas socialists frequently promise, under their coercive system, 'a new socialist man' of a virtuous sort the world has never seen before, democratic capitalism (although it, too, depends upon and nourishes virtuous behavior) promises no such thing. Its political economy, while depending upon a high degree of civic virtue in its citizens (and upon an especially potent moral-cultural system separated from the state), is designed for sinners. That is, for humans as they are.

   "Most social revolutions promise a reign of the saints. Most promise a new type of moral man. And most intend to produce this higher type of morality through the coercive power of the state. This is precisely the impulse in the human breast which democratic capitalism finds to be the most productive of evil.

   "There are, in this respect, two main traditions of revolutionary thought, the utopian and the realist. Utopian revolutionaries imagine that the source of human evil lies in social structures and systems and that in removing these they will remove evil and virtue will flourish. By contrast, realists hold that the source of human evil lies in the self and in the necessary limitations of every form of social organization. Realists hold that no real or imagined social structures and no system, however ingeniously designed, will banish sin from the field of human liberty. . . . For the utopians, morality flows from structures and systems. . . . For the realists, morality flows from individual will and act" (Michael Novak, *The Spirit of Democratic Capitalism* [New York: Simon and Schuster, 1982], 85–86).

39. Lord Acton, "Letter to Bishop Mandell Creighton, 1887," Online Library of Liberty, http://oll.libertyfund.org/index.php?option=com_content&task=view&id=1407&Itemid=283.

40. Deut. 10:17; 2 Chron. 19:7; Job 34:19; Acts 10:34; Rom. 2:11; 1 Pet. 1:17.

41. John Adams, quoted in John Eidsmoe, *Christianity and the Constitution: The Faith of our Founding Fathers*, 4th ed. (Grand Rapids: Baker Books, 2002), 372.

42. When the Brazilian legislature was established, one of its first acts was to exempt legislators from all laws! Thankfully, this exemption has since been eliminated.

43. Rom. 13:1–7.

44. Acts 5:25–29: Peter argues before the Sanhedrin that we are to serve God rather than people. Acts 17:6–9: Christians defy Caesar's decree by saying Jesus is a king. Acts 17:11: Desire for truth leads to the questioning of religious authorities. Acts 19:23–40: Paul's preaching has an economic impact on Ephesian artisans, which leads to civil unrest.

45. Jonathan Mayhew, "A Discourse Concerning Unlimited Submission and Non-Resistance to the Higher Powers," 1750, http://www.lawandliberty.org/mayhew.htm.

46. Roy Moore and John Perry, *So Help Me God: The Ten Commandments, Judicial Tyranny, and the Battle for Religious Freedom* (Los Angeles: WorldNetDaily, 2005), 208.

47. Martin Luther King Jr., "Letter From Birmingham Jail," April 16, 1963, http://www.mtholyoke.edu/acad/intrel/mlkbirm.htm; emphasis added.

48. Harold Berman, quoted in Amos and Gardiner, *Never Before in History: America's Inspired Birth* (Dallas: Haughton, 1998), 63–64.

49. Ibid., 43.

50. Ibid., 41.

51. Thomas Hooker, quoted in ibid., 40.

52. Joseph G. Lehman, "Civil Society: Moral Arguments for Limiting Government," *Indivisible: Social and Economic Foundations of American Liberty*, The Heritage Foundation, 15, http://thf_media.s3.amazonaws.com/2010/pdf/Ind.Ch1.Lehman.pdf.

53. On the sacredness of work and stewardship in the Bible, see chapter 10.

54. Kenneth Hopper and William Hopper, *The Puritan Gift: Reclaiming the American Dream amidst Global Financial Chaos* (New York: I.B. Tauris, 2009), 3.

55. Ibid., 7.

56. For more on this, see chapters 11 and 12 of Darrow L. Miller, *Discipling Nations: The Power of Truth to Transform Cultures*, 2nd ed. (Seattle: YWAM Publishing, 2001) and chapter 15 of *LifeWork: A Biblical Theology for What You Do Every Day* (Seattle: YWAM Publishing, 2009).

57. Exod. 20:15, 17.

58. The parable of the minas (Luke 19:11–27) and the parable of the talents (Matt. 25:14–30).

59. For more on this, see Scott Allen and Darrow L. Miller, *The Forest in the Seed* (Phoenix: Disciple Nations Alliance, 2007).

60. Matt. 25:34–36; James 1:27.

61. For more on the creation and stewardship of wealth, please see chapters 15 and 16 of my book *LifeWork: A Biblical Theology for What You Do Every Day* (Seattle: YWAM Publishing, 2009).

62. John Adams, quoted in Mark Levin, *Liberty and Tyranny: A Conservative Manifesto* (New York: Threshold Editions, 2009), 126.

63. 2 Cor. 8:2; Eph. 4:28; 1 Tim 6:18.

64. The Virginia Declaration of Rights, May 15, 1776, http://www.constitution.org/bcp/virg_dor.htm; emphasis added.

16. Goodness: The Moral Order

Epigraph: Russell Kirk, *The Roots of American Order* (Washington, DC: Regnery Gateway, 1991), 27.

1. Prov. 20:27; Rom. 2:14–15; 7:15–23; 1 John 3:19–21.

2. Matt. 5:17–18; Rom. 10:4.
3. Matt. 5:18–20; Rom. 10:3.
4. Matt. 5:21–48.
5. Michael Metzger, "Clickers," DoggieHeadTilt, June 6, 2011, http://www.doggieheadtilt.com/clickers/.
6. I have selected some of Washington's rules and updated the spelling. The full list of rules can be seen at the Colonial Williamsburg site: http://www.history.org/almanack/life/manners/rules2.cfm.
7. Charles G. Finney, "Lecture 20: Human Government," *Systematic Theology* (1878 edition), Wesley Center Online, http://wesley.nnu.edu/related_traditions/finney/systematic/lecture20.htm.
8. In *Discipling Nations*, 176, I noted that several Asian cultures "have elements that are functional equivalents of the biblical ethic. Confucianism, for example, has a work ethic similar to the [Protestant work ethic]. . . . It works both ways, too. The West's current orientation to the now, with little thought to the future, is a functional equivalent of animist thought."
9. Fyodor Dostoyevsky, *The Brothers Karamazov*, part 4, book 11, chapter 4 ("A Hymn and a Secret").
10. George Grant, *Carry a Big Stick: The Uncommon Heroism of Theodore Roosevelt* (Elkton, Md.: Highland Books, 1996), 99.
11. "Impact of Drugs on Society," *National Drug Threat Assessment 2010*, National Drug Intelligence Center, http://www.justice.gov/ndic/pubs38/38661/drugImpact.htm.
12. "Report: Drug abuse costs $215 billion," *United Press International*, March 26, 2010, http://www.upi.com/Top_News/US/2010/03/26/Report-Drug-abuse-costs-215-billion/UPI-43111269583190/.
13. "Mexico says 28,000 killed in drugs war since 2006," *BBC News*, http://www.bbc.co.uk/news/world-latin-america-10860614.
14. "Facts on Induced Abortion in the United States," Guttmacher Institute, August 2011, http://www.guttmacher.org/pubs/fb_induced_abortion.html.
15. Ibid.
16. "Abortion Common among All Women," Guttmacher Institute, 1996, http://www.guttmacher.org/media/nr/prabort2.html.

17. Beauty: The Aesthetic Order

Epigraph: John R. Sachs, "Beauty," in *The New Dictionary of Theology*, ed. Joseph A. Komonchak, Mary Collins, Dermot A. Lane (Collegeville, Minn.: Liturgical Press, 1991), 84.
1. Gen. 1:1ff.; Ps. 33:6; Isa. 40:26; John 1:3; Acts 17:24; Heb. 11:3; Rev. 4:11.
2. Ps. 4:6; 27:1–2; 104:2; Ezek. 1:27; Matt. 17:1–7; John 1:6–9, 14; 2:11; Heb. 1:3; 1 John 1:5.

3. Gen. 1:3–5, 14–19; Rev. 21:23–26.

4. 1 Chron. 16:27; 29:11; Isa. 58:8; 60:1; 60:19.

5. Deut. 32:3–4; 2 Sam. 22:31; Job 37:16; Ps. 5:4; 119:96; 1 John 1:5.

6. Matt. 17:1–6; Col. 1:15; 2 Pet. 1:16–18.

7. John 1:14; 2:11; 2 Cor. 4:6; Heb. 1:3.

8. Ps. 48:1–3; 50:1–2; 96:4–6.

9. Ps. 29:1–2; 96:7–9; 2 Chron. 20:21.

10. Ps. 27:4; 90:17; Matt. 17:1–2; 2 Cor. 3:17–18.

11. Cynthia Pearl Maus, *Christ and the Fine Arts: An Anthology of Pictures, Poetry, Music, and Stories Centering on the Life of Christ* (New York: Harper & Brothers, 1938), 8.

12. W. M. O'Hanlon, *Walks among the Poor of Belfast: and Suggestions for Their Improvement* (Belfast, Ireland: Mayne, 1853), 102.

13. Rev. 22:1–2.

14. Thomas Dubay, *The Evidential Power of Beauty: Science and Theology Meet* (San Francisco: Ignatius, 1999), 77.

15. Bonaventure, *Bonaventure: The Soul's Journey into God, the Tree of Life, the Life of St. Francis*, Ewert H. Cousins ed. (Mahwah, N.J.: Paulist Press, 1978), 30.

16. Gen. 2:15; 2:19–20.

17. Thomas of Celano, *Second Life*, cxxiv, 165, http://www.hnp.org/who/francis.cfm.

18. J. R. R. Tolkien, *Tree and Leaf* (London: Unwin Books, 1964), 61–62.

19. C. S. Lewis, "Christianity and Literature," *Genesis: Journal of the Society of Christians in the Arts, Inc.* 1, no. 2 (1975): 22; emphasis added.

20. Frank E. Gaebelein, *The Christian, the Arts, and Truth: Regaining the Vision of Greatness* (Colorado Springs: Multnomah, 1985), 59.

21. Dr. Elizabeth Youmans, "The Fine Arts and Literature," *AMO Training Manual*, Chrysalis International 2003, 2.

22. Dubay, *The Evidential Power of Beauty*, 58.

23. Cynthia Pearl Maus, quoted in Elizabeth Youmans, "The Fine Arts and Literature," 2.

24. John R. Erickson, *Story Craft: Reflections on Faith, Culture, and Writing by the Author of Hank the Cowdog* (Perryton, Tex.: Maverick Books, 2009), 109; citing Phil. 4:8.

25. Ibid., 82.

26. Tolkien, *Tree and Leaf*, 61–62.

27. Paul Davies, *God and the New Physics* (New York: Simon and Schuster, 1983), 220–21.

28. Archibald Russell, quoted in Francis A. Schaeffer, *How Shall We Then Live? The Rise and Decline of Western Thought and Culture* (Wheaton, Ill.: Crossway Books, 1976), 196.

29. Dubay, *The Evidential Power of Beauty*, 116.
30. Edith Schaeffer, *Hidden Art: Ideas for Creating Beauty in Everyday Life* (Wheaton, Ill.: Tyndale, 1971). This book has also been published under the title *The Hidden Art of Homemaking: Creative Ideas for Enriching Everyday Life.*

18. The Consummation of the Kingdom

Epigraph: G. B. Caird, *A Commentary on the Revelation of St. John the Divine* (New York: Harper & Row, 1966), 279–80.
1. *Enhanced Strong's Lexicon*, s.v. "idou."
2. Matt. 28:18; Rev. 17:14; 19:16.
3. Matt. 1:22–23.
4. Gen. 12:3; 18:18; 22:18; 26:4; 28:14; Ps. 72:17; Acts 3:25.
5. Isa. 60:11; 62:10; Rev. 21:25.
6. Isa. 2:4
7. Gen. 1:3.
8. Gen. 1:14–19.
9. Num. 14:21; Neh. 9:5; Ps. 72:19; Isa. 6:3; Mal. 1:11; Matt. 6:10 (the fulfillment of "thy kingdom come, thy will be done on earth as it is in heaven"); Rev. 5:13.
10. Zech. 2:4–5; 14:6–7; Isa. 60:19–20; Rev. 21:11, 23; 22:5.
11. Isa. 2:5; 55:5; 60:3; 62:1–3; 66:18–20; Rev. 21:24.
12. Isa. 2:2–5; 11:6–9; 25:6–9; 61:2–3; 65:18–19; Jer. 31:13; Hos. 13:14; 1 Cor. 15:26, 54–58; Rev 20:14; 22:3.
13. The Hebrew word *yada,* "to know," does not mean simply to know about something (i.e., know about God) but to know something or someone personally and intimately (Exod. 33:13, 17; Isa. 43:10; 53:11; Jer. 9:23–24). The Greek equivalent in the New Testament is *ginosko* (John 17:3; Phil. 3:7–10; 2 Pet. 1:3). We are to know God's love, goodness, beauty, compassion, and veracity, and we are to enjoy his presence and engage with him in his mission.
14. Ps. 22:27; Isa. 45:22; 49:6, 12; Zech. 2:11; 8:22–23; Rom. 15:10–12.
15. Eph. 2:11–22.
16. *Strong's Enhanced Lexicon*, s.v. "yalad."
17. Isa. 26:2; 35:8; Matt. 13:41–43; Eph. 5:5; Rev. 22:14.
18. Ps. 47:1–7; 67:3; 86:9; 102:15; 148:7, 11–14; Isa. 24:15–16; 42:10–12; Rev. 7:9–10; 15:4.
19. Ps. 46:4; 84:6; Rev. 7:17.
20. Ps. 45:10–16; Matt. 22:2; 25:1–10; Eph. 5:32; Rev. 19:6–10.
21. Gen. 24:10.
22. Exod. 25:1–8.

23. 1 Kings 10:1–13.
24. Matt. 2:2.
25. Matt. 2:11.
26. W. E. Vine, *An Expository Dictionary of New Testament Words,* s.v. "honour."
27. See also Mal. 3:2–4.
28. *Dictionary of Biblical Languages with Semantic Domains: Hebrew (Old Testament),* s.v. "sarar."
29. Rev. 19:6–10.
30. Rev. 21:1–4.
31. Ps. 72:10–11; 86:9; Isa. 35:2; 56:7; 60:5–13; 66:11–12; Ezek. 7:27.
32. Richard J. Mouw, *When the Kings Come Marching In: Isaiah and the New Jerusalem* (Grand Rapids: Eerdmans, 2002), 108.
33. Anthony Hoekema, *The Bible and the Future* (Grand Rapids: Eerdmans, 1994), 286.
34. Isa. 60:5–9, 13.
35. G. B. Caird, quoted in D. B. Hegeman, *Plowing in Hope: Towards a Biblical Theology of Culture,* 2nd ed. (Moscow, Idaho: Canon Press, 2007), 90–91.
36. The Latin phrase *coram Deo,* "before the face of God," reminds us that we are to live continually in the knowledge of God's presence.
37. The Bible uses "the bride of Christ" as a metaphor for both the church and the New Jerusalem. Paul compares the union of Christ and the church to that of husbands and wives (Eph. 5:22–33). John, the author of Revelation, describes the bride as the New Jerusalem (Rev. 21:2, 9–10) and speaks of the bride wearing fine linen, that is, the righteous acts of God's people (Rev. 19:7–8).
38. Two recent popular books by analysts of Western culture are pessimistic about the future: Mark Steyn's *After America: Getting Ready for Armageddon* and Patrick J. Buchanan's *Suicide of a Superpower: Will America Survive Until 2025?* Neither of these authors fully appreciates the reality of *Christus Victor.*
39. Rom. 8:17–18; 2 Cor. 1:5–7; 4:10; Phil. 3:10; 2 Tim. 2:12; 1 Pet. 2:21; 4:13.
40. Matt. 16:18.

SUBJECT AND NAME INDEX

SCRIPTURE INDEX

Only quoted references are cited here. See notes section for additional references.

ABOUT THE AUTHOR

For over thirty years, Darrow L. Miller has been a popular speaker on Christianity and culture, apologetics, worldview, poverty, and the dignity of women. He has traveled and lectured in over seventy countries, and his books and publications have been translated into twenty languages.

Darrow has a master's degree in higher and adult education and has pursued graduate studies in philosophy, theology, Christian apologetics, biblical studies, and missions. He and his wife, Marilyn, studied at the Institute for Holy Land Studies in Jerusalem and studied and worked with Francis and Edith Schaeffer at L'Abri Fellowship in Switzerland from 1969 to 1971.

For twenty-seven years, Darrow served as a vice president of Food for the Hungry International (FHI) in the area of recruiting, staff development, and the creation of curriculum in worldview and development. While at FHI, he and Dr. Bob Moffitt founded the Disciple Nations Alliance (DNA). The DNA is a nonprofit organization seeking to spread a school of thought—a virus, if you will—through training, publishing, and mentoring. The global DNA network comprises likeminded organizations and people in over sixty countries who are "equipping the church to transform the world."

Darrow and his wife live in Blue Ridge, Arizona. They have four children and thirteen grandchildren.

Baptism 940